T0390466

OVERLANDING
101

A FIELD GUIDE TO VEHICLE-BASED ADVENTURE TRAVEL

OVERLANDING 101

SCOTT BRADY

and the Editors of *Overland Journal*

ADAMS MEDIA

NEW YORK   AMSTERDAM/ANTWERP   LONDON   TORONTO   SYDNEY/MELBOURNE   NEW DELHI

Adams Media
An Imprint of Simon & Schuster, LLC
100 Technology Center Drive
Stoughton, MA 02072

First Adams Media trade paperback edition May 2025

ADAMS MEDIA and colophon are registered trademarks of Simon & Schuster, LLC.

Simon & Schuster strongly believes in freedom of expression and stands against censorship in all its forms. For more information, visit BooksBelong.com.

For information about special discounts for bulk purchases, please contact Simon & Schuster Special Sales at 1-866-506-1949 or business@simonandschuster.com.

The Simon & Schuster Speakers Bureau can bring authors to your live event. For more information or to book an event, contact the Simon & Schuster Speakers Bureau at 1-866-248-3049 or visit our website at www.simonspeakers.com.

Interior design by Sylvia McArdle
Interior photographs by Scott Brady unless otherwise noted

Manufactured in the United States of America

1 2025

Library of Congress Cataloging-in-Publication Data
Names: Brady, Scott, 1972– author. | Overland Journal, editor.
Title: Overlanding 101 / Scott Brady and the Editors of Overland Journal.
Description: Stoughton, Massachusetts: Adams Media, [2025]
Identifiers: LCCN 2024058387 | ISBN 9781507223659 (pb) | ISBN 9781507223666 (ebook)
Subjects: LCSH: Automobile travel--Guidebooks. | Adventure and adventurers. | Outdoor recreation.
Classification: LCC GV1021 .B62 2025 | DDC 796.7--dc23/eng/20250108
LC record available at https://lccn.loc.gov/2024058387

ISBN 978-1-5072-2365-9
ISBN 978-1-5072-2366-6 (ebook)

DEDICATION

To my mom, Janice Brady (1944–2022), for her unwavering support, but especially for encouraging me to explore.

CONTENTS

PART 2: The Fundamentals of Overland Travel 63

PART 4: The Overland Journey 203

PREFACE

Adventure is an undertaking with an unknown outcome. In the community of overland travelers, it is all about adventure, turning left instead of right or driving just a few more miles to see what is over the next hill. The unknown and uncertainty are what make an overland journey so appealing; it is a roulette wheel of outcomes just waiting to be discovered.

I was first exposed to the joys of travel in 1995 when I landed in southern Italy as a United States Air Force serviceman. Completely out of my element, I slowly adjusted to the unfamiliar language, the jet-lag, and the challenging dance with officials and bureaucracy. Over the months that followed, my apprehension transitioned into a deep love for the Italian people and their generosity, family values, and, of course, their cooking. That first trip had me hooked and once I was back in the United States, I set the goal of making travel my avocation. Travel was invigorating for me, but what really captured my passion was the process of overlanding. The thrill of exploring from border

to border, from point A to Z, and from coastline to coastline was intoxicating. I knew immediately that this was the path I was meant to take.

Despite the hundreds of thousands of miles I've seen since that first experience, vehicle-based travel is an endless learning and discovery journey for me. The deeper I get, the more I realize that I still have so much to learn and experience—and that is all part of the adventure of overlanding. I have developed my overlanding skills over several decades (and numerous failures) and throughout this book, I will share those skills with you—along with the stories of how I became the overlander I am today.

From my first expedition to Tuktoyaktuk, Canada, in some of the harshest elements in the country, driving via the precarious ice roads that were once the Peel and Mackenzie Rivers, to my crossing of Central America to the harrowing Darién Gap, my early explorations instilled in me a desire to venture farther afield. During this period, *Overland Journal* was born, as was the curious idea of traveling all seven continents. That plan was further inspired during my crossing of Europe and Central Asia in 2010, and then finally came to life during a breakfast conversation with my friend Greg Miller. During that morning, Expeditions 7 (E7) and a four-year adventure to take the same Land Cruiser to all seven continents was born.

Greg and I took delivery of the Land Cruiser VDJ78s in Japan, and then shipped them to North America and Europe before embarking on our crossing of Asia via Russia and the infamous Road of Bones. Australia was next, with our goal being to cross the Canning Stock Route, the longest unsupported overland track in the world. The year 2013 would usher in the continent of Africa and exploration of the Skeleton Coast of Namibia, known for its harsh climate, fog, and shipwrecks, before loading the Land Cruiser onto a Russian Ilyushin Il-76 bound for Antarctica. We would not only drive the Land Cruiser on Antarctica, but we would become the first Americans to complete a double-crossing of the continent via four-wheel drive (4WD), including two stops at the South Pole and saving Prince Harry along the way. The final continent was South America in 2014, arriving in Ushuaia, the world's southernmost city, still savoring the asados that the gauchos prepared along Route 40.

In subsequent years I would join E7 again for the first long-axis crossing of the Greenland Ice Sheet. With international travel halted during the pandemic, I transitioned to a sailboat and crossed the Pacific in 2021 with the Kailani Expedition. I had managed to cross six of the seven continents, but Africa remained. Starting in 2023, I shipped a newly minted INEOS Grenadier to South Africa and began my journey from Cape Town to north Africa, arriving in Djibouti just as war erupted in the region. When I finally pulled my vehicle to the water's edge at the Gulf of Aden, I had completed my decades-long goal of becoming the first person in history to cross all seven continents by vehicle.

With each accomplishment came the longing to share my story and the skills I learned along the way. Yet in 2006, when *Overland Journal* was founded, the term "overlanding" was only familiar to Australians and a few weather-worn international travelers. Still, my team and I were guided by the goal of inspiring others to see the world by vehicle, and we ventured forth into the world of publishing with that one goal in mind. Our journal started as an employee-owned publication and remains so nearly twenty years later. From its humble beginnings, the publication now reaches more than 200,000 readers in print and digital form, each year inspiring new overlanders to embark on their own adventures.

Overlanding is an adventure that will deeply change you by revealing the world and the vast diversity it contains. As Mark Twain so astutely observed, "Travel is fatal to prejudice, bigotry, and narrow-mindedness, and many of our people need it sorely on these accounts." By becoming a guest in another land, you can experience and better understand different cultures, political beliefs, religions, cuisines, family units, and art. Through that process, you learn that despite any differences, we are all far more alike than different. You learn how safe the world is and how generous and hospitable people are everywhere, from the nomadic Himba of Namibia to the dedicated scientists of the South Pole station.

Join me on this journey of exploration as we venture into the 101 of overlanding.

INTRODUCTION

Welcome to the joys of overland travel—the world unfolding in miles of remote vistas, cultural discoveries, culinary delights, and natural wonders. While the typical weeklong vacation makes you a tourist, the overlanding journey helps you become a traveler, immersed in experiences and connections that last a lifetime.

Overlanding is often perceived as a way to travel the world and see exotic international destinations—and it certainly can be that. But an overland adventure can also be found just a few hours from home. With countless available route planning and mapping tools, it is possible to discover new roads and trails that lead to high mesas, narrow canyons, or abandoned ghost towns. Over a long weekend, it is possible to retrace a historic wagon route to a remote destination and experience a location rarely visited. By being self-sufficient and prepared, you can travel close to home and still experience the rewards of overlanding.

Overlanding 101 will help you discover what overlanding is, its history and first explorers, and how to prepare yourself and your vehicle for the trip of a lifetime. This useful guide breaks down the aspects of overlanding into manageable and realistic steps, giving you multiple options and routes to choose from. You'll find information on all aspects of overland travel like planning your trip, packing your gear, choosing your communication and navigation equipment, outfitting your emergency kit, picking the right vehicle for your type of trip, and staying safe on your journey.

Each chapter also includes an overlanding story from individuals who've experienced their own unique adventures, whether it's getting stuck in Australia's Great Sandy Desert, crossing the Greenland Ice Sheet, adventuring on El Camino del Diablo in Arizona, or helping fellow explorers in Antarctica. These stories will show you the real-life expeditions of overlanders who went out there and pushed the limits. You'll learn about their successes and failures, including how they overcame challenges when things went awry.

Whether you have overlanding experience already or are ready to start on your first journey, *Overlanding 101* will give you the confidence, advice, and information you need to embark on your own adventure!

PART 1

Vehicle-Based Adventure Travel

Welcome to the overland journey! Motorcycles and four-wheel drive vehicles have ventured to every corner of the globe and across every continent in pursuit of scientific discovery, cultural awareness, and adventure—and now you can be a part of it all. In this first part you'll learn what overlanding is and the differences between overland travel, four-wheeling, road-tripping, and expeditions. In addition, you'll discover the history of overland travel and its legacy of adventure that continues to inspire countless journeys.

After reading about overlanding and the pioneers who brought it into being, you'll find out how to start planning an overlanding journey of your own. With details on picking your destination, finding the necessary items to bring with you, and choosing the right vehicle for the terrain you'll encounter—you'll find all you'll need to begin planning your first overnight journey and then advance to longer, more distant travels from there. Overlanding opens a world of discovery for solo travelers, couples, friends, and families—it's time to see what is just beyond the next horizon.

←

Vehicle-based adventure takes many forms, from discovering new cultures to exploring remote and challenging landscapes.

CHAPTER 1

WHAT IS OVERLANDING?

Turning the key, the diesel engine in the old Land Cruiser purrs to life, the gentle clatter of a trusted friend ready to embark on the next journey. Shifting the transfer case into low range and selecting first gear, the Toyota slowly climbs the grade up Elephant Hill, a sandstone and rock trail in Canyonlands National Park. This area is extremely remote, and the challenging obstacles limit the number of visitors. The trip can take days or weeks; there is no cell coverage, and it requires complete self-reliance. While this route is not located in the wilds of South America, it is everything an overlander dreams of—travel, adventure, culture, wilderness, and self-discovery.

In this chapter, you will learn what overlanding is and gain a helpful foundation for learning the requisite skills of vehicle-based travel, while also clearing the air around how many ways you can go about an overland journey. You'll also discover a glossary of terms and the rewards of supporting scientific and geographic goals. The chapter wraps up with a few examples of trip budgets and vehicle builds before diving into the important principles of Tread Lightly, Leave No Trace, and the Overlander's Code.

The Joys of Overland Travel

Over fifteen years ago, the team at *Overland Journal* defined overlanding as "vehicle-based adventure travel" in an effort to help future explorers differentiate from off-roading, car camping, and road-tripping. With the primary goal of travel, overlanding will also typically include one or more of the following:

- Remote destinations that often require days or weeks of fuel, food, water, and supplies.
- Navigation, route finding, weather tracking, and consideration of seasonal closures.
- Interactions with cultures other than your own, including indigenous peoples, cultural sites, and historic routes.

- Travel to under-explored or under-documented regions, allowing for the serendipity of the unknown. (It is the departure from the overshared social media hotspots to find the unexpected, getting the traveler out of the rut.)
- Self-reliant travel for days, weeks, or months. Overlanding has an undertone of both distance and time, allowing the journey to uncouple you from the day-to-day to help you change and grow.
- A healthy amount of time. Overlanding generally takes time and is difficult to achieve in a night or two. This is not to say that a weekend trip cannot be overlanding, but the rewards really start to reveal themselves over weeks, months, and years.

↑ **The Toyota Land Cruiser 70 Series** is still the vehicle of choice for most long-distance overland adventure due to the durability and simplicity.

Overlanding Fundamentals

The following is a glossary of terms to help you understand the remainder of this book. It's important to know, however, that these terms are not set in stone; for example, it is possible to overland without even putting tires on a dirt road or spending a night camping. Overlanding is not just four-wheeling and camping (although it can be). Adventurous travels with your vehicle are truly the goal.

- **Overland(ing):** Vehicle-based adventure travel, most often over weeks, months, or years across countries and continents. Its primary purpose is exploration and adventure travel.
- **Overland duration:** Typically, an overland adventure lasts a week to many years. However, more journeys on technical or infrequently traveled routes may be only a few days long due to the challenges of fuel or water resupply.
- **Logistics:** Detailed planning is required for the environmental, geographic, and geopolitical contingencies you will face while overlanding.
- **Route finding:** Navigation can be easy or complicated. Many areas you may want to overland in may not have detailed mapping available, thus requiring extensive research and route finding.
- **Camping:** Camping in overland terms is usually remote camping. Some travelers may use a self-contained unit due to weather conditions, security concerns, or the duration of travel, though most will camp in a roof tent or high-quality ground tent. There may also be limited camping available (like in many parts of Asia), requiring the use of local accommodations, hostels, and so on.
- **International borders:** Overlanding often includes crossing international borders. Some overlanders may cross dozens of borders and even entire continents in a trip.
- **Risk:** There is risk involved in overlanding. In particular, there is a potential for moderate risk to personnel and equipment due to security issues or the extreme remoteness and difficulty of the journey.
- **Terrain:** The terrain in overlanding can vary depending on environmental and use conditions, but it can be highly technical, such as in jungles and remote deserts. The vehicle and driver must be prepared for the unknowns.
- **Car camping:** Using a car to access an established campground for one or more nights of sleeping in, on, or around the vehicle.
- **Van life:** The lifestyle of using a van to live in and often work from the road.

- **Four-wheeling (off-roading):** Recreational driving sport with a four-wheel drive (4WD) vehicle on unimproved trails where overcoming obstacles is the primary goal.
- **Vehicle-dependent expedition:** An organized, vehicle-supported journey with a defined purpose, often geographic, philanthropic, or scientific.

OVERLANDING VERSUS FOUR-WHEELING AND ROAD-TRIPPING

The easiest way to distinguish overlanding from four-wheeling is that four-wheeling (or off-roading) is a recreational sport. It is about overcoming obstacles with a 4WD vehicle, often requiring a marshal (spotter), advanced recovery, and even aftermarket modifications to the vehicle. The challenge is most of the fun, and the activity can be a great way to spend a day honing your driving skills. While overlanding *can* include technical terrain, those challenges are overcome in pursuit of the journey between points A and Z. Four-wheeling is vehicular sport while overlanding is vehicular travel.

A road trip has all the trappings of hauling a family across the country to see relatives, the world's most giant ball of twine, or the expanse of the Grand Canyon. While a family road trip can feel like an adventure, the goal is often to arrive at a specific tourist spot or holiday gathering with relatives. A road trip is a journey *to* a destination instead of the remote meanderings of the overlander, where the journey *is* the destination.

OVERLANDING VERSUS CAR CAMPING

Car camping can be some of the most fun you can do with a vehicle, transporting your friends and yourself into nature with all the comforts of home. Having a car allows the camper to bring items that would be difficult to bring with a backpack, like larger tents, thicker air mattresses, larger chairs, hygiene (shower) solutions, and elaborate cooking equipment. A vehicle can also provide access to remote camping for those with limited mobility or special medical needs. Car camping can also be done close to home for just one night. On the other hand, overlanding can eschew camping entirely. However, it is common for overlanders to camp as their routes often include trails without accommodation, or the traveler prefers to be away from it all. In some countries or regions, the overland destinations have limited camping availability, or the adventurer chooses to experience the vibrancy and culture by staying in villages and cities to enjoy local cuisines, museums, and festivals.

WHAT MAKES AN EXPEDITION?

While it has become popular to call a week's trip with friends into the desert an "expedition," it might be helpful to understand what the term means regarding overlanding. While you may never embark on an official overland expedition, you should know that an expedition is a vehicle-supported journey that meets one or more of the following criteria:

1. An overland journey to a rarely visited or documented remote and harsh location with limited (or no) infrastructure and support—for example, the Empty Quarter of Oman or the Summit Station near the apex of the Greenland Ice Sheet. These trips should be documented for the benefit of future travelers and generations.
2. An overland journey that significantly supports a remote or challenging philanthropic need—for example, transporting medical supplies and doctors to a remote village in Bolivia or delivering equipment for clean water infrastructure on the Skeleton Coast.
3. An overland journey that contributes to scientific discovery, data collection, or logistics, such as measuring snow depth on a glacier, transporting a biologist to a remote research station, or assisting with an observational census.

Sample Trips and Budgets

It is possible to overland with minimal expenses. On a limited budget, travelers can start on a bicycle with a backpack or a rack with a few panniers (on-bike packs). I remember encountering a lone cyclist along the Silk Road in Kyrgyzstan who managed to see all of Central Asia for less than $10 per day. Other travelers have explored for less and many have traveled for more, but overall, overlanding can be affordable. As another example, Luisa and Graeme Bell have traveled for over ten years with their two children in their Land Rover Defender for about $2,000 per month ($65 per day). They sleep in the vehicle nearly every night, cook meals, and do maintenance themselves. They have been able to drive the length of the Americas and Africa, showing their son and daughter the real world.

In reality, a $120,000 vehicle loaded to the gills with modifications and gear is unnecessary, and the expense often complicates or constrains the adventure. For example, temporary importation duties or the bond on a Carnet (import/export document) can be two to four times the value of the vehicle, along with the challenges of obtaining comprehensive insurance, and so on. The car and modifications should only represent a third of the travel budget over the lifecycle of a 4WD/car/motorcycle. As an alternate approach, look at the $120,000 investment as the total cost of travel, which will allow for the purchase of a used but reliable overland vehicle, a few basic modifications, and a daily travel budget to drive from Prudhoe Bay in Alaska to Ushuaia in Argentina.

←
A simple motorcycle like the Suzuki V-Strom can provide efficiency, comfort, and reliability for remote exploration.

Following are some sample budgets, trips, and vehicles to give you some ideas about the process and expense of overland travel. These sample trips are not intended to discourage the purchase of a new or even expensive vehicle, as those vehicles have their place for those with the financial means to justify the investment. In fact, a newer vehicle has the advantage of (often) improved reliability, safety, and performance. Many new original equipment manufacturer (OEM) overland offerings are well-suited to international and backcountry use, requiring almost no modification to travel the world. The goal here is to prioritize travel, so again it is recommended that you only spend 30 percent or less of your travel budget on the vehicle and modifications. Individual incomes, budgets, and goals vary widely, so the percentage can change for more affluent travelers.

↑ **Supremely reliable** and internationally serviceable, the Toyota Land Cruiser 200 Series remains one of the best around-the-world options for North American travelers.

Example: A 2-Year Travel Budget of $120,000: 4WD Vehicle

- **Vehicle:** Used 2012 Toyota Land Cruiser 200 Series: $28,000
- **Basic modifications:** $3,500 (springs/shocks, rack, and interior storage platform for sleeping)
- **Support and camping equipment:** $2,200 (sleeping, cooking, self-recovery, and tools)
- $86,300 travel budget for North, Central, and South America: At $100 per day average and associated shipping and visa fees, it would allow for a full two years of travel.

Example: A 100-Day Travel Budget of $45,000: 4WD

- **Vehicle:** Used 2016 Nissan Frontier PRO-4X 4WD: $17,000
- Used Go Fast Camper: $5,000
- **Basic modifications:** $2,000 (rear helper spring, shocks, and portable power pack)
- **Support and camping equipment:** $2,200 (sleeping, cooking, self-recovery, and tools)
- $18,800 travel budget to drive through the western US and Baja California, Mexico. At $85 per day (mostly camping in the camper), the budget would allow for one hundred days of exploring the Backcountry Discovery Routes of New Mexico, Colorado, Wyoming, Idaho, Washington, and Oregon before embarking on Sinuhe Xavier's challenging Utah Traverse and even a few months camping on the beach (and eating tacos) in Baja California, Mexico.

Example: A 1-Year Travel Budget of $25,000: Motorcycle

- **Vehicle:** Used 2020 Kawasaki KLR 650 motorcycle: $5,400
- **Basic modifications:** $1,200 (rack and side luggage)
- **Support and camping equipment:** $2,300 (tent, sleeping, cooking, GPS, tools, and spares)
- $16,100 travel budget to cross the TransAmerica Trail (TAT), up to Alaska, and through the Sierra Madre of Mexico before arriving at the Mayan ruins in Tikal, Guatemala. At $50 per day average (which requires a lot of camping), the budget would allow 300-plus days to cross the US and ride an ambitious foray in Copper Canyon, Mexico, before crossing into Belize and Guatemala.

The Land Cruiser, Frontier, and KLR650 motorcycle in the previous examples will still have considerable resale value at the end of these adventures. They can then be sold to offset the travel expenses and adjust the total vehicle and modification costs well below the optimal 30 percent of travel expenses.

Conscious Overlanding

One of the most critical responsibilities of the overland traveler is to preserve the places you visit for future adventurers and generations. You can minimize and even eliminate most of the impact of your travels by using Tread Lightly, Leave No Trace, and Overlander's Code principles. Also, you can consider supporting nonprofit organizations like Tread Lightly and Leave No Trace by donating your resources or time. Following are the principles and codes of those organizations and how you utilize them while overlanding.

THE T.R.E.A.D. PRINCIPLES

Tread Lightly began in 1985 as an off-highway vehicle program for the US Forest Service before becoming an independent nonprofit in 1990. Led by a committed team of multiuse professionals, the organization has evolved to support user education, vehicle-manufacturer responsibilities (primarily around advertising responsible use), and the preservation of public land access. Their principles are:

- **Travel responsibly** on land by staying on designated roads, trails, and area. Go over, not around, obstacles to avoid widening the trails. Cross streams only at designated fords. When possible, avoid wet, muddy trails.
- **Respect the rights of others**, including private property owners, all recreational trail users, campers, and others, so they can enjoy their recreational activities undisturbed. Leave gates as you found them. Yield right of way to those passing you or going uphill.
- **Educate yourself** prior to your trip by obtaining travel maps and regulations from public agencies. Plan for your trip, take recreation skills classes, and know how to operate your equipment safely.
- **Avoid sensitive areas** on land such as meadows, lake shores, wetlands, and streams. Always ride with caution any time water is present. Wet soils are more susceptible to damage. Riding along river and stream beds causes erosion and habitat destruction. Stay on designated routes.

This protects wildlife habitats and sensitive soils from damage. Don't disturb historical, archaeological, or paleontological sites.

- **Do your part** by modeling appropriate behavior, leaving the area better than you found it, properly disposing of waste, minimizing the use of fire, avoiding the spread of invasive species, and repairing degraded areas.

THE LEAVE NO TRACE PRINCIPLES

As outdoor recreation expanded in popularity during the mid-twentieth century, there became increased awareness of the impact of backcountry use on the environment. In 1990, the US Forest Service and the National Outdoor Leadership School (NOLS) created the Leave No Trace (LNT) curriculum and outreach campaign. By 1994 the program morphed into a 501(c)(3) nonprofit, and the seven LNT principles were established with the goal of leaving the wild places of the world unchanged by human presence.

Plan Ahead and Prepare

- Know the regulations and special concerns for the area you'll visit.
- Prepare for extreme weather, hazards, and emergencies.
- Schedule your trip to avoid times of high use.
- Visit in small groups. Split larger parties into smaller groups.
- Repackage food to minimize waste.
- Use a map and compass to eliminate the use of rock cairns, flagging, or marking paint.

Travel and Camp on Durable Surfaces

- Durable surfaces include established trails, campsites, rock, gravel, or snow.
- Protect riparian areas by camping at least 200 feet from lakes and streams.
- Good campsites are found, not made. Altering a site is not necessary.
- Use existing trails and campsites.
- Keep campsites small. Focus activity in areas where vegetation is absent.

Dispose of Waste Properly

- Pack it in, pack it out. Inspect your campsite and rest areas for trash or spilled food. Pack out all trash, leftover food, and litter. Burning trash is never recommended.
- Deposit solid human waste in catholes dug 6–8 inches deep at least 200 feet from water, camp, and trails. Cover and disguise the cathole when finished.
- Bury toilet paper deep in a cathole or pack the toilet paper out along with hygiene products.
- To wash yourself or your dishes, carry water 200 feet away from streams or lakes and use small amounts of biodegradable soap. Scatter strained dishwater.

Leave What You Find

- Preserve the past: Observe cultural or historic structures and artifacts, but do not touch them.
- Leave rocks, plants, and other natural objects as you find them.
- Avoid introducing or transporting non-native species.
- Do not build structures, furniture, or dig trenches.

Minimize Campfire Impacts

- Campfires can cause lasting impacts on the environment. Use a lightweight stove for cooking and enjoy a candle lantern for light.
- Use established fire rings, pans, or mound fires where fires are permitted.
- Keep fires small. Use only sticks from the ground that can be broken by hand.
- Burn all wood and coals to ash, put out campfires completely, then scatter the cool ashes.

Respect Wildlife

- Observe wildlife from a distance. Do not follow or approach them.
- Never feed animals. Feeding wildlife damages their health, alters natural behaviors, and exposes them to predators and other dangers.
- Control pets at all times or leave them at home.
- Avoid wildlife during sensitive times: mating, nesting, raising young, or winter.

Be Considerate of Others

- Respect others and protect the quality of their experience.
- Be courteous. Yield to other users on the trail.
- Greet riders and ask which side of the trail to move to when encountering pack animals and those on horseback.
- Take breaks and camp away from others.
- Let nature's sounds prevail. Avoid loud voices and noises. (Note: This was a minor edit of the Leave No Trace principles to avoid confusion between human-powered and mechanized backcountry use.)

THE OVERLANDER'S CODE

As overlanders, we have a unique ability to interact with remote cultures and environments. As travelers, it is our responsibility to be kind, patient, and gracious guests, while also taking care to minimize our impact on the environment and local communities. With responsible overlanding, we can preserve these experiences for future generations.

- **Kindness is key:** Overland travel inevitably leads to challenging situations and encounters, so it is our responsibility to limit conflict, be patient, and be good ambassadors for travelers who will follow in our footsteps.
- **Respect the unique cultures you visit:** As guests of the countries and regions we visit, we often encounter unique traditions, beliefs, values, and norms that are different from our own. Researching these differences and assimilating as much as possible is important to help minimize conflict and misunderstanding.
- **Take responsibility for your actions:** Accidents can happen during travel, so it is essential to take responsibility if livestock is injured or killed or a vehicle accident occurs. Have sufficient currency available to resolve those incidents ethically and generously.

↑ **Slow down, observe,** always be kind, and let the journey take you.

- **Do no harm:** Research the regions you are visiting and understand the implications of your actions. Harmful actions include giving treats or money to children at the roadside, as this encourages them to run into the street with the possibility of being hit. Avoid driving on remote tracks in heavy rains to limit trail damage and dispose of all waste properly. Travel as a solo vehicle or in small groups to minimize campsite damage and impact on local infrastructure.
- **Avoid paying bribes:** In most situations, proper planning, research, and patience will all but eliminate the likelihood of paying a bribe to officials and law enforcement. There are exceptions, such as when a bribe is paid unknowingly or if personal safety is threatened. Paying bribes increases the likelihood of pressure for similar kickbacks from locals and future travelers.
- **Help other travelers:** Help fellow travelers and locals along the journey, including getting a vehicle unstuck or fixing a flat tire. Ask walkers, bikers, and motorcyclists if they need water or other support. Give back on community forums and apps with updated road and border crossing reports.
- **Give back when possible:** As travelers, we gain so much from our experiences that finding ways to give back during our journeys is deeply rewarding. There are ways to volunteer or use your professional skills in every country you visit, so make time to honor the local communities and conservation organizations that make the experience possible. When feasible, spend money with locally owned businesses and guides.

Traveling Well

By considering what overlanding is and understanding the terms of the pursuit, you can better communicate and plan your travel goals. In the case of an overland adventure, there are numerous forums and communities that can help you refine the itinerary or equipment, and the members may even have a few secret spots to share. If you have determined that your trip serves as a vehicle-based expedition, there are nonprofit organizations like The Royal Geographical Society and The Explorers Club that can provide professional consulting, introductions, and access to journals from previous travelers.

Even though vehicle-based travel only represents 137 years of history, it has become a powerful component of the human experience, but the mechanized nature also demands a steward's mindset. With the rapid growth of overlanding, the negative impact on trails, campsites, and cultures continues to expand, requiring large-scale cleanups, education programs, law enforcement, and even route closures. If we all do our part and employ the principles of Tread Lightly, Leave No Trace, and the Overlander's Code, we can protect multiuse access and pass on these experiences to future travelers.

The Horn of Afar

Despite the close confines, the Harar market exploded with life and the smell of roasting coffee beans and frankincense. Bryon and I negotiated the maze of stalls, open baskets, and teetering bags of raw spices. The spice porters announced, "Welbel, Welbel," as they vaulted 80-pound sacks over their shoulders and pushed through the chaos. We were purchasing provisions for our journey through the Afar Triangle and facing the uncertainty of the border with Djibouti at the start of Ramadan. The Horn of Africa is slowly being torn away at the tectonic confluence of the Arabian, Nubian, and Somali plates, forming the Afar Triangle and the start of the Great Rift Valley. This region is one of the planet's hottest, lowest, and driest places. We would need to navigate this region to arrive at the Gulf of Aden, including a border crossing into Djibouti just as war in the Middle East erupted.

With the vehicle loaded with fuel and equipment, we departed the historic Harar for the borderlands of Ethiopia, Somalia, and Djibouti. Despite this being the main route to the coast, it was nearly devoid of traffic—the fuel shortage and an impending port agreement with Somaliland flaring tensions. With the specter of the border looming, we drove slowly to conserve fuel and navigate this region known for banditry and trucking accidents. Once we arrived at Ethiopia's Dewele border post, the challenges began. One official after another was disinterested in closing out our vehicle documentation or was unwilling to assume responsibility for our being able to leave. Hours passed, and we were given a reprieve with the changing of the guard and an official more sympathetic to our plight, and the fact that we were stuck at his border with no means of forward or return prospects—he would be the first of our patrons of kindness in the coming days.

Having cleared the Ethiopian border late in the day, we rolled up to the Djiboutian post just as darkness fell. The border was a haphazard congregation of confiscated Land Cruisers, blowing trash, and decaying buildings. It seemed that everyone was yelling, jockeying for the attention of the few officials still on duty. Bags were being searched, and ramshackle buses filled with Somalis from Mogadishu poured into the dirt lot chased by a sea of dust. We found a parking spot for the Grenadier and made our way, gingerly, toward the outpost. Within minutes our visas were validated, passports stamped, and vehicle carnet verified. But I sighed relief too soon, as just as we were pulling away, a customs official yelled in our direction, "Show me your papers!"

This would begin nearly four days of detention at the border, including hours of desperate communications over satellite messenger and restricted cellular calling to escalate our plight to the highest reaches of the Djibouti government and even the US State Department. Frustrated and surviving on little sleep and dwindling supplies, one of the police officers approached in broken English, "Do you need any water or food?" Our second patron of kindness had arrived.

As the days passed, word of our detention had reached a local overlander and retired French Foreign Legionnaire, Ali. We connected on the phone, and plans were made for him to drive several hours to the border to advocate for our release. He arrived with a beaming smile and bags of food, hot coffee, and tea. After handing us the food, he stormed off to the customs hut like a man on a mission. Emotions welled in my chest as I took that first sip of coffee. Kindness had prevailed yet again, and freedom was within our grasp.

→

The border crossing with Djibouti and Ethiopia was alive with buses, cars, and travelers during Ramadan. This group had just arrived from Mogadishu with piles of goods and luggage.

CHAPTER 2

THE HISTORY OF VEHICLE-BASED TRAVEL

The history of overlanding is a storied past, starting in the 1200s with the word's origins coming from the Middle English term *overlond* and then entering regular use by the 1700s to describe journeys over the land. Overlanding was best captured by legendary cattle drovers of Australia that crossed vast distances in Oceania to open new grazing lands or transport herds to lucrative stockyards in the south. Then, in 1888, Bertha Benz changed history with the first overland journey by vehicle.

This chapter delves into the history of overlanding, including many of the pursuit's most colorful characters and luminaries. From the first overlanders to modern explorers, there are innumerable lessons to be learned about the benefits of a simple vehicle and the desire for adventure. This chapter ends with a review of the biggest game changers in overland travel today, including satellite communication and the advent of the electronic visa.

The First Overlanders

Bertha Benz captured all the core attributes of future overlanders, including a desire to explore, a fierce self-sufficiency, and an indominable determination to drive the world.

Overlanding started with Bertha Benz, the business partner (and wife) of Karl Benz, the inventor of the Benz Patent-Motorwagen. Bertha is impressive for many accomplishments beyond that first road trip, including being the financier (before their marriage) of Karl's patent efforts with the motorized horseless carriage. She was an astute businesswoman, but German law in 1885 did not permit a woman to hold patent rights. By all measures, her contributions and business acumen turned the first Benz from idea to reality. So, it is no surprise that in August 1888, without anyone's permission or approval from the authorities, Bertha climbed aboard the Benz Patent-Motorwagen No. 3 with her two teenage sons and drove 106 kilometers (over 65 miles) from Mannheim to Pforzheim. Bertha's journey was the world's first long-distance road trip by an internal combustion engine vehicle. Thank you, Bertha, for inspiring all who would overland after you.

THE RACE TO CROSS CONTINENTS

After Bertha's impressive feat, the race was on to undertake longer and more ambitious adventures with the horseless carriage. On a bet, Dr. Horatio Jackson left San Francisco in 1903 and became the first person to drive an automobile across the United States. Researching his journey, it was clear that the good doctor had no idea what he was in for, but he left nonetheless. He had only received driving lessons the week before, and he blew his only spare tire within 15 miles of Oakland. Calamity continued, but Horatio and his mechanic Sewall Crocker persevered, arriving in New York City on July 26, 1903, sixty-three days after starting their journey. Along the way, they adopted Bud, who was likely the first overlanding bulldog. Even back then, trips were just better with a best friend along for the ride.

In 1922, Aloha Wanderwell (born Idris Galcia Hall) captured the world's attention by departing for a global journey at age sixteen after answering an advertisement; she took on many roles throughout the expedition, including serving as a translator, driver, and film editor. The adventure took about seven years and was partially sponsored by the Ford Motor Company. She fell in love with her co-driver Walter Wanderwell, who headed the expedition, and the two married in 1925 during the American leg of their expedition. Incredibly, her overland driving expedition included forty-three countries and gave Aloha the title of the first woman to drive around the world.

Around 1955, Land Rover was eager to demonstrate the durability of their indomitable Series I station wagons, so they partnered with Oxford University and Cambridge University to undertake the Far Eastern Expedition. The six expedition members had just graduated from their respective institutions and departed from London's Hyde Park on September 1, 1955, with the end goal of Singapore. The six travelers in their two Land Rovers would journey through France, Monaco, Germany, Austria, Yugoslavia, Greece, Turkey, Syria, Iraq, Iran, Afghanistan, Pakistan, India, Nepal, Burma, Thailand, Malaya, and Singapore. Over six months and 18,000 miles, they had achieved the seemingly impossible, which the world watched in rapt attention as BBC played their *Travellers' Tales*, produced by David Attenborough.

↑ **The Far Eastern Expedition** traveled from London to Singapore and into the imagination of every overlander since.

Tom Sheppard and the 1975 Joint Services West-East Sahara Expedition

There are few overland travelers that I respect more than Tom Sheppard. In addition to his distinguished career as a pilot in the Royal Air Force, Tom began a second career as a desert overlander, completing 110,000 miles of expeditions in over fifty-plus years. Tom is also the author of the preeminent *Vehicle-dependent Expedition Guide*, a 620-page tome on the art and practicalities of conducting significant vehicle expeditions. At ninety years old, Tom still rides his BMW adventure motorcycle to the gym every day and continues to inspire generations of wide-eyed adventurers.

In January 1975, squadron leader Tom Sheppard and his Joint Services team departed London across the Westminster Bridge, driving four Land Rover 101 Forward Controls. After shipping to the African continent, they departed Dakar, Senegal, with 1,100 gallons of fuel and 410 gallons of water. Over the subsequent one hundred days, the expedition crossed 7,500 miles of Northern Africa through much of the Sahara. With the excursion happening before the invention of the Global Positioning System (GPS), the route finding required hundreds of navigational stops, often satisfied with a universal sun compass to validate longitude. In support of geography, the team would take over 600 gravitational readings and conduct numerous zoological and geophysical studies.

Overlanders in Support of Science and Geography

Overlanders have supported scientific and geographic expeditions since the early 1900s, providing travel efficiency and payload for carrying personnel and equipment into the field. They are also well-suited to extremely remote conditions and can often support research during their own excursions. For example, in my 2018 crossing of the Greenland Ice Sheet, our Expeditions 7 team supported research on snow depth using highly accurate GPS units while also taking snow samples for later testing throughout the crossing.

THE ROYAL GEOGRAPHICAL SOCIETY

The Royal Geographical Society (RGS) in the UK is one of the best examples of an organization that supports and receives support from overland explorers. RGS was founded in 1830 to advance geographical science, with a list of notable fellows and accomplishments. Members like David Livingstone, Henry Morton Stanley, Robert Falcon Scott, Sir Ernest Shackleton, and Sir Edmund Hillary have all walked the hallowed halls of the

RGS. RGS worked closely with Tom Sheppard on several expeditions and published several works helping overland explorers plan a safe and successful project. RGS also helps budding overland expeditioners with their annual RGS Explore event, where Land Rover Bursary also presents a vehicle and financial stipend for an upcoming RGS-supported expedition.

THE EXPLORERS CLUB

Since 1904, The Explorers Club has been headquartered in New York City and supports scientific expeditions of all disciplines. *The Explorers Journal* is also one of the finest executions of a nonprofit periodical we have encountered. For 120 years, The Explorers Club has supported significant expeditions, including many that included overland vehicles and overlander support. The Explorers Club members include Sir Edmund Hillary, who reached the summit of Everest in 1953; US Navy Lieutenant Don Walsh; and Swiss Engineer Jacques Piccard, who arrived at the bottom of the Mariana Trench. Their Explorers Cubs program helps to support future generations of explorers.

Modern Explorers

Lois Pryce has traveled solo across the length of the Americas and Africa, along with a notable motorcycle journey across Iran.

Thankfully, overlanding continues to expand into new demographics. The grizzled explorer is now sharing the map with young families, solo female travelers, and adventurers of all races, genders, nationalities, incomes, and beliefs. The segment's rapid growth has introduced the joys of overlanding to more travelers. The availability of better information, higher-quality products, and a global community have all helped foster the growing tide of modern explorers.

For example, one of my heroes, Lois Pryce, has crossed the length of the Americas and Africa solo on a small, affordable motorcycle. In later travels, she also overlanded Iran and shared her experiences in the brilliant account *Revolutionary Ride*. It is exciting to see what these new generations of modern explorers will accomplish as they embark on their travels around the globe.

Expeditions 7 and Crossing Continents

With humility and reservation, I include my expeditions in this chapter to add context to my experiences reflected in this book and highlight the realities of twenty-first-century overland expeditions. From 2011 to 2018, Greg Miller and I worked to plan and execute driving the first vehicle on all seven continents. Through that process, we would cross North America, drive to Nordkapp in Europe, cross the Road of Bones in Russia's Far East, the Canning Stock Route of Australia, and the Skeleton Coast of Africa before putting the Land Cruiser VDJ78 on an Ilyushin IL-76 transport plane for Antarctica. While on the frozen continent, we would drive the Land Cruiser and also cross the continent twice in a Toyota Hilux, including two stops at the Amundsen-Scott South Pole Station. The final continent was South America, where we completed the goal by driving to the southernmost city of Ushuaia and becoming the first people in history to drive the same vehicle on all seven continents.

In 2018, the E7 adventures continued with the first south-north crossing of the Greenland Ice Sheet by four-wheel drive. Through Expeditions 7 and my dozens of other long-distance journeys, I have crossed all seven continents. Still, I wanted to drive Africa south to north, crossing from the Southern Hemisphere to the Northern Hemisphere along the eastern side and ending above the Horn of Africa and the gateway to the Red Sea in Djibouti. On March 14, 2024, I completed the journey and became the first person to cross all seven continents by vehicle.

↑ **In 2014,** Greg Miller and the author became the first people in history to take the same 4WD to all seven continents.

A Timeline of the History of Overlanding

Every corner of the globe has been explored by vehicle, including the South and North Poles, and across every continent. From Bertha Benz's first overland journey in 1888 to Julie and Chris Ramsey driving from the North Pole to the South Pole in 2023, history continues to be made and drivers continue to test their mettle around the world.

- **1888:** Bertha Benz completes the first long-distance road trip in an automobile.
- **1903:** Dr. Horatio Jackson is the first person to drive across the United States.
- **1908:** George Schuster becomes the first person to drive around the world.
- **1927:** Aloha Wanderwell becomes the first woman to drive around the world.
- **1946:** Len Beadell begins overland road surveys into the interior of Australia.
- **1958:** Sir Edmund Hillary is the first person to reach the South Pole by vehicle.
- **1972:** Colonel John Blashford-Snell completes the first north-south crossing of the Americas, including the Darién Gap.
- **1975:** Tom Sheppard completes the west-east crossing of the Sahara.
- **1980–1998:** The Camel Trophy events (an off-road vehicle-orientated competition) inspire millions to explore the world by vehicle.
- **1982:** Sir Ranulph Fiennes completes the first land and sea circumnavigation of the planet, from Pole to Pole, using human power, a ship, and Land Rovers.
- **1997:** Turtle Expedition completes the winter crossing of Russia (and circumnavigation).
- **2009:** Vasily Elagin drives to the North Pole (airlifted after reaching the Pole).
- **2014:** Expeditions 7 is the first in history to drive the same vehicle on all seven continents.
- **2023:** Julie and Chris Ramsey complete the first electric vehicle (EV) journey from the 1823 Magnetic North Pole to the South Pole in Antarctica.
- **2024:** Scott Brady completes the first crossing of all seven continents by vehicle.

The Top 10 Overlanding Game Changers

Significant engineering and communication advancements have transformed domestic and international overlanding in the past few decades. These changes have made the process safer, easier, and more connected than ever, facilitating a lower cost of travel and the ability to work remotely in a vehicle from anywhere on the planet. Here are some of the biggest changes in the field of overlanding:

1. FACTORY OVERLAND VEHICLES

The original equipment manufacturers have embraced overlanding and have started to deliver factory-ready 4WDs and adventure motorcycles to travel the world. These new vehicles have larger tires, more robust suspensions, steel bumpers, locking differentials, raised air intakes, and winches. Examples like the Chevrolet Colorado Bison AEV, INEOS Grenadier, Toyota Trailhunter, Jeep Wrangler Rubicon, and Ford F-150 Tremor have all reset the expectation of what is possible from the dealership—all with a warranty. Adventure motorcycles like the Ducati DesertX Rally, BMW GS Adventure, and Triumph Tiger 900 Rally Pro are impressive offerings.

2. STARLINK

SpaceX has transformed remote work as we know it by delivering Starlink—broadband Internet—to nearly every inch of the planet. For the overlander, this can provide additional income through content creation or even permit a "work-from-home" career. Starlink also improves connectivity and safety so travelers can stay in touch with family or facilitate support during illness or breakdown.

3. GARMIN INREACH

The Garmin inReach has been a boon to remote travelers, providing two-way messaging access

↑ **There are more factory overland vehicle options** than ever before, like this GMC Canyon AT4X engineered in partnership with American Expedition Vehicles.

to the Iridium satellite network for 100 percent global coverage. The unit is only a few hundred dollars, and the service is a reasonable $12–$64 per month, depending on the services and number of messages you wish to transmit. These compact communicators provide a layer of safety, security, and connection that was previously never available in this price range.

4. iOVERLANDER

There are many smartphone apps available, but iOverlander has proven to be the most widely adopted, respected, and up-to-date app for vehicle-based travelers. While it has limited mapping capabilities, the offline database of campsites, accommodations, fuel, repair shops, and border crossing information is unparalleled. Travelers can also provide their own updates and new locations to help spread the impact over more points of interest.

5. SMARTPHONES

Since the first iPhone, smartphones have changed personal device use forever. Nearly every traveler has a computer in their pocket with accurate GPS positioning, detailed mapping, translation, currency conversion, research, email, and even high-quality cameras. These devices allow the overlander to solve problems quickly and accurately with the assistance of online searches, calls, texts, Short Message Service (SMS), Multimedia Messaging Service (MMS), WhatsApp, and other tools. You can even use them as a level to make sure the camper is positioned properly for sleeping.

6. ALL-WHEEL DRIVE VANS

The availability of all-wheel drive (AWD) vans has changed the overlanding landscape forever, for better or for worse. They are easy to drive, reasonably capable, and supremely comfortable boxes on wheels available to a wide audience. They can be configured or modified to the owner's delight and, with sufficient modification, can be made capable of driving moderately challenging backcountry roads. An additional advantage is that these platforms are available globally and can be repaired and serviced almost anywhere. For example, a Mercedes-Benz Sprinter AWD can be serviced or repaired at Mercedes dealerships in nearly every country.

7. SMALL, AFFORDABLE CAMPERS

One of the challenges of using a small, capable 4WD truck like the Toyota Tacoma or Hilux is the available payload. As a result, campers like the AT Overland Equipment Habitat or the Go Fast Camper (GFC) with a hardtop lifting roof and tent sides have exploded in popularity. These campers can be purchased for under $10,000 and weigh less than 500 pounds. Campers like these are excellent for three-season use and for maintaining the off-highway capability of lighter-duty trucks.

8. FACEBOOK GROUPS AND FORUMS

Within the last twenty years, the availability of online forums and Facebook groups has completely changed the overland planning process. It is now possible to quickly search for and ask questions to a large group of active travelers. These communities can provide immediate assistance and support for travelers struggling with bureaucracy, route guidance, or mechanical failures in a particular country. This development has even extended to WhatsApp groups for travelers actively moving together through the region.

9. LITHIUM BATTERIES

All this new technology requires power to keep running, with Starlink consuming up to 10 amps per hour. The development and improvement of lithium batteries have brought more capacity and less weight and space for the overland camper. Lithium power allows the traveler to allocate less of their payload to the house battery systems, even allowing for 12-volt air conditioning, induction cooking, and more.

10. E-VISAS

Within the last five years, the availability of electronic visas has significantly improved the international overland experience. The online application and approval process makes it possible to apply for the visa from anywhere and receive it for download in your email or even by adding it to your Apple wallet. Paper visas require going to an embassy or consulate in person or sending the passport to a visa service and waiting days or weeks for it to return. E-visa adoption is spreading quickly, with many African countries now promoting their use.

Greenland, by Way of the Wolf

This story relates a moment during my involvement with the historic south-north crossing of the Greenland Ice Sheet with Expeditions 7.

I clipped the 10-millimeter static line to my harness, the carabiners and ice screws clanking as I moved in my seat, the other end of the rope secured to a massive plate on the floorboard of the Toyota Hilux. The action felt like a duty, a promise I had made to those I love back home, a token to alleviate their fear. Sure, there were crevasses on this glacier, but what were the chances? I grabbed the door handle and opened it to swirling snow and biting cold, my feet descending to the surface of ice—but the purchase did not come, my left leg punching through the snow bridge, gravity unchecked by the illusion of safety. My right foot was just at the lip of the crevasse, but it held and arrested my descent. I was lucky, this one was no wider than my leg, and I felt grateful for that leash and for promises. Looking at Emil, I yelled, "I just fell knee-deep into one." His reply, with typical Icelandic brevity, was "Scott, we are in a minefield."

Steadying myself, I looked into the hole my boot had opened, and all that showed was darkness. I pulled on the Prusik knot, slowly moving to the side of the vehicle to examine the terrain ahead. It was a labyrinth, a sea of frozen valleys and cliffs, the hollows filled with snow and the ridges glistening with azure ice. As the scout vehicle, Emil and I had already spent several hours attempting to discover a weakness in the maze, but it had grown dark, the shapes playing tricks in the light of our headlights and headlamps. Small obstacles seemed massive, while real challenges appeared benign. We needed to see; we needed sunlight to gauge distance and scale.

Over the previous weeks, the Expeditions 7 team had struggled against the elements, fuel logistics, and even the specter of failing entirely. Despite my optimism, my body was slowly fading from a lack of sleep, constant cold, and limited calories. While photographing the aurora borealis, I had a lapse of judgment and spent dangerous minutes with only a glove liner on my hands. My error only became evident when the fingers on my left hand stopped moving—entirely. Through a process of slow rewarming most of the movement returned, but my middle finger remains numb even as I type this years later.

We had made history by crossing the Greenland Ice Sheet from south to north, but would I make a fatal mistake in the final moments even as land was visible in the distance? My legs trembled as I looked into the abyss where I had just plunged. Steadying myself, I reverted back to the things I knew, starting with a deep breath, the cold air entering my lungs as I drew in one long inhale after another. Soon, clarity came back to my mind and the world around me. I studied the glacial ice around the vehicle and could see a deep blue ridge extending to my right. With a smile at Emil, I closed the Hilux door and stepped forward, my crampon striking home on a secure surface, each step more settled than the last. Onward.

←
Just when the Expeditions 7 crossing of Greenland seemed in our grasp, we encountered deep snow and an even deeper crevasse.

CHAPTER 3

JUST GO! YOUR FIRST OVERLAND JOURNEY

Reading about historic expeditions and following travelers on social media will certainly get your imagination going for your first overland journey. However, the problem is these stories can also give you the impression that an expensive 4WD filled with the newest gear is necessary for you to explore the world. As you've seen in prior chapters, significant adventures have been accomplished with only simple vehicles and a rucksack of supplies. This chapter will discuss the basic considerations of planning your first overland journey, with the impetus to "just go" locally while using what you already have.

Think about Why You Want to Go

My advice for your first journey will not start with what kind of roof tent to buy but rather with the softer side of planning—a conversation. You first need to ask yourself, "Why do I want to overland?" and then pose the same question to each of your travel companions. All too often, one person is an enthusiastic explorer, ready to take on the jungles of Borneo, but is everyone else? And if not, will the relationship survive such a foray? Having a conversation with your companions gives everyone some agency in the process, and you might be surprised with the ideas and compromises that come through that process. You may find that one person enjoys rock climbing while another enjoys rock hunting. It may also be that your partner enjoys the technical aspects of driving. Having everyone sit down in the comforts of home and decide *before you go* leads to a great opportunity for having fun and the possibility of future trips. Here are some example questions to ask travel partners (and even yourself) to help fuel conversation:

- What are your favorite foods on the road?
- Do you love deserts, mountains, or water?
- Are you more interested in navigation, cooking, mechanics, or driving?
- Would you rather see animals or ghost towns?
- What about history do you like most?
- Would you rather be in the vehicle or walking during a challenging section?
- What item from home would you most want to bring along?
- What helps you get a good night's sleep?
- What are you most excited to experience while traveling?
- What do you feel is your best strength as an overland traveler?
- What are you most afraid of encountering while traveling?
- Can you speak up if something is worrying you?
- What should our code word be if anyone feels uncomfortable with a situation?
- Should marshmallows be toasted or burnt before making s'mores?

← **There are more factory overland vehicle models** than ever before, with trucks like the GMC Sierra 1500 AT4X providing excellent capability while still being a comfortable daily driver or even towing the boat to the lake.

Plan a Day Trip

Now that you have discussed the needs, interests, and strengths of the family or group, it is time to start dreaming up where to go. For your first journey, it is best to begin in stages, starting with a few hours' drive that might include some light 4WD challenges and a scenic destination. This will familiarize you and the group with route finding, testing the vehicle systems, and evaluating everyone's tolerance for the rough and tumble path. Does the 4WD system engage properly? Are the GPS and smartphone apps working for offline navigation? Do you need more snacks, drinks, or ice in the cooler? A few hours' drive into nature can be a wonderful escape for the new overlander and companions, dipping your toes into the backcountry. Keep it close to home, make it only a few hours, and choose an easier route than the vehicle is rated for (more on trail ratings later).

Planning this first day trip should start with research, learning what routes are nearby and gaining some insights into how difficult the road or trail is; if permits are required; and what

↑ **The overlander is rewarded with views like this,** achieved after a long day on the trail.

government agencies may manage the area. This process usually starts online with a search, typing in something like, "overland routes in Southern Arizona" or "where to overland in Sedona?", which yields thousands of results (as of this writing). This initial scan will help you find a day trip that matches your vehicle and inspires your companions. Writing down a top five list will give you enough options to match your requirements and prompt further planning.

Using the Sedona example, you select Schnebly Hill Road, a US National Forest Scenic Byway that meanders nearly 20 miles of dirt from Oak Creek to Interstate 17, making it a simple day trip from the city of Phoenix. You will want to purchase a guidebook or print the route details from a comprehensive web resource. The map should have sufficient resolution and scale for navigation should your GPS or phone stop working (see Aids for Navigation later in this chapter). The guide

↑ **It is possible to drive on roads like this** in Sedona with a high-clearance crossover vehicle like the Jeep Compass, which is both affordable and compact for driving around a city.

should also reflect the difficulty of the trail so that you know if it aligns with your vehicle's capabilities and driver's skills.

Overland Route Difficulty Guide (0–10)

As overlanders, we typically travel on roads, tracks, and trails. *Roads* are engineered for all vehicles and all-weather travel and are typically paved. *Tracks* are well-traveled and maintained dirt routes that have limited surface engineering, fewer bridges, and are more susceptible to weather closure and damage. *Trails* are only suitable for 4WDs and lightweight adventure motorcycles.

The following overland route rating system is intended as a guide, acknowledging that driver training and skill will be the most significant predictor of success. When you are researching places to go on your first overland journey, it is important to note the difficulty level of the route you are planning on taking. For the first few overland trips, you should consider ratings from 1 to 4, with the higher numbers reserved for more capable 4WDs and motorcycles. Also, while it may

seem that technical trails rated 7 or higher are outside of the scope of overlanding, it is important that you learn and practice those advanced driving and recovery techniques, as road conditions can degrade without warning in remote areas of the world.

Note: While many guidebooks prescribe to the 1–10 scale, some use a 1–5, which can still be used by halving the following reference points and using some judgment in the overlap. It is also important to note that taller vehicles or expedition campers should use extreme caution traveling on anything more advanced than a 3 or 4, as regular maintenance and tree trimming are unlikely. It is the responsibility of the camper traveler to not exceed bridge ratings, as this may cut off entire communities should the span fail under the excess weight.

0 RATING: Paved Road

An all-weather paved road intended for all passenger vehicles and motorcycles.

1 RATING: Engineered, Maintained, and Graded Dirt Road

An improved dirt road that is passable by most standard vehicles and motorcycles, excluding those with low hanging body panels and low-profile tires. Improved dirt roads will have regular maintenance and will be wide enough for two-way traffic. They will also have good signage, proper crown and drainage, and bridges and guardrails.

2 RATING: Graded Dirt Road

A graded dirt road receives regular maintenance and is passable by most 2WD vehicles and motorcycles. However, caution is required, and lower speeds may be necessary, for vehicles with less clearance as the road will be narrower and lack adequate drainage and signage. Small rocks may

be embedded in the surface. There will be sufficient room for passing on most of the road, but some steep grades are possible. All-wheel drive (AWD) may be required in some weather conditions like snow, ice, or heavy rain.

3 RATING: Maintained Track

An AWD or 4WD vehicle is required, along with an upright seating position motorcycle. Steep grades will be present, along with larger rocks of up to 7 inches embedded infrequently in the track. Some loose surfaces and shallow water crossings will be present, requiring proper driving techniques. Sand and dry washes may challenge

available traction, requiring an all-terrain tire with lower air pressure on some vehicles. The track will be regularly maintained but may be narrow with fewer opportunities to pass and signage will be limited. Level 3 is not suggested for standard passenger vehicles and touring motorcycles.

4 RATING: Unimproved Track

An AWD or a 4WD with higher clearance is required for unimproved tracks, with low-range gearing preferred. The motorcycle should be an adventure or dual-sport model with a sump guard. Rutted, crossed-axle terrain is possible on the track, along with loose and steep climbs. Deep sand, mud, ruts, and ledges are also likely, along with loose and embedded rocks up to 8 inches in diameter. Some larger rocks may be present, requiring a spotter on the most challenging portions to prevent body damage on vehicles with

less clearance. Expect water crossings of up to 12 inches. Loose surfaces will be present, often with tight clearance and smaller margin for error. The track will be maintained enough to allow through traffic and to control erosion but is subject to flooding and seasonal closures. AWD crossover vehicles will struggle and may suffer damage due to lack of low gearing and insufficient underbody protection.

5 RATING: 4WD Trail

A high-clearance 4WD with low-range gearing is required for formed trails. Some models of 4WDs may require modification to complete the route. Adventure and dual-sport motorcycles should have larger wheel diameters and crash protection, along with all-terrain tires. The trail will be well-traveled but rough and possibly eroded, with large, loose rocks present and steep climbs requiring good traction and driver skill to negotiate. The trail may have bridges or other improvements to control washouts and allow regular travel for both commercial and recreational purposes. Skid plates and larger diameter tires will be required for ground

clearance and protection. Deeper water and mud crossings are possible, up to 24 inches. Parts of the trail may be entirely in a wash, with deep sand and large rocks present. Good suspension articulation, lower tire pressures, and traction-aiding devices may be required to maintain progress through cross-axle obstacles and over large rocks. Taller all-terrain tires, along with a rear traction device or traction control system, are recommended to limit trail and vehicle damage.

6 RATING: Recreational 4WD Trail

For recreational 4WD trails, a high-clearance vehicle with differential locks or advanced traction control is required. These trails generally require sub-500-pound adventure and dual-sport motorcycles with long-travel suspension and larger wheels with aggressive all-terrain tires. Rocks, ledges, and roots exceeding 12 inches may be present throughout the trail, requiring a spotter or modified vehicle to traverse. The trail will often have loose and cambered climbs with deep ruts and washouts, requiring good suspension articulation and tire placement. Lower tire pressure, skid plates, and self-recovery may be necessary, and some obstacles will have little margin for error. Most 4WDs will require a rear locking differential and 33-inch or taller tires with strong sidewalls and a full-sized spare.

7 RATING: Technical 4WD Trail

A high-clearance vehicle with large-diameter tires and at least one differential lock is required for technical trails. Few stock 4WDs are suitable for these conditions. Only the lightest (sub 450

pounds) and most trail-worthy adventure motorcycles are appropriate, with a 21-inch front and 18-inch rear wheel, crash protection, appropriate tires, and advanced rider skills. The trail will likely traverse a river or wash bottom with large rocks and boulders present. Deep mud is possible, requiring aggressive tires and higher speeds. Water crossings may be deeper than 30 inches. Heavily rutted and cross-axle terrain will be present, with large ledges and steep climbs. Body protection will be required to prevent damage, with good skid plates and strong (or modified) steering components necessary. Advanced self-recovery and driving skills are often required. Thirty-five-inch tires and front/rear locking differentials are recommended, with 37-inch tires for larger vehicles.

8 RATING: Extreme 4WD Trail

Modified vehicles are required for extreme trails unless the driver and spotters have advanced skills. Only light (less than 400 pounds) dual-sport motorcycles with experienced riders should attempt these trails. This type of route typically includes rock crawling, with large boulders and ledges present, requiring winching for shorter wheelbase vehicles. Body and drivetrain damage is possible, and cambered terrain may cause rollovers. Water crossings may be hood height, and mud will be deep and heavily rutted. Roll cages or a full metal roof are required, along with spare parts and a working knowledge of field repairs. Extreme trails are rarely encountered during overland travel and are typically considered for sport and the joy of overcoming the challenge itself.

9 AND 10 RATINGS: No Trail or Competitive Rock Crawling

Routes rated a 9 or a 10 are outside the scope of most overland travelers, except for high-latitude polar travel or specialized expedition conditions.

The First Overnight

↑ **The first overnight** can be close to home and with a few friends along to help set up camp. This campsite is just a few hours from the city of Johannesburg in South Africa.

With the day trip out of the way, an overnight adventure is in order. As a piece of advice, you should hope for the best and plan for the worst. Take the vehicle you already own (or rent a 4WD from a local rental agency) and pack it with the camping gear you already have. If you don't own any, consider borrowing the basics from family or friends or renting from a local outdoor store to determine what you like and don't like. A few people can easily sleep in the back of most SUVs and pickups, with extra blankets for a pad and pillows and sheets from your own bed. A simple butane stove can be purchased for less than $20 and utensils and pans can be absconded from the kitchen.

There is some serious fun in using what you already own and making it work, then beg, borrow, or rent the rest if necessary. The goal here is to do it cheaply and find what works and what doesn't, and then slowly make quality purchases once you determine what suits you. Keeping that first overnight trip *really* close to home makes it possible to break camp and head back to civilization if the air mattress goes flat, someone forgets their medications, or dad burns the chicken.

Planning Your Overland Journey

After a few overnights and trail drives, your team will understand what they like and don't like, what gear is becoming essential, and what can be left in the garage. With good communication, these discussions can take place at the end of each outing to help build a framework for what a successful overland trip looks like for you and your team. The next step is to plan your first overland journey, which will probably take place over a long weekend and within a half-day's drive from home base. The goal is to drive to an established and popular overland route to ensure there are good community resources available to ask questions and a greater likelihood that other travelers will also be on the route should you need help.

Here are a few recommended regional overland routes:

- **Southwest:** Death Valley National Park
- **Northwest:** The Steens Mountains and Alvord Desert
- **Central:** The Alpine Loop
- **South Central:** Big Bend National Park
- **East:** Mid-Atlantic Backcountry Discovery Route
- **Northeast:** Northeast Backcountry Discovery Route

This stage of the planning process is also a great opportunity to engage with the local overland community about places to visit, suggested routes, and even the right equipment to bring along. Connecting with local overlanders will provide a point of contact that may serve as an emergency contact. For overland journeys, it is important to share your itinerary and expected return date with a trusted source and friends or family. This way, someone can report your absence to the authorities should you become lost or stranded.

↑ **Planning can be kept simple** with a ground tent and some basic cooking supplies.

The Basic Overland Gear Everyone Should Have

← **A well-organized vehicle** will always pay dividends in the backcountry with less stress and more time to watch the sunset.

The following critical ABCs and essentials form the foundation of the basic equipment needed for overland travel. These useful tools are just as appropriate for an overnight campout as they are for an around-the-world sabbatical, and many overlanders keep these items with their vehicle despite how long the trip is. This checklist forms the baseline from which to add more advanced systems, camping equipment, and cooking gear. More detailed gear lists will be covered in Chapters 8 and 10.

I am covering these items early in this book because of my own experiences, having been stranded, broken down, or lost while traveling. There were times I got in a rush and left without going through the list or told myself, "It is only a few hours' trail ride." Despite my numerous failings, I either got lucky or a kind passerby came to my aid, but the lessons finally stuck and now I go through this list every time, no matter the trip, country, or vehicle.

The basic overland gear you should always carry is:

The Critical ABCs

1. **A**ids for Navigation
2. **B**asic Emergency Supplies
3. **C**ommunication in Remote Areas

For the ABCs, you should focus on equipment that should be taken as responsible backcountry travelers. These items allow you to avoid getting lost (or traveling on private property), sustain life in an emergency, and call for help when you are outside cell coverage.

AIDS FOR NAVIGATION

Most problems occur from a cascade of events, often after a wrong turn or traveling down a route that exceeds the vehicle's or driver's capabilities. By having a primary, secondary, and contingent

↑ **A quality GPS** will form the foundation for effective overland navigation.

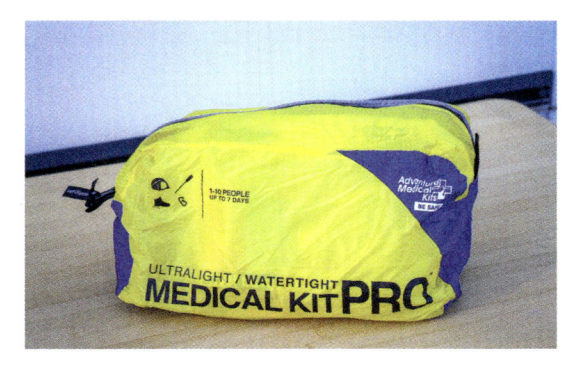

↑ **A small medical kit** will be useful in day-to-day travel as well as more significant emergencies.

navigation method, you can reduce the chances of ending up in the wrong place and increase the likelihood of returning to civilization.

A typical primary navigation method is a reliable and easy-to-read GPS unit with detailed base maps of local trails and topography. The GPS should be supported by a secondary application on a smartphone or GPS-enabled tablet that provides multiple map layers along with information on trail difficulty and points of interest (examples include onX, iOverlander, and Gaia). All modern smartphones include a built-in GPS chip that provides accurate location services to the applications. The third form of navigation should consist of a set of paper maps, guidebooks, and a compass. While traveling, take breaks to record your location on the paper maps in case the devices stop working. (You'll find more on navigation in Chapter 7.)

BASIC EMERGENCY SUPPLIES

For basic emergency supplies, it is important to have a small bag of medical and survival equipment easily accessible to the driver (this is often known as a ditch bag). In addition to first aid supplies, backup medications, and sunscreen, the bag should include a form of shelter, insulation (which can even be a down jacket), and a method for making fire to provide warmth and signaling. This is also where you should store your remote communication device(s) and practical items like a headlamp, water, hard candy, and even a backup GPS. (I also include a backup driver's license,

credit card, and a bit of cash for my bag.) It is easy to dismiss a kit like this, but a fire, one of the most common causes of vehicle loss, will give you only a few minutes to grab these essential items before the car is engulfed in flames. These items make sense in the vehicle, so why not concentrate them in one easy-to-access ditch bag? In addition to the ditch bag, it is important that the vehicle is fitted with a fire extinguisher, emergency triangles, and a safety vest. These items are often a requirement in many countries. (See Chapter 5 for more information on emergency preparations.)

COMMUNICATION IN REMOTE AREAS

There have never been more options to communicate in remote areas. Even the newer iPhones have a built-in satellite emergency SOS feature that

↑ **A robust satellite communicator** like the Iridium GO! exec will provide quality voice and data connections anywhere on the planet.

works in many countries, including Australia, Austria, Belgium, Canada, France, Germany, Ireland, Italy, Luxembourg, the Netherlands, New Zealand, Portugal, Spain, Switzerland, the UK, and the US.

For emergency communications, it is worth having primary, secondary, and contingent means of calling for help. The primary may be a cell phone connection (with emergency SOS available), followed by an Iridium-network-enabled two-way messenger (like a Garmin inReach or Iridium GO! exec) or Starlink as a secondary communicator. Contingency communications can be an amateur radio (HAM), a personal locator beacon (PLB), and various long-distance analog methods like smoke or a signaling mirror. (You can find more information on communications in Chapter 6.)

Other Overlanding Essentials

In addition to the critical ABCs, you'll also need the following items. These will form the basis for your overland equipment, ensuring that the essentials are covered without breaking the bank or adding too much payload to the vehicle. Once you have these items purchased, rented, or borrowed,

↑ **The essentials for a local trip** are the same that are needed for an international sojourn, remembering that less is always more.

take a few day trips and see what else you really need. It is surprising how little is actually needed to travel around the world, and the more stuff you bring, the more that stuff can own you.

1. Tools and basic spare parts like filters, belts, hoses, and known failure points.
2. Self-recovery equipment, including gross vehicle weight rating (GVWR) recovery points.
3. Quality tires and a full-sized spare. (Additionally, tire repair and inflation equipment.)
4. Loading and lashing points with proper straps.
5. Minimalist camping gear.

TOOLS AND BASIC SPARES

Once the critical items are addressed, it is important to assemble these essentials to help solve problems and be safer and more comfortable in the field. This starts with repairing the vehicle and supporting equipment using tools and basic spares. The best way to determine the tools you'll need to bring is to ask other owners of the same make and model vehicle what items they pack. In addition to a basic mechanic's tool roll, there will also be bolt sizes and specialty items unique to the model you drive. It's a good idea to try using your vehicle tool roll while performing upgrades and service at home to check the kit for suitability before you travel.

There are also some common service and repair items worth bringing along, like fuses, filters,

↑ **Quality tools** help you better solve problems or provide the equipment to someone else who can.

belts, hoses, and fluids. How much you bring will depend on your experience and how new or reliable the travel vehicle is. But even if you have no mechanical experience, these items are helpful, as a good Samaritan passing by might know how to fix it if you have the supplies.

SELF-RECOVERY EQUIPMENT

↑ **Traction boards** are an easy addition for self-recovery and can be moved from vehicle to vehicle.

Unfortunately, getting stuck can happen to anyone, so it is valuable to have self-recovery equipment to save the day. You should have:

- Shovel
- Gloves
- Traction boards
- Recovery kit
- Possibly a vehicle-mounted winch

The recovery kit for your first overland journey can be simple, so start with the basics and pack a pair of leather gloves, a spade shovel, and a recovery strap with shackles. Before leaving home, ensure that proper recovery points are available on both ends of your vehicle. This may require researching the model or even buying a screw-in recovery eyelet or transit cluster, which includes specialty hooks for connecting to vehicles without recovery points. Having rated recovery points helps to ensure you have a safe attachment point for extraction.

QUALITY TIRES

The one component of the vehicle that is always in contact with the terrain is the tires, so a good set of all-terrain tires is considered an overlanding essential. These can be the stock tires on the car, but they should have sufficient tread life and traction to support backcountry use. It is also important to ensure you have a full-sized spare that matches the diameter of the other tires on the vehicle. An all-terrain tire with a heavy-duty construction will help reduce punctures and improve performance. Upgrading the tires on an overland vehicle to light truck (LT) all-terrain tires is not critical, but it is certainly recommended. In addition to quality tires, the automobile or motorcycle should have a tire gauge and compressor, along with a tire repair kit to fix punctures.

LOADING AND LASHING POINTS AND STRAPS

All support equipment and camping gear must be loaded properly into the vehicle and lashed securely. Most modern 4WDs have lashing points in the load area, which should be used to secure all items in the passenger compartment. This helps prevent the load from shifting unexpectedly or causing injury to the passengers in the unlikely event of an accident or a rollover. Proper straps should be used with a cinching cam or mechanism, and bungee cords are not recommended for anything but soft and lightweight goods.

CAMPING GEAR

Even if camping is not on the agenda, bringing basic equipment is a good idea. This allows for the serendipity of staying at an idyllic beach on a whim or being able to sleep properly if the vehicle becomes disabled. It is better to have the camping equipment available and not need it than to spend a bitter cold night curled up in the driver's seat. While these critical items and essentials provide the basics, complete packing lists for long-term camping and cooking will be covered in later chapters.

↑ **An all-terrain tire** with a heavy-duty sidewall will always be a worthwhile upgrade.

↑ **Nothing beats sleeping under the stars** on a cool desert night.

Dancing with the Devil

My first overland journey was a laughable affair. I put in months of preparations, weeks of packing, and countless sleepless nights getting ready to cross El Camino del Diablo, the Road of the Devil, a 140-plus mile backcountry sojourn along the border of Arizona and Sonora, Mexico. At the time, I felt as if I had been overlanding for years, but I was just an enthusiastic newbie with a serious case of impostor syndrome.

Most of my trips to that point were 4WD trails or car camping weekends. For this endeavor, I would be crossing uncharted territory. At places, the trail runs within a few meters of the border wall and the only cell coverage is from Telcel, complete with international roaming charges. There had been stories of drug runners, smugglers, and even armed conflict with the US Border Patrol in the region. It was 2002, and I had never done anything like this before. I had a knot of anticipation in my stomach, but I also knew I must go.

Over several days, our ragtag group of travelers bounced and meandered our way across the Mojave and Sonoran desert ecosystem, including a camp at the fabled Tinajas Altas tanks. This remote natural cistern was the only water for 25 miles in any direction. A young couple was with us, their Nissan barely loaded with backpacking gear. Mark and Brooke Stephens were having an easy time of the whole endeavor and seemed to lack a care in the world. They rock climbed and laughed; their camp was set up in minutes, while I toiled for hours with the tent trailer, shower, privy, kitchen, and gear. It became quickly apparent that they were doing it right, and I was doing it horribly, laughably wrong.

The trip continued and was a proper adventure, but I felt oppressed by all the stuff I had brought along and the things that didn't work or broke. Soon, I was bumbling more than I was bouncing or even meandering. All the junk I brought along had started to rule me, but I was too frustrated to notice and too prideful to change it. Eventually, we made it to the other end of the trail, and I had enough fuel in cans to drive all the way home. I hadn't touched a third of the water I brought along, and I likely annoyed my partner to no end as well. Heck, I had annoyed myself to no end. In my effort to be super "overlandy," I had completely jumped the shark. In all the buying and grasping, I missed the point of going in the first place.

After that first trip, the adventures became more extreme, but it easily took me a decade to embrace a modicum of minimalism. In 2022, I crossed El Camino del Diablo for the fourth time, but I had finally evolved (some), driving a stock GMC Canyon diesel with all my camping gear fitting in the back seat, and a single can of diesel lashed in the bed (I didn't need it). I bounced and meandered, rock climbed and laughed my way for the entire 140 miles—Mark and Brooke would be proud.

←
Before I started overlanding, I was mostly *overloading*, my poor Isuzu Trooper loaded well past its payload.

PART 2

The Fundamentals of Overland Travel

Overlanding benefits from building strong travel skillsets and confidence in driving, vehicle recovery, navigation, mechanical repairs, and medical emergencies. For me, the start of my travels began with too much error and not enough training, so the subject of overland education begins this part of the book.

This part will also cover how to set up your critical ABCs with the right medical, communication, navigation, and survival equipment. You want to plan for the worst even though serious issues are rare.

Next, you'll learn how to assemble your tools and recovery kit for keeping your vehicle running and for getting unstuck. Even if your skills are still developing, having the right equipment will let you work with other travelers and local drivers to solve issues that arise. An essentials packing list is also included to help make sure no important items are left behind.

Finally, you'll discover all about overland camping, including how to pack a kit for preparing hearty meals in nature and choosing the right sleeping accommodations for your vehicle and location.

←

A robust vehicle and comfortable way to camp
is often all that is required to explore the remote landscapes of the world.

CHAPTER 4

4WD, MOTORCYCLE, AND RECOVERY TRAINING

I remember my first performance driving course where the lead instructor spent the first minutes of the class telling all of us that we couldn't *really* drive. How dare he! His verbal lambasting was followed by throwing each of us keys to a Ford Mustang Cobra and pointing in the direction of an open skid pad filled with precisely arranged cones. Hilarity ensued, cones were scattered, and all in attendance proved him right. We had all driven "fast" before taking the course, but not a single student on that track could drive with the control, precision, and smoothness needed to complete the exercise.

The reality is that a significant percentage of overlanders lack the skills required to safely operate their heavy and tall vehicles at speed and in technical terrain on the trail. Since overlanding has so many unique and unrelated skillsets, proper training helps to accelerate the process of gaining experience and knowledge. This starts with having the awareness that everyone, despite their travels, has something to learn. Because of the nature of vehicle-based travel, you should consider starting with basic medical training, followed by driving and riding training, and then recovery training, navigation, mechanics, and possibly even a complete overland training class. This chapter helps you prioritize training and prepares you to be a good student to maximize learning; it also includes some important questions to ask a trainer before selecting a course.

Train for the Journey Ahead

People often overestimate their knowledge, experience, and competence on a subject. For example, Ola Svenson's study published in *Acta Psychologica* found that 93 percent of drivers rated themselves as "better than average," which is statistically impossible and dangerously overconfident. Unless the driver can demonstrate effectiveness through third-party assessment or competitive ranking (like racing), it is important to approach the process of skills development with humility and enthusiasm. If you want to *know* that you are a good driver, start by getting training.

Operating an adventure motorcycle and 4WD is the same as high-speed precision driving. It requires a mastery of input, modulating each driver motion with control and smoothness. Balance, threshold, and effectiveness all come with practice, which results in muscle memory and experience. Experience will directly relate to confidence in the field or when, for example, things go pear-shaped on the Death Road in Bolivia.

While technical four-wheel-drive skills and advanced recovery principles are important, the reality is that most overland miles are spent on paved and dirt roads. Can you recover from a skid? Do you know the difference between understeer and oversteer, and what inputs are required to counteract both? Most trips that are cut short are due to road accidents and rollovers. As a result, performance driving training is the foundation of a safe and competent overland driver.

In my travels around the world, all my close calls with driving have benefited from my commitment to advanced performance driving skills.

↑ **Premium adventure motorcycle training** like the D.A.R.T. School gives new riders the confidence to explore on two wheels.

Those skills have helped me avoid more accidents than I can count while (thankfully) keeping the vehicles shiny side up. If I could only choose one training course to recommend (even though they are all valuable), it would be a three- or four-day rally driving school. For example, the Vittorio Caneva Rally School in Italy, the Team O'Neil Rally School on the US East Coast, or the Dirt-Fish Rally School on the US West Coast are all excellent choices. These programs will provide a foundation for accident avoidance while traveling. These classes will also teach skills that you will use daily, like threshold braking, throttle modulation, steering precision, and much more. It might also be some of the most fun you will have on four wheels.

The motorcycle equivalent of these classes are flat track courses, like the one MotoGP Champion Valentino Rossi operates in Italy called the VR46 Riders Academy or the US-based Moto Anatomy Slide School. Feeling comfortable when a motor-cycle is skidding or sliding is a critical component of safe overland riding. It is common for global

↑ **A rally driving school** will pay dividends while traveling and in your daily commute by practicing the skills necessary to avoid accidents and correct for a skid.

motorcycle travelers to encounter mud or oil on the road or hundreds of miles of loose gravel, even combined with high wind (for example, on Route 40 in Argentina). Advanced dirt riding schools or flat track courses give you the tools to stay upright when things go sideways.

How to Prepare Yourself for Training

Overland training courses can be expensive and highly condensed, so a bit of preparation goes a long way. This starts by creating the mindset of learning and acknowledging that even the most experienced driver still has something to learn. Prior to the class is also the best time to schedule routine maintenance and do a complete inspec-tion of the vehicle to ensure that it (and all of the modifications) are working properly. In the lead-up to a course you should also make sure you are eating healthy, exercising, and getting good sleep—all those actions will help ensure the best possible knowledge transfer.

HAVE A BEGINNER'S MINDSET

Your job is to have a student's mindset, as everyone still has something to learn. Listen to the instructor and conduct each exercise with deliberate action and focus. Even if the exercise appears beginner or simplistic, it will likely build toward more complex actions. The more humility and open-mindedness you bring to the process, the better your learning will be.

INCREASE YOUR FITNESS LEVEL

As a trainer, I have worked with military and civilian clients, and the differences in advancement are often marked by physical fitness. If you invest hundreds (or thousands) of dollars in driver and recovery training (particularly on a motorcycle), develop a fitness baseline that will help keep fatigue from being a distraction. You will be walking over uneven terrain, operating a vehicle for hours, pulling winch cables, lifting heavy items like a Hi-Lift jack or a motorcycle, and so on. Students who attend with a basic fitness level excel because they have the reserves to maintain focus on the task at hand while also developing the fine motor skills of driver/rider inputs.

KEEP YOUR VEHICLE IN GOOD CONDITION

It is important to arrive at the training course with a well-maintained and thoroughly inspected vehicle. It is surprising how many students will attend a class with an inoperable winch or broken suspension components. Having a motorcycle or 4WD in good repair and with good tires is far more important than buying a set of expensive LED lights. Arriving ready to go helps protect your investment in the training and shows respect to the instructor and your fellow students.

KNOW YOUR EQUIPMENT

Make sure you have a basic tool and recovery kit at the course. Ask your instructor what equipment you need for the course in advance, as they should have a detailed checklist. Did you pack the winch remote? Is your spare tire a matching size, and do you have the correct lug wrench? Avoid overpacking or bringing complex and unusual products to a training session (unless it is a custom course). Keep the 4WD under payload and the motorcycle as light as possible. An overly laden vehicle can make the course more difficult and might limit the exercises you can perform.

HAVE FUN!

You are in this class to learn skills critical to your chosen passion, so it is important to enjoy the

ASK QUESTIONS

Any good training program will be foundational, building on concepts and skills throughout the session. Some intermediate courses also assume a basic understanding of mechanical systems and vehicle operation. It is important to ask your instructor to explain if a concept doesn't make sense or a term is unknown to you. You are there to learn, and other students might be wondering the same question. Questions are also a big help to the instructor, aiding them in crafting the course toward the areas of need in that particular class.

process too. Learning about performance driving or riding a motorcycle through the sand is a blast, and you will leave with lasting friendships and important new skills. Your mindset will determine the benefits of the training. Be positive, listen, and ask questions. It is normal to make mistakes or retry a few things to gain confidence. It is also important to turn off your smartphone, as it can be a major distraction to you, your fellow students, and the trainer.

Selecting a 4WD Trainer

Qualified overland trainers are rare, but there are ways to find and vet them properly before engaging their services. Overland trainers need to have a combination of specific knowledge, academic acumen, and relevant travel experience. While there are many 4WD trainers to choose from, have they had recent exposure to the regions of the world you plan to travel? For example, a trainer without that regional experience may suggest modifications that are regulated in the country you are visiting. An overland trainer's instruction will emphasize risk reduction, road building, terrain assessment, and controlled self-recovery.

Here are some important questions to ask a prospective trainer:

- **What advanced driving or riding experience do you have?** Like higher education, you want the instructor to have driving experience several levels higher than the curriculum. This may include motorsports racing, competitive 4WD events, or well-documented crossings of technical overland routes. You want the BMW instructor who competed successfully in the GS Trophy, not the one with the newly embroidered polo shirt. Use caution in selecting an instructor purely on "years of experience," as the depth,

breadth, and frequency of the skills make the difference, not the years. Just like in higher education, getting a tenth associate's degree does not yield someone a PhD. Find the Doctor of Driving who has just completed a significant expedition through the Darién Gap or recently won a regional Sports Car Club of America RallyCross Championship.

- **Please share your recent continuing education experience.** Technologies and best practices change, so the instructor must attend regular continuing education courses. For example, the International 4WD Trainers Association (I4WDTA) requires its members to receive ongoing training and update their training standards regularly. Continuing education also shows humility as an educator, understanding that there is always something to learn despite the experience gained to date. The more isolated the instructor is from the industry and continuing education, the more likely they are to be siloed in their expertise and ineffective as an educator.
- **Do you have experience instructing on my specific vehicle?** While most riding, four-wheeling, and recovery techniques translate across multiple platforms, it is still important that the instructor has experience with your specific vehicle or is willing to research the unique systems of your model. As motorcycles and 4WDs become more complex, many of the systems are buried in screen menus or require specific operating techniques to engage. With sand driving as an example, some vehicles have a dedicated sand mode. In contrast, other manufacturers call it "off-road" mode, while others even require turning off vehicle stability control to achieve the same results. Work with your instructor to ensure that you both have a good working knowledge of the systems prior to the training.
- **Do you have experience in the region of the world I am traveling?** For overland training, regional experience is more important than most people think. It will help inform the instructor on recommended modifications, tools, spares, and regulations. For example, spare alternators are recommended in Botswana due to the depth and length of water crossings in the Okavango Delta. In Australia, there are regula-

tions and random police inspections that check if the vehicle is over payload, and some Australian states have strict rules on suspension lifts. While this regional knowledge is not a requirement for good training, why not find an instructor who can help you through all aspects of the process? If the instructor has yet to gain specific regional experience, make sure they have recent and relevant experience in the type of environments you are traveling, like jungle, glaciers, or dunes.

- **Does your course provide vehicle inspection and repair instruction?** Often absent from traditional 4WD instruction is an overview of vehicle inspection principles and a review of daily and weekly check sheets (see Chapter 8 for a working example). Even if your mechanical experience is limited, it is important to gain familiarity with checking fluid levels and inspecting systems for what is "not normal." An experienced instructor can answer questions and help you identify components that need to be checked. This type of inspection is hands-on learning, so it is best done in person and on your specific vehicle.
- In addition to vehicle inspection, **an overland instructor will train you** in how to change a tire, repair a tire, and conduct basic field repairs. They will know which systems are most likely to fail (like tires) and show the steps necessary to fix the problem. You will want to leave the training having operated the vehicle jack, removed a tire/wheel, and accessed the spare. It is also common for an instructor to bring along a training tire that can be punctured and repaired multiple times to learn the process of plugging and patching. There are also training courses that focus only on inspection and repair, like the D.A.R.T. School Shop Days program.
- **Can you provide a copy of your insurance and permits?** Many instructors operate without land use permits or sufficient insurance, so it is a good idea to confirm those ahead of time. The US Forest Service and other agencies require use permits for commercial training, and not having them can result in expensive tickets for the students and a disruption of the training session. Also, is there insurance coverage if another student accidentally slides their vehicle into yours?

↑ **Even the author gets stuck** . . . often. It is all part of the fun and helps keep the skills fresh.

Photo by Joseph Fleming

Preparing Mentally for Getting Stuck

Now that you have received driving, riding, or recovery training, it is important to acknowledge that getting stuck is all part of the adventure, and planning mentally for its eventuality is important. Acknowledging that getting stuck will most likely happen and may even occur many times on a long journey helps shift the incident from frustration to opportunity. Getting stuck can feel embarrassing, but everyone (yes, everyone) who pushes the limits of exploration eventually has it happen to them. In my journeys, I have been "momentarily unable to make forward progress" more times than I can count. Ultimately, I cherished the memories and opportunities to keep my skills sharp. The old saying goes, "If you haven't been stuck, you haven't really been anywhere."

Each stuck or breakdown is a chance to work on overcoming the challenges, often collaborat-

ing with your companions and other travelers to resolve the issue. It can feel stressful in the moment, but these mishaps are rarely an emergency, so take a few minutes and make a cup of tea or coffee and assess the situation. Think about the training you received, and the steps required for a safe and effective recovery. What is the safest and simplest solution to the problem? Look under the vehicle to see if a log has wedged against the cross member or take a few minutes to air down the tires for more flotation. This is called *the stuck assessment*, which applies as much to a breakdown as it does to being frame-deep in mud. Stopping for a moment helps to limit overreaction, while taking a few minutes (or hours) to look and assess aids in good decision-making. Part of the training investment is to keep those skills sharp, so go out and get stuck!

Wilderness Medical and Survival Training

Alongside training for performance driving, trail driving, and recovery skills, it is important to consider emergency preparedness. While traveling in remote areas, wilderness medical and survival training may become more important than any driving or riding skillset. Once you leave proximity to a city, the standard and availability of care often diminishes, requiring you and your companions to render aid in an emergency. As with driver training, education and experience serve you in emergencies far more than the gear you bring. Have you been trained in emergency communications and how to articulate the symptoms to a medical professional? Do you know how to use the contents of the first aid kit?

These skills can be built in stages, starting with basic first aid and CPR certification, which can be taken through most Red Cross chapters. They offer a classroom-based CPR/AED/First Aid course that can be completed in a few hours. The next step is a Wilderness First Aid (WFA) course, which is the level most often recommended for overland travelers. It is a sixteen-hour class conducted in the field to take advantage of basic equipment and natural materials to assess and stabilize medical scenarios in the backcountry. It teaches primary and secondary assessment in addition to treating allergies, heat- and cold-related emergencies, burns, wounds, and other injuries.

WILDERNESS FIRST RESPONDER (WFR) TRAINING

Advanced backcountry medical training includes the Wilderness First Responder (WFR) course, which is an intensive eighty-hour curriculum that builds on the foundations of WFA but includes more complex scenarios and hands-on skills necessary for longer-term patient care and transportation. This training is more common for overland guides or teams undertaking remote expeditions, but it is useful for anyone with the interest and aptitude. Some explorers will even complement their WFR with a Wilderness Emergency Medical Technician (WEMT) license and other advanced care certifications. If deciding between the WFR and WEMT levels, the WFR provides more flexibility, as it is not bound by the limited acts allowed by state regulations, which can reduce the options for care provided to a patient. WEMT is more commonly pursued as a requirement for employment, for example for ski patrol. Meanwhile, a WFR can give a larger scope of care as provided in the training or as approved by a physician (often over satellite communication), including many pharmaceuticals, physical interventions, and procedures.

BUSHCRAFT

Beyond medical emergencies, basic survival and bushcraft training are worth considering. These can help sustain travelers encountering severe weather or if they are separated from their vehicle in the backcountry. Bushcraft training is a fascinating pursuit that teaches the traveler to understand the natural world better and how best to thrive in it. Both survival and bushcraft knowledge can start with books like *Bushcraft 101* or similar, which will help create a foundation of understanding around the use of wild foods and natural materials. Survival skills can extend beyond bushcraft, including using the contents and components of the vehicle. Think of bushcraft as thriving in the backcountry with limited supplies. In contrast, survival training is about enduring extreme scenarios in an emergency (which can include populated areas during a coup or a natural disaster). Both are valuable skills for the overland traveler.

My Fourteen-Hour Mistake

We were four days into the Canning Stock Route, the longest unsupported overland road on the planet. Our Expeditions 7 team attempted the 1,800-kilometer crossing in late summer, and ours were the first tracks of the season through the 1,000-plus dunes that bisect Western Australia's Great Sandy Desert.

The track weaved through thick groves of brush and scrubby trees, occasionally interrupted by higher sand areas and short water sections. While navigating a curve between two trees, I entered what I thought would be another short water crossing, but it ended up being a rather lengthy seasonal lake. Though it was only knee-deep, I'd passed the point of return and was now fully committed. Progress was slow as we churned along, making every effort to stay on course. Luck ran out when I zigged around a tree instead of zagged. The heavy Land Cruiser listed to the left and stopped. I engaged both locking differentials and slid the transmission into reverse. Hoping the tires would bite, I slowly modulated the clutch just off stall to apply minimum torque to the wheels. Nothing.

Knowing better than to spin the wheels and bury the 3.5-ton vehicle, we deployed a winch line to a forward tree, but the ground was too soft and the Troopy sank farther. To compound matters, the second Cruiser had slipped slightly off-line and bogged. Fortunately, our trusty Sherpa II, the third vehicle, had not entered the water and was waiting on hard ground about 150 meters back.

The plan was to use the second Troopy to recover the first, which went well until the winch line snapped. We repaired the line and repeated the process until the motor failed—winch number two out of the fight. Unable to reach the Sherpa, there was only one solution: shovels, manpower, and a small mountain of traction boards. The digging began, and down went the tracks, twelve in total. Slowly, the Land Cruiser started to inch rearward one track length at a time. Once I was back on the solid surface (though still in several feet of water and

far from dry land), attention shifted to the second Land Cruiser, which we called Fernweh. Out came every piece of recovery gear in our kit. We were glad to be well stocked with extensions, tree straps, and replacement lines, and by some miracle, they stretched back to the Sherpa's winch hook. It never faltered and dragged Fernweh rearward through the frame-deep mud and back to terra firma. The process took over two hours and required nearly every piece of recovery equipment we had.

My Land Cruiser (known as Mateship) was next. I began slowly backing toward the section of churned-up soup from the first recovery while the team sloshed through the bug-infested muck, illuminating the path of least resistance with their headlamps. When we reached the bog, the crew built a Roman road of traction boards. The guys found a rhythm and were soon as efficient as an Indy pit crew. Within 20 minutes, we'd backed out of the bog without ever receiving the business end of a winch line.

↑ **On Expeditions 7,** we spent most of a day and nearly all of a night stuck in mud and deep water. It was one of the best adventures in my life!

CHAPTER 5

Emergency, Medical, and Survival Equipment

The unknowns of overland travel can seem risky, but on average, travelers and adventurers outlive their homebound peers. This improved lifespan could be influenced by many factors, but generally, overlanders are more physically active, spend more time outdoors (getting vitamin D), and develop skills that make them less accident-prone and more resilient. Outside of known terrorism zones or regions with particularly dangerous diseases like malaria, Zika, or Ebola, overlanding is no more deadly than the daily commute.

In my discussions with new travelers, most of them fear the unknown. Understanding that travel is not statistically more dangerous helps you identify the real risks associated with overlanding. However, accidents can happen, so this chapter focuses on the basic skills and equipment required to manage emergency scenarios, including vehicle accidents, medical aid, and how to survive being stranded with a breakdown or stuck in inclement weather.

Be Prepared

According to the US Department of State, transportation accidents are the most common reason for loss of life for travelers (over one-third), with vehicle accidents being number one. However, when overlanders are asked what they are most afraid of, it is being murdered by bandits. Fortunately, outside of Honduras and Haiti, the chance of homicide is near zero, particularly if you don't drive at night and completely avoid illegal drug transactions. Preparation for the real (not imagined) risks starts by putting on a seat belt or helmet and slowing down.

With the real risks understood, several important planning steps help reduce the chance of an emergency. Risk mitigation starts at home by scheduling a physical exam (preferably a sports physical) with your doctor to complete a full range of movement assessments, along with a review of your skin, ears, eyes, mouth, heart, lungs, abdomen, feet, and nervous system. Additional procedures include a complete blood count, EKG, stress test, urinalysis, and lipid panel. It is also the time to ensure that you have the vaccinations required for the countries you plan to visit, which typically includes a yellow fever card. Your doctor may recommend other vaccinations like hepatitis, typhoid, cholera, and the like, but make sure you know which ones the local officials will check for your vaccination record.

Before departure, it is also important to ensure that you have enough prescription medications and that you have checked that the drugs are legal in the country you are visiting. (That physical exam you scheduled with your doctor would be a great time to request specific travel prescriptions.) It is surprising how many medicines prescribed in the United States (like sleep aids or some pain medications) are not legal in other parts of the world. Transportation restrictions can also apply to over-the-counter medications like Sudafed. Keep the medicines in their original containers and bring a printed copy of the prescription. It is often possible to get replacement medications in other countries with the original doctor's prescription document.

The final step before departure is to consider remote medical, evacuation, and possibly kidnapping and ransom (K&R) insurance. Does your health insurance cover you while traveling abroad? If you have a medical emergency while traveling, do you have the funds or insurance to cover air evacuation to a well-equipped hospital? These items will be covered in detail later in the chapter, but they need to be secured before your departure, and it is critical to research the fine print to ensure that your insurance will protect you when you need it the most.

Emergency Contacts and Coordination

When an emergency occurs, timing and coordination are essential. As an overlander, you should designate a primary point of contact back home that can track your location via a mobile phone app (like Apple's Find My) and a satellite tracker like the Garmin inReach. This person becomes your guardian angel for reporting you missing to government officials. I have a primary point of contact back home, a family member as a backup, and someone to call in the country I am visiting.

As a US citizen, you should also enroll in the Smart Traveler Enrollment Program (STEP) through the consular department at https://step .state.gov. The STEP program informs the consulate of your travel plans in the country you are visiting, which allows the US Department of State to contact you in the case of natural disaster or civil unrest. Other countries have similar programs, so it is important to research ahead of time and add those phone numbers to your contacts.

Assuring Through Insuring

If an emergency happens, you will want insurance to facilitate a quick response and to help protect against significant expenses. Insurance should be considered in the following order of importance:

1. Vehicle insurance
2. International medical insurance and evacuation coverage

Vehicle insurance protects you from financial liability in the event of an accident. Third-party liability insurance is required in most countries, and it is common to be asked for proof of insurance during a traffic stop. You should do your research before traveling to secure vehicle insurance, as it may be purchased online, through a broker, or even at the border crossing.

The next most important policy is international medical insurance and evacuation coverage. These protections are typically purchased together and are often the most confusing or subject to borderline scams. For example, we have seen claims denied because the person had an accident on an unpaved road, which was the major road in that part of Namibia! The coverage only insured if the accident occurred on a paved road. Some countries even require proof of travel medical insurance when you arrive at the border, so do your research ahead of time. The challenge is finding a policy that covers preexisting conditions and a large enough coverage limit to pay for significant injuries. The good policies are expensive, with only Ripcord, World Nomads Travel Insurance, and Divers Alert Network (DAN) providing acceptable restrictions and reviews.

←
Rollovers are an unfortunate possibility when driving on remote dirt roads. While there were some injuries, the driver and passengers of this accident survived.

Photo by LR Workshop

In remote areas, it may be necessary to administer backcountry care and procedures, which can be supported by a medical professional via a satellite phone or Starlink video conference. Calls like these are often included as part of a 24/7 hotline with the emergency evacuation membership, and critical assistance with assessment, diagnosis, and treatment is provided. Most of these services are called "memberships" due to insurance regulations. A backcountry-trained doctor can assess many medical emergencies quickly, will know which questions to ask, and will make the best of your training and tools with the vehicle. The diagnosis from the hotline will help inform the course of care and determine if evacuation is required.

Building a Medical Kit

The first item on a medical kit list should be training in wilderness first aid, which was covered in detail in Chapter 4. Often you will hear the advice to match your medical kit to your level of training, but that excludes the opportunity of support from telemedicine or the emergency room doctor who just might be riding by on his BMW. Your kit should be comprehensive, according to your budget and available space. Once an appropriate level of instruction is addressed, you should make the decision between a first aid kit and a medical kit. *Overland Journal*'s medical editor, Dr. Jon Solberg, summarizes it best:

"The act of rendering first aid involves providing medical care to the victim of sudden illness or injury and attempting to promote recovery or prevent a worsening condition until professional help can be obtained. Thus, a first aid kit is a collection of supplies assembled to address acute problems. However, a first aid kit should not be confused with a medical kit, the latter of which is more comprehensive and often addresses prophylaxis of altitude sickness or malaria, emergency water purification, immunization records, and usually contains spare prescription medications, eyeglasses, and articles of a more personal medical nature. These items are too specialized to be included in a generically fabricated first aid kit; however, a solid first aid kit is the foundation for a solid medical kit."

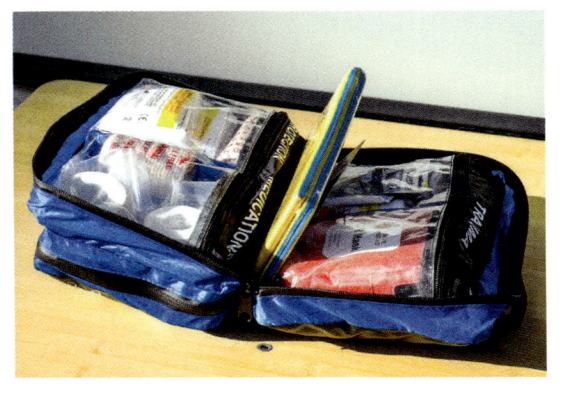

↑ **Comprehensive solutions** like this Adventure Medical Kits Pro Series Guide 1 are designed to support one to twelve people over two-week-long excursions.

↑ **Small medical kits** are best allocated to either ditch bag or motorcycle use.

↑ **Offerings like the Rescue Essentials Motorcycle Operator's Kit** are intentionally minimal yet are tailored to the injuries riders tend to suffer.

Building a medical kit combines first aid contents, pharmaceuticals, trip-specific items, CPR aids, dental aids, and other essentials. The challenge is to bring the important items, but not so many things that it contributes to an overloaded motorcycle or 4WD. Fortunately, there are organizations like the National Outdoor Leadership School (NOLS) that set standards for kit contents or work with first aid companies like Wilderness Medical Systems to sell comprehensive solutions.

NOLS Med Kit 5.0 weighs 25.3 ounces and measures 10 inches × 7.5 inches × 4.5 inches, making it appropriate for 4WDs but a bit bulky on a motorcycle. Consider the NOLS Med Kit 3.0 for motorcycle travel, which weighs 11.2 ounces and measures only 5.5 inches × 7.5 inches × 2.5 inches.

The NOLS Med Kit 5.0 contains:

Wound Care/Burn/Blister

- 4 dressings (gauze, sterile, 4 inches × 4 inches, Pkg./2)
- 4 dressings (gauze, sterile, 2 inches × 2 inches, Pkg./2)
- 3 dressings (non-adherent, sterile, 3 inches × 4 inches)
- 2 bandages (conforming gauze, non-sterile, 3 inches)
- 1 bandage (stockinette tubular, 1 inch × 4 inches)
- 8 bandages (adhesive, fabric, 1 inch × 3 inches)
- 5 bandages (adhesive, fabric, knuckle)
- 1 tape (1 inch × 10 yards)
- 2 cotton tip applicators (Pkg./2)
- 1 syringe (irrigation, 10 cc with 18 gauge removable tip)
- 1 wound closure strip (1 inch × 4 inches, Pkg./10)
- 1 povidone iodine (1 ounce)
- 2 moleskins (pre-cut and shaped, 14 pieces)
- 2 dressings (GlacierGel, rectangle, 2.5 inches × 1 inch)
- 6 antiseptic towelettes
- 4 triple antibiotic ointments ($\frac{1}{32}$ ounce)
- 2 Skin-Tac topical adhesives

Bleeding

- 2 gloves (nitrile (pair), one hand wipe)
- 1 trauma pad (8 inches × 10 inches)
- 1 trauma pad (5 inches × 9 inches)
- 1 dressing (gauze, sterile, 4 inches × 4 inches, Pkg./2)

Fracture/Sprain

- 1 bandage (elastic with Velcro closure, 3 inches)
- 1 bandage (triangular)
- 3 safety pins
- 1 ibuprofen (200 milligrams, Pkg./2)

Medications

- 4 ibuprofen (200 milligrams, Pkg./2)
- 4 acetaminophen (500 milligrams, Pkg./2)
- 4 antihistamine (diphenhydramine, 25 milligrams)
- 4 Diamode (loperamide HCL, 2 milligrams, Pkg. 1)
- 1 aspirin (325 milligrams, Pkg./2)
- 2 After Bite sting and itch relief wipes

Instruments

- 1 CPR breathing barrier
- 1 EMT shears (4 inches)
- 1 splinter picker/tick remover forceps
- 1 duct tape (2 inches × 5 yards)
- 1 pencil
- 1 patient assessment form
- 3 thermometers (disposable)
- 2 plastic vials (flip-top, large)

PHARMACEUTICALS

Only you and your doctor can determine which medications are appropriate for the trip and your experience level, but there are some important ones to discuss with a doctor. Your kit should include antibiotics for wound care, pneumonia, abdominal infection, parasitic infection, allergic reactions, UTIs, fungal infections, tooth infections, and even radiation exposure. A noteworthy example of a common emergency is appendicitis, which can often be treated or managed using high-dose antibiotics until medical care can be accessed.

The more remote the trip, the more medications will be important to consider. For example, an EpiPen can be a critical lifesaving drug for an allergic reaction when help is a long way away. Medical kits can be expensive, so the investment should balance risk, weight, and expense. In our research, companies like Duration Health specialize in supporting overland expeditions by providing a comprehensive kit with medications and prescription copies, a doctor consultation, a field guide, and access to their medical team via email/text. I worked with my local concierge doctor (thank you, Dr. Blum) to fill the required prescriptions for trips like Expeditions 7 and when I crossed the Pacific on a sailboat.

TRIP-SPECIFIC ITEMS

Different regions of the world lend themselves to unique trip-specific items, like mosquito netting and malaria treatment kits. You will also want items that treat hypothermia or heat stroke in cold or hot environments. Other overland routes can be at extreme altitudes, like Umling La, the highest motorable pass in the world at 19,024 feet (5,799 meters), and so you would want to bring acetazolamide to treat acute mountain sickness (AMS).

CPR AIDS

In addition to current CPR training for all team members, there are some other items you may consider. For longer overland trips or where team members are vulnerable to cardiac conditions, it might be worth investigating having an automated external defibrillator (AED). An AED can be particularly useful in electrocution and drowning incidents (unfortunately, both are common for travelers). I have also included a bag valve mask in my kit.

DENTAL AIDS

Unfortunately, you cannot escape the dentist, even while traveling. I have learned this the hard way and suffered the effects of delayed treatments, root canals, and abscesses. The best dental aid is an up-to-date treatment and cleaning schedule before you travel. However, issues can still arise, so it is important to travel with basic dental treatment items like dental wax, loose filling repair (like Dentemp), oral antiseptic, floss, and clove. These are small items that can be easily added to any first aid kit.

OTHER ESSENTIALS

Besides the items previously mentioned, I suggest a blood oxygen monitor and/or heart rate monitor, a tourniquet, and a package or two of Quik-Clot. I also bring several Water-Jel burn pads, as burns are a common overlanding injury. Personal items should include SPF lip balm, sunscreen, eye drops, antacids, and over-the-counter pain medications like acetaminophen (anti-fever), and an NSAID like ibuprofen (anti-inflammatory). It is important to talk with other team members about items that bring them comfort while traveling, including melatonin for jet-lag, allergy relief tablets, or nose sprays.

Real-World Backcountry Survival Story

Preparing and training to survive unexpected and challenging incidents is not just in the realm of those in uniform. It is an essential exercise in self-reliance and preservation for the overland traveler as well. Survival scenarios are more common than expected and may include needing to evacuate a vehicle that just caught fire, a truck that is flooded during a water crossing, or even a simple breakdown like in this real-world example.

Journal Entry *(33°17'24"N, 109°15'25"W)*
by Mark Stephens

When the Jeep stopped moving, I had a hunch we were in trouble. I tried to restart it, but I knew better—I knew exactly what a dead fuel pump felt like. It was a little pointless to hope, but hope was all we had—since Brooke and I were totally alone, and over 40 miles from the nearest town on a solitary road that went nowhere.

Based on the GPS, we knew we had at least a 10-mile hike to reach the nearest residence. While we hiked, it rained. Then it hailed. Then it rained harder. The only option we had was to keep walking since we were limited to the food and water we carried.

And after those 10 miles? A ranch house, complete with chickens, horses, dogs, and a Ford pickup, yet no one was home. We were soaked, cold, out of water, but had two containers of yogurt and a half-package of beef jerky—a blessing? I felt like a criminal poaching a night's bivouac in the dusty bunkhouse while the owners were away, but surely there was nothing else to do in that weather.

We finished our rations the following day while making the push toward the highway, another 18 miles away. We removed our shoes, hiked up our pants, and waded across the Blue River. At least it was sunny. The thing we never spoke about, but kept thinking to ourselves, was, "What if we don't find help today?"

It was early in the afternoon when we came upon another ranch, this time with a person. Sharon was her name, a kind cowgirl who sniffed out that we were in trouble from a hundred yards away. "Oh my God, what happened to you?" she asked.

Sharon's ranch was still about 40 miles from town, so she let us make a call with her cell phone, with which I made short, spotty contact with my family and managed to pass off our coordinates. We'd made it.

Mark's story came to a happy ending. However, with a few additional pieces of equipment, they could have communicated their problem to the outside world, set up an effective shelter, and remained dry, warm, well-fed, and hydrated. One way to ensure this equipment is always available is to carry what sailors call (for obvious reasons) a *ditch bag*.

Building a Ditch Bag

The goal of a ditch bag is to have a self-contained, life-sustaining kit instantly accessible to the driver. Its sole purpose is to ensure comfort and survival should the occupants be required to evacuate or abandon the vehicle. *Evacuation* can happen for many reasons, the most common being a vehicle fire; a failed water crossing, resulting in a hydro lock of the engine in a dangerous current; or breaking through an ice road over deep water. *Abandonment* is less abrupt, usually due to a non-repairable breakdown or a non-recoverable stuck vehicle, when contact cannot be made with rescuers and passersby are extremely unlikely (such as the previous situation faced by Brooke and Mark). In an abandonment, much more time is available to retrieve supplies from the vehicle; nevertheless, having a basic kit already prepared puts you one step ahead. Following are the four critical requirements of a ditch bag.

PREVENTION

Risk is often unavoidable during an expedition, but that risk must always be balanced with preparation and good judgment. Keeping an accessible ditch bag in the vehicle is wise and leaving it forever unused should be your goal. In addition to having the right equipment, taking certain precautions to prevent risk will help you to (hopefully) never need it. For example, spend an extra few minutes to speak with the locals, or use a drill to determine the thickness of the ice

Photo by Douglas Hackney

↑ **Flooded rivers** can create an unexpected evacuation scenario where you have moments to grab a ditch bag.

road you are crossing; you can also recce ahead on foot to gauge the depth and current of a river crossing. And you should always make an effort to travel with multiple vehicles, as there is safety in numbers. However, accidents happen, plans fail, people take solo vehicle trips, and unforeseen dangers can result in you being completely separated from your vehicle.

COMMUNICATIONS

While we will review communications in detail in Chapter 6, whatever device you use should be immediately accessible and preferably in your ditch bag—the ability to quickly and reliably communicate in an emergency is paramount to a positive outcome. The best way to resolve a vehicle separation incident is to have a method of summoning rescue. If you are 200 miles from help, the meager rations and water in the ditch bag will only last for three to seven days (possibly a bit longer, depending on environmental conditions). You might be injured and unable to trek. The goal is to plan for the worst eventuality, and the best chance for rescue is to be able to call the authorities or trained personnel and organize a recovery. The communication device can include a personal locator beacon (PLB), satellite messenger, satellite phone, or other compact remote communication device that fits in the ditch bag.

SHELTER

Once any medical emergencies have been stabilized and the call for assistance has been initiated, everyone must have adequate shelter from dangerous environmental conditions, including rain, snow, extreme cold, extreme heat, sun exposure, and so on. Stay near the abandoned vehicle if possible (even if it is just a burned-out hull) since a vehicle is much easier than a person to spot from the air.

In a survival situation, you're not concerned with comfort, simply protection from exposure, so forgo the weight of a heavy tent and use an ultralightweight tent, bivvy, or tarp. Make sure your sleeping bag has an extreme temperature rating to suit your expected conditions. My kit typically includes a compact, 20°F NEMO Equipment sleeping bag with a lightweight, insulated pad. Additionally, my kit consists of a heavy-duty space blanket, which can be used as a tarp, and a SOL bivvy bag, which adds a bit of warmth to the sleeping system and additional weather protection. I could eliminate the sleeping bag and pad in warmer environments and carry just the bivvy and blanket.

WATER AND FOOD

Once communications have been established and shelter from the elements is resolved, your situation becomes a waiting game. With help on the way, staying calm, dry, hydrated, and well-fed is your priority. Even just a few warm meals and a hot chocolate can greatly improve morale.

On the other hand, if you have not been able to summon help and are faced with a hike out, food and water become even more important. Many variables affect when and if you should leave a vehicle and walk for help, but should the need arise, you must have sufficient water and high-calorie foods available. Meals should be either ready to eat or require an absolute minimum of preparation. It is best to have 100 ounces of water per traveler, a compact filter, and water treatment tablets. For energy, you will want a minimum of 3,000 calories per person, comprised of a combination of electrolyte energy drink powders and solid food calories. Most emergency ration bars will keep for five years and have 2,000 calories per bar. I prefer a combination of energy bars, jerky, and backpacking meals.

TYPICAL DITCH BAG CONTENTS

Here are some sample contents of a well-equipped ditch bag:

- ☐ Garmin inReach Explorer GPS with preloaded maps
- ☐ Dual hemisphere compass
- ☐ LED headlamp
- ☐ Lighter
- ☐ MSR Dromedary 4-liter bag with hydration kit
- ☐ MSR Thru-Link inline water filter
- ☐ Water purification tablets

↑ **A quality backpack** filled with the right equipment can help ensure your survival in the backcountry.

- ☐ Notepad/pencil/pen
- ☐ Signal mirror
- ☐ Adventure Medical Kits Mountain Series Day Tripper Lite
- ☐ SOL Escape Bivvy Orange
- ☐ SOL all-season blanket
- ☐ Compact butane backpacking stove
- ☐ Compact pot and pan kit (holds stove and fuel canister)
- ☐ Documents (copy of passport and a spare driver's license)
- ☐ Cash ($60, small bills, stashed in several locations)
- ☐ Insulated gloves
- ☐ Poncho
- ☐ Electrolyte drink packages (10)
- ☐ Hard candy
- ☐ Meal bars (4)
- ☐ Good To-Go backpacking meals (2)
- ☐ Blister kit
- ☐ Medications (NSAID, antibiotic, antihistamine)
- ☐ 50 SPF sunscreen
- ☐ Sunglasses (polycarbonate lenses double as safety glasses)
- ☐ Bandana
- ☐ Multitool
- ☐ Parachute cord
- ☐ Wool socks
- ☐ Optional for cold climates: NEMO sleeping bag and insulated pad

RENEW, INSPECT, AND DON'T MESS WITH IT

Once you have determined your ditch bag kit contents and stocked it with the required gear, don't mess with it. Other than a periodic inspection and renewal of perishable items, the kit should stay with you in whatever vehicle you drive (even for that "short" day trip to the mountains) and remain unmolested unless a genuine emergency arises. For example, you shouldn't be using the multitool, flashlight, or matches for day-to-day needs, and you shouldn't be snacking on the jerky.

Planning, education (medical and survival training), and prevention are the keys to surviving a vehicle separation incident. Overlanding takes the traveler to remote, challenging, and unpredictable environments. Preparation, communicating your route plans, and having a properly outfitted ditch bag can make the difference between an epic adventure story and a tragedy. Be prepared!

TRY A 24-HOUR SURVIVAL TEST

After assembling a solid complement of ditch bag contents, consider doing a 24-hour survival test. Several years ago, I did this to ensure all the equipment, my assumptions, and even I was up to the challenge. I decided to test the ditch bag in a real-world scenario. I enlisted the help of several friends who came along for a trail drive on a snow-covered route just south of Prescott, Arizona. I only wore standard clothing and light boots to make it as realistic as possible. My goal was to spend the night in the forest with the ditch bag and trek 11 miles into Prescott the next morning. For additional safety, I carried a 2-meter VHF radio and a satellite messenger with tracking enabled.

The scenario was a vehicle fire, so I only had a few moments to gather my ditch bag and other items. Walking off into the forest, a small backpack and my wits would get me through the night. Everything worked, and I was more comfortable than I had anticipated. It was reassuring to know that my ditch bag would be the lifeline I need it to be in a real emergency.

Dodging Gunboats

Sinuhe, Mauricio, Felipe, and I had just spent days riding motorcycles across the vast expanse of Los Llanos, Colombia, a high savanna stretching from the Andes to Venezuela. We had battled deep mud for days, ran out of water, and our strength was sapped. Arriving at the Meta River, we discovered that the ferry was disabled, and our only option was the long narrow boats of llaneros.

Felipe was the first of our team to cross. The narrow canoe rocked hard from the heavy chop, and Felipe strained against the weight of his Triumph as it shifted between the gunwales. Sweat poured from his forehead, the heat of the midday sun pounding his back, any breeze impeded by thick riding gear. The canoe, filled with three motorcycles and four people, had just crossed the main channel of the Meta River, and everyone felt fatigued from the passage. Felipe's grip tightened on the handlebar when the bark of a megaphone broke his focus. "Alto! Alto!" punctuated the rattle of the outboard motor, and he turned his head left to see a .50 caliber machine gun aimed directly at him. The gunboat was only 20 meters away and closing fast. The canoe operator chopped the throttle in response to the order, immediately destabilizing the small vessel. Felipe fought against the loss of balance and braced himself for impact. The gunship was upon them within moments, turning only slightly before slamming into the canoe. The force of steel and wake crushed the side of the narrow boat and sent everyone into the river's piranha-infested depths.

Felipe crashed into the water. The momentum of the falling Triumph forced him under, and he opened his eyes to a murky underworld of sinking bikes and thrashing bodies. He struggled back to the surface to see the canoe lifting skyward like the Titanic, being pulled under by the weight of the outboard and fuel tank. Feverishly he looked about, seeing the soldiers with carbines brought to bear, yelling at him to show his hands. To his right, he felt the Triumph, which miraculously did not sink immediately. It was most likely spared by the air in the fuel tank and luggage, but it was going down. Felipe grabbed for the

↑ **Felipe arrives at the shore** after recovering his lost motorcycle, his gear still soaked from nearly drowning.

Photo by Sinuhe Xavier

handlebar and kicked with all of his strength toward the side of the gunship. With his free hand, he managed to grasp a strap dangling from the side of the boat and thrust his mouth skyward, pulling in a long breath. The relief was only momentary before the weight of the motorcycle dragged him under again, and he fought against it, kicking and struggling to bring it back to the surface. His head completely underwater, he thought, "I either let go of the boat, or I let go of the bike." His grip relaxed off the handlebar, and the motorcycle slipped free into the deep. He pulled himself skyward again, directing all his ferocity at his attackers. "What in the *hell* have you done?" Felipe foamed, his blue eyes glaring directly at the closest contact. He gasped for another breath but could immediately see that the soldier's countenance had changed from suspicion to confusion.

When the rest of the team and I arrived in the next canoe, we found Felipe alive and his motorcycle dragged up from the deep. He was muddy, sodden, and shaken. The situation was only getting worse; the other victims were now looking for restitution from anyone they could blame. Tempers were flaring, and our options were dwindling when a local Samaritan arrived with his Land Cruiser pickup and offered to drive Felipe and his bike to the next town. We looked at each other and grinned. Remember, it isn't an adventure until something goes wrong.

CHAPTER 6

BACKCOUNTRY COMMUNICATIONS

For the modern explorer, many communication options exist, from sending a postcard to low-orbit satellites with broadband connectivity and everything in between. As an overlander, there are practical and professional reasons to maintain a degree of connectivity. Many people now work remotely, choosing their place on the map based on the view and not the access to Wi-Fi or cellular coverage. Improved communications allow you to stay remote for longer periods while still allowing for the ability to earn a living. The practical considerations are even more critical, as a reliable connection gives you the confidence to explore more remote areas—especially as a solo traveler, as there are means to get support from fellow travelers or rescue personnel (with every effort made to travel responsibly and not put rescue workers at unnecessary risk). With two-way messaging, it is now possible to specifically request the items you need, like extra fuel, a driver's-side CV axle, and so on.

While it is true that you don't need comms to travel, they can certainly improve the efficiency and safety of the journey. This chapter will explore your backcountry communications options in order of simplicity and accessibility. You'll also discover the pros and cons of each one.

Cell Phones

It has been said that humans are more likely to have a cell phone than a toilet. The smartphone is ubiquitous and accessible and used by two-thirds of the world's population. The upside is that 97 percent of the world's population lives within cellular coverage, but the downside is only 34 percent of the landmass has cellular coverage. Limited backcountry towers leave a lot of area where overlanders travel without a network. The smartphone is cost-effective, highly portable, and rich with functionality (via apps), but it has limited connectivity in remote areas.

Cellular phone communications are extended in the backcountry via boosting technologies and antennas like the weBoost, which offer two advantages:

1. They improve reception by allowing the antenna to be mounted outside the vehicle at a higher position relative to the phone and surrounding terrain.
2. They boost the transmission power to the maximum legal wattage (from 200 milliwatts in the phone to a full 1 watt with the booster), combined with the antenna gain of 50 decibels (the legal booster limit).

It is common for premium boosters to improve cellular calling and data performance by up to ten times.

The most important thing to understand about cellular boosters is that while they do work as advertised, they cannot *create* a signal where one does not exist. Products like weBoost improve cellular performance in multiple ways, resulting in better call quality and faster download and upload speeds.

The most important feature is the antenna, which should be mounted high on the vehicle and above the tallest solid object mounted to the roof or rack. The weBoost Drive Over the Road (OTR) antenna has numerous mounting options and extension rod heights. It can be mounted on a spring or on a hinged base, which allows the traveler to

↑ **The weBoost Drive Reach** is compact and powerful, adding range to your smartphone in most conditions.

either leave the antenna up all the time or fold it down to limit tree or overhang damage. It draws 1.5–2 amps at 12 volts, which is manageable by most house electrical systems or smaller power stations.

In general, systems like weBoost are the best first step toward remote communications, as they solve the needs of most travelers and work across all of the mobile phones and hotspots in the travel party. They are best paired with a hotspot device or a mobile phone that can be left on the interior antenna. Most complaints about cellular boosters stem from a need for more understanding about how the amplification works, expecting the boost to work in a large area or the entire interior of the vehicle or camper. I like to use a mobile hotspot set directly next to or on top of the interior antenna and then have Wi-Fi broadcast to the broader network of devices, phones, tablets, and laptops. During my several months traveling the western United States, this was the primary data solution for my needs, and it worked well in motion. The added benefit is the lower long-term cost, as there are no monthly fees for its use. Only the most remote locations will demand a satellite connection.

Radio Communication

For overlanding, radio communications have two jobs: to provide efficient localized dialogue among a group via simplex (in which the mobile or handheld radios have only one frequency assigned to them and the radios talk directly to each other), and for longer distance emergency communications using simplex, repeaters, or high frequency (HF) bands. Travelers most often use General Mobile Radio Service/Family Radio Service (GMRS/FRS) radios like the Rocky Talkie or Midland or less frequently Citizens Band (CB). HAM radio communication using very high frequency (VHF) or ultra-high frequency (UHF) in simplex or via repeater is another option that requires a license.

The second means of radio communication is high frequency (HF), which can travel extreme distances by bouncing off the ionosphere. HF requires a large antenna and a HAM license. Although it does not require service fees, the communication is unpredictable and requires large antennas with specialized (and often internationally restricted) equipment. In recent years, apps and other tools have helped to improve the outcomes, but even with the right frequency and path, you are just as likely to have an amateur operator in Singapore answer you as anyone else. Forty years ago, this was the best option, but now, other solutions provide remote communication

↑ **Multiband HAM handheld transceivers** (HTs) and robust GMRS radios are both good solutions for group communication or maintaining contact with a fellow traveler walking through the local market.

for a fraction of the cost of a suitable HF radio and array. In most cases, it is best to use GMRS for simplex communication and leave the long-range emergency work to the satellites.

Basic Communication Devices

As discussed in Chapter 3, it is important to have a means of communication in remote areas, which should include a primary and secondary means of calling for help, with the recommendation of a contingent and emergency method. For most travelers, two or three communication devices are

sufficient, typically a smartphone (hopefully with built-in satellite SOS) and a satellite messenger. This redundancy is important, as the ability to connect with emergency services or designated contacts can often be the difference between a great story and a tragedy.

SATELLITE MESSENGERS

Without question, the most prolific form of remote communication is the satellite messenger, which permits two-way communication of text messages. These systems typically use low-earth orbit satellites, and some units, like the Garmin inReach, work globally, while others, like SPOT, only have regional coverage (i.e., not the Poles). These units also permit SOS functionality and tracking, so the product can report a location trail without sending text messages. This tracking function is a critical feature should you ever be involved in an accident and unable to send messages. Those following you will have a record of your last known location. These compact and affordable units give travelers and family members peace of mind worldwide. We have used inReach on all seven continents and have relied on the technology to keep in contact with loved ones, business contacts, and support personnel. The system allows for 160-character SMS, prestored messages, OK check-ins, SOS emergency messaging, tracking, and weather updates.

↑ **The Garmin inReach Messenger** is small enough to fit in your pocket yet adds powerful satellite communication, SOS, and location tracking for the overlander.

While the inReach is available in many configurations, we recommend and use the compact models most often because they can be carried everywhere, even on your person, while walking around a market or city. We use two, one always on and stored discreetly in the vehicle and another kept on our person and powered off except when out on foot, thus ensuring active tracking of the vehicle and the occupants. You could also option

the on-person unit to a less expensive plan, as the in-vehicle inReach will be used for regular tracking and SMS. Personally, I use the inReach Mini 2 in the vehicle, and I carry the new inReach Messenger on my person. It charges via USB-C, and the battery lasts up to forty-six days, with location pings sent every 30 minutes. The inReach Messenger permits reverse charging of your phone from the 1,800-milliampere lithium internal battery, so I swapped my usual power brick for the inReach Messenger in my daily carry kit. I now take the inReach Messenger everywhere, as it is only 3.1 inches × 2.5 inches, weighs 4 ounces, and easily tucks into a pocket or shoulder bag. Its diminutive sunlight-readable display allows SMS and SOS functionality without a smartphone.

There are very few downsides to the inReach as it represents a near-perfect confluence of value and capability. However, a few considerations are worth noting, including the lack of voice communications. Depending on the nature of the emergency and the proximity to rescue, it may be critical to engage in voice-based telemedicine for assistance with effective diagnosis and rapid treatment. SMS is better than nothing when communicating with an emergency physician, but active video or voice comms are superior. There are limitations with the small units, particularly with sending messages without a smartphone paired. Messages can be sent, but they take time to construct one character at a time. Compact satellite communicators like the inReach should be considered secondary or contingent solutions and part of your safety procedure for remote travel.

SMARTPHONE SATELLITE POSITIONING AND SOS

In the past few years, even the humble smartphone has joined the satellite communication game. Since the launch of the iPhone 14, all new Apple phones can communicate SOS messages via the Globalstar network and on to an emergency dispatch. As of January 2024, SpaceX launched their first direct-to-cell phone capable satellites and has announced an agreement with T-Mobile to offer Starlink remote coverage as part of their Coverage Above and Beyond program. While late to the game, Google has launched dual-band Global Navigation Satellite Systems (GNSS) satellite two-way communication in their Pixel lineup. The downside is that these communications are *only* for requesting an emergency response like a medical or life-threatening rescue. These services are also restricted to a few select regions, so it is important to verify availability before relying on them for emergency use. Cell-based SOS is a tertiary (contingent or emergency) communication method.

Advanced Communicators for Remote Travel

As your overland adventures get more remote or the conditions amplify the risk, you must consider more advanced communication tools. Does your remote travel include working a few hours a day? Do you want to be able to speak directly with telemedicine while crossing the Canning Stock Route in the outback of Australia? This is where solutions like the satellite phone, Broadband Global Area Network (BGAN), and Starlink make all the difference. Reliable communication is a normal part of life nowadays, but it's important to remember that most phone apps require a connection to operate properly. I still remember when the audiobook I was listening to stopped playing because it had only downloaded to 68 percent before I lost coverage while ascending the Greenland Ice Sheet. That was a minor inconvenience, but it is important to acknowledge how ubiquitous technology is in the modern day.

SATELLITE PHONE WITH DATA

Satellite phones (satphones) have been used for nearly fifty years; the first models marketed to commercial ships were known as the Mobile Satellite Service (MSS), which used the International Maritime Satellite Organization (INMARSAT) constellation. Satellite phones can be geostationary orbit (GEO) like INMARSAT or low-earth orbit (LEO) like the more popular Globalstar and Iridium, which permit two-way voice communications and low-speed data connectivity (email without attachments). While they have lost popularity with overlanders due to the advent of messengers like the inReach, they still offer the vital function of expedient dialogue with support personnel— for example, during a medical emergency where telemedicine provides real-time coaching for diagnosis and treatment. They also provide the opportunity for family members to hear their loved ones speak. For others, the satphone allows them to call for help in an emergency yet remain blissfully disconnected otherwise, without any apps, notifications, or inboxes to be found.

↑ **The Iridium GO! exec** is a significant advancement in Pole-to-Pole communications, providing two lines of voice calls and up to 88 kilobits per second (Kbps) data connection.

We use units like the Iridium Extreme 9575 with data dongle or the recently impressive Iridium GO! exec with improved data rates and up to two lines of voice calling. The Iridium GO! exec takes advantage of Iridium's new NEXT satellites with up to forty times faster data rates of 88 Kbps download and 22 Kbps upload. The new exec now permits additional app integration like WhatsApp, Gmail, and light web browsing. Most notable is that this new service works everywhere, even at the Poles. It also permits two active calls at the same time. This solution is best for travelers who need robust connectivity or improved portability. The exec is larger than the Iridium GO! and weighs 2.6 pounds (1,200 grams). The monthly data plans can range significantly, with some options exceeding $500 monthly. Satellite phones like the Iridium Extreme 9575 or Iridium GO! exec would be considered a primary or secondary remote communication device.

BROADBAND GLOBAL AREA NETWORK (BGAN)

A review of remote communications would be complete only with the inclusion of BGAN, currently the only compact, portable, low-power broadband technology with global coverage (excluding the highest latitudes). Since 2005, the BGAN has provided up to 492 Kbps across the planet, nearly to the Poles. Given the satellite orbit altitude and hardware limitations, the latency can be around one second. While governments and industries most commonly use BGAN, it is appropriate for some overland travelers who require a data connection for their style of travel or professional needs. The BGAN may be the only way a prominent CEO can escape into the backcountry, as she has the budget to support the connectivity expense.

The BGAN terminal is typically the size of a laptop and combines the antenna, battery, and Wi-Fi router into a single unit. The terminals cost between $2,000 and $8,000; data rates are about $7 per megabyte. Voice call fees vary on the data package but should be budgeted at $1 per minute. Download speeds vary based on the connection, with the High Data Rate (HDR) providing rates up to 800 Kbps or even 1 megabits per second (Mbps) with terminal bonding. I have used BGAN for select trips, including the Silk Road and the

↑ **Until the advent of Starlink,** the BGAN was the de facto remote data solution for governments and media.

South Pole, and consider it a primary or secondary means of remote communication.

LOW-ORBIT, LOW-LATENCY BROADBAND (STARLINK)

Currently, over 6,000 Starlink satellites are sitting 550 kilometers above Earth. Plans are in place for up to 42,000 satellites, ten times more than all other satellites in orbit, from every other company, space agency, or country, resulting in unimaginable performance, accessibility, and low latency to the company's 1.5 million subscribers worldwide. Once Starlink access is available on a smartphone, that number will be even higher, and remote travel will forever change. *Overland Journal* utilizes two Starlink antennas for fixed, mobile, and maritime connectivity.

↑ **In just a few years** Starlink antennas have shrunk in size to one-third of the surface area and now have integrated power supplies and Wi-Fi routers. The future is now.

As with many emerging technologies, SpaceX has upended, reshuffled, and universally disrupted the remote data provider sector and (soon) the telecommunications sectors. Until 2021, there were limited and highly siloed satellite options, and none worked perfectly. By February 2021, Starlink had 10,000 subscribers; and in just three years, the company surpassed 3 million subscribers. The technology uses thousands of low-earth orbit satellites, and they are adding to the constellation regularly, expecting to be at over 7,000 in a few years. This capacity and low-orbit positioning results in unimaginable speeds, often exceeding 200 Mbps download. The low latency also allows for video conferencing.

When Starlink first launched, *Overland Journal* was on the beta waiting list and we took a gamble that it would allow for mobile use. That was not the case, and we were restricted to testing within 40–50 miles of our offices. That soon changed, and the new residential/mobile antenna was released, allowing for stationary use or roaming service within the home continent. Within the past year, global roaming has become an option with a $200 monthly fee. During the summer of 2022, I used the new antenna with my Scout Camper and lived/worked throughout the western United States. In all candor, it changed everything, as I could do my work virtually anywhere, including video meetings, podcast recordings, large file uploads, and so on. And it worked—every time.

The original Starlink dish was round and large, making it difficult to mount or store in a vehicle. Fortunately, the new antenna changed to a rectangle, with much smaller overall dimensions. The unit includes a mounting rod and internal motors for positioning and stowing. Fortunately, Starlink launched their new flat high-performance antenna, which costs $2,500 and still uses 120-volt power and an external router. In a further boon for travelers, the Global Mobile service was launched, which (theoretically) works on land anywhere outside the polar regions. Ocean and air models are also in final development. The service fees vary, but the around $200 per month Global Mobile package is ideal for our purposes, providing 5–50 Mbps download speeds. Third-party options like Unique Componentry offer a $1,000 conversion to an ultra-flat, 1-inch thickness, 12-volt operation, and we have tested the modified antenna throughout Africa and Europe with excellent results, including making calls or listening to podcasts while in motion.

Overall, finding fault with Starlink for vehicle-based connectivity is difficult. The hardware is less expensive than most of the competition, and the monthly service fees are a fraction of BGAN's costs. However, power consumption can tax 12-volt vehicle electrical systems. Fortunately, the new Starlink Mini has been launched, is sized like a laptop, and is capable of running on 12–48 volts with a 12-volt consumption of around 60 watts.

Staying Connected with Family

Communications play a role in multiple outcomes, including safety, remote work, sharing your experiences with friends, and staying connected with family. One of the most rewarding results of remote connectivity tools is the joy and peace of mind that comes from touching base with family. Often, your family members feel fear or anxiety around your overland travel, so sending messages and active track logs can boost their confidence in your safety.

Family can also support your travels, report your last known locations, or advise the consulate if communications have stopped for a few days. Those regular updates help them feel a part of the journey and better connected to the experience. It is common for travelers to change profoundly during long-term exploration, so keeping that emotional and experiential lifeline active is an important component of the "reentry" process.

Remote Work

While it can be a romantic notion to stop working and overland into the sunset, many travelers either prefer, or need, to keep working while traveling. Remote work has become a common practice in today's world and can be accomplished with a laptop and a reliable Internet connection. I work a few hours nearly every day while traveling, helping to produce content and coordinate with the team from remote locations or foreign countries.

Remote work can help extend travel by providing a recurring income stream or even allowing for perpetual travel for some fortunate digital nomads. You should have a primary, secondary, and tertiary means of getting work done, typically starting with a laptop and moving to a tablet and then a phone in emergencies. Unfortunately, electronic devices can fail or be pilfered, so backups are important.

The scheduling of remote work can vary widely while overlanding, but I prefer the tempo of two days traveling, then one day stationary to finish the bigger project. I can manage basic emails, calls, and updates during the travel days. Stopping at an Airbnb or campground for two nights will allow for an uninterrupted day of addressing deeper work. Working while traveling is a genuine solution, and scores of overlanders do so successfully. The key is to slow the travel pace down to allow for the work schedule and place clear distinctions between driving time, content capture, and work blocks.

Saving a Prince

We had been driving across the Antarctic Plateau for weeks, my audiobook of *Unbroken* interrupted by the satellite phone ringing. After so many days of the same sounds, the tires crunching against the snow, the diesel motor's purr, the ring broke us out of the stupor of monotony like a 4:00 a.m. wake-up call. The phone call was from Emil Grimson, an Icelandic explorer and the vehicle lead of the Walking With The Wounded team skiing to the South Pole. Impossibly, he was calling on a satellite phone from the middle of Antarctica, and we were also receiving the call in the middle of Antarctica.

Emil was calm on the call but stressed the sense of urgency needed by their team. Walking With The Wounded had a team of twelve veterans from the UK, Canada, Australia, New Zealand, and the US, all working together to ski to the South Pole. The problem was . . . they weren't going to make it. The conditions were proving to be more difficult than they had anticipated, and the extreme cold was compounding their war injuries (which included amputations). They were nearly 100 kilometers behind schedule and needed our help transporting everyone and their equipment closer to the Pole.

Fortunately, we were just a few kilometers from their bearing to the Pole, so we decided to deviate from our course and help. We had space in our two Toyota Hiluxes for additional passengers and room on the racks to store hundreds of kilograms of equipment. When we arrived at their camp, we were greeted with big smiles, hand waving, and the embrace only fellow adventurers could give. Prince Harry, the Duke of Sussex, walked up to thank us as well, taking the time to meet each one of our team and see if we needed anything. Then he proceeded to work, catching bags and cases on the top of the Hiluxes, using care to assemble each piece into an interlocking gear tower. We had a long way to drive them, and the path was one of the most abusive of the route.

Through the whiteout we plodded, each truck grossly overloaded, the drivers taking care to

↑ **The author standing on the Antarctic Ice Sheet** with Prince Harry and a Walking With The Wounded team member.

preserve these mechanical lifelines. We had already broken a spring and needed to replace it in the field at -30°F, the cold oppressive at nearly 11,000 feet elevation and getting worse as we closed in on the Pole. With visibility limited, we needed to communicate our positions regularly with the other trucks, using our two-way radios due to proximity. The radio chatter was minimal, and most of the Walking With The Wounded group was exhausted and stoic from the realities of suspending their race. But we knew their success at reaching the Pole was nearly guaranteed, given the 100-kilometer boost they needed. This effort also got Expeditions 7 closer to the Pole, and we could feel the anticipation, too, recognizing that our goal was also within reach.

Within a few days, we would reach the South Pole and ultimately cross the continent to the Ross Ice Shelf. We were thousands of miles from where we had begun but needed to turn around and drive it all again. Returning to the South Pole, I called my dad and shared the news of our success. Communication was critical to our safety and allowed us to talk with our families. In a fitting example, the satellite phone even helped us save a prince.

CHAPTER 7

OVERLAND NAVIGATION

Wayfinding is not only an essential part of being an overlander but of being human. Numerous rites of passage include a walkabout not only physically to find your way but intellectually, emotionally, and socially too. Navigating effectively translates to confidence in the world around you and finding your true north despite the challenges travel may throw your way. Wayfinding also improves your memory and your ability to solve other complex problems.

As a traveler, you may embrace the serendipity and randomness of adventure, the paper map unfurled on a dusty hood, each direction yielding a wonder. However, planning and technology can complement

adventure, even if your romantic ideals of exploration rebel against them. There are tools available today that make overlanding safer and more connected than ever before, allowing you to plug in while simultaneously unplugging.

Navigation is a key component of both planning and traveling. In this chapter you will discover several tools for finding your way, such as primary navigational tools like a GPS, secondary applications on a smartphone or tablet, and contingent navigation devices like a backup GPS (often serving as the satellite messenger).

Honing Your Instincts

Have you ever noticed that some people have a natural sense of direction even in an unfamiliar place, while others seem unable to navigate themselves out of their neighborhood? The reality is that we all have an innate ability to navigate our surroundings. Creatures of every order present an incredible ability to navigate long distances, from the Arctic tern's impossible journey (25,000 miles annually) to the monarch butterfly (3,000 miles) or the Chinook salmon (1,900 miles). Humans have impressive natural navigation and tracking skills, too, with legends of wayfinding cultures ranging from the Inuit of the Arctic to the seafarers of the Marshall Islands. Humans will use everything at their disposal to help solve the direction puzzle, including the wind, celestial bodies, currents, scents, and even other animals.

Getting better at navigating first stems from observing. During your next commute, notice the landmarks, the meandering rivers, or even the In-N-Out Burger restaurant at the corner where you need to turn left. Many vehicles have a built-in compass, so test yourself by guessing your direction and then looking at the gauge to confirm. Ask a friend to give you verbal directions to the concert and then try to drive there by memory. If you get lost, Google Maps isn't far away, but fight

↑ **Camel trains** are led by desert nomad wayfinders, who can read the sand, wind, and stars to find water and their destination.

the urge to look until you need to. The same can be done on a short hike in a city park or in an area where truly getting lost isn't possible. Use a map to go one direction and then your senses to bring you back. The mind loves the challenge of wayfinding. For your next overland journey, you could only use a paper map. Many years ago, my friend Sinuhe Xavier challenged us to do a long weekend trip without any phones or GPS. Using only paper maps, we embarked on one of our best trips, finding the nuances and even new tracks of a place so close to home.

Tools for Finding Your Way

Effective navigation begins at home when you first start planning your route. Start with a list of highlights you hope to visit in a particular region, state, or country. Add those to Google Maps by clicking on the point of interest (POI) and selecting save, then add it to the custom directory for that trip. I like saving all these planning directories for future use, including sharing favorite spots with friends. Once all the POIs are entered, you can zoom out and get a sense of the route or what destinations need to be excluded. I then use Google Maps or Google Earth to create an informal route to determine distances and estimated travel times. This serves as a framework to discuss the trip with your travel companions and make decisions around pacing and alternate destinations.

With the rough outline complete, you can start the deep dive into specific overland tracks and trails or determine which campsites have vacancies or which national parks require advanced bookings. In North America, I recommend onX, as it shows the trails suitable for your vehicle and the land ownership information. If you enjoy finding the less traveled road, this is one of the best resources for the task. This kind of research can be more difficult in other parts of the world, but there is Tracks4Africa in Africa and Hema Maps in Australia. Navigation planning is an important part of overlanding and will save you countless frustrations when tires hit the dirt at your destination.

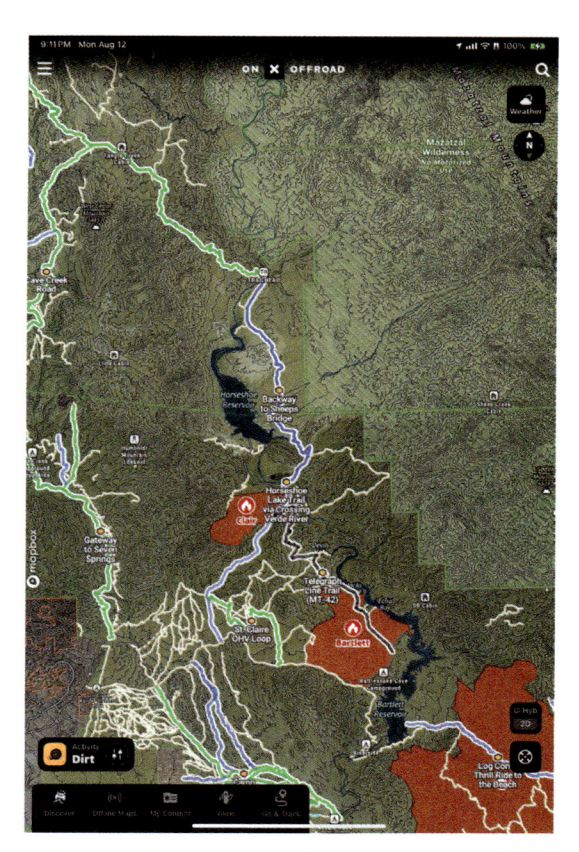

↑ **onX** is a powerful planning and navigation tool for overland travel, providing customization for the type of vehicle you are using and desired trail difficulty.

GPS Unit (Primary Navigation Tool)

For navigation, a dedicated GPS is the most reliable and effective tool for the job. Phones overheat, tablet apps crash, and sometimes you need to multitask with your smartphone. Having a robust, vibration-resistance device that has an ingress protection (IP) rating of at least IP67, IPX6, or IPX7 will help to prevent failures. These ratings protect the unit from dust and submersion should the GPS be used outside the vehicle. The dedicated GPS space has been reduced to Garmin and Lowrance, along with a few robust factory-installed options.

It is tempting to purchase a GPS with the largest screen possible, but this has numerous downsides, including blocking driver visibility, cost, and theft. In my testing, we found a unit in the 5–8-inch range, which results in the best compromise between obstructing your view and having enough screen area for scale and resolution. I recommend the Garmin Montana 700i, Garmin Tread, or Garmin Overlander. Lowrance makes numerous race and side-by-side units, but their Elite FS 7 is particularly well suited to overlanding and has the capability of an external antenna for increased gain and an unobstructed view of the sky.

↑ **Even a smartwatch like the Garmin fēnix** can provide GPS and mapping data to the traveler, this one showing that I was 591 feet below sea level at the lowest point in Africa.

Photo by Paula Burr

↑ **A GPS gives the traveler confidence** in their route while allowing for continuous track recording (should you need to retrace your steps.) This Garmin Overlander is complemented by a portable unit with inReach.

Navigation Applications
(Secondary Navigation Tool)

The most useful programs are navigation applications, which allow physical progress (via the smartphone or tablet GPS) to be rendered over a map layer, shown alongside XML data like waypoints, tracks, and POIs. What started ten years ago as simple topographical applications displaying 7.5-minute scanned and raster paper maps on an iPhone (Topo Maps app) has become feature-rich navigation and planning tools with base layers from open and curated sources. Most importantly, they have started to become more reliable for track recording.

Navigation apps fall into three categories: the juggernauts, tracking and mapping apps, and support applications.

THE JUGGERNAUTS

It is easy to dismiss the most popular (and even native) applications like Google Maps, Google Earth, Apple Maps, and Waze, but they are widely used for compelling reasons. Most notably, their access to user data helps indicate traffic patterns, closed roads, or the newest routes.

The most useful of all of these juggernauts is Google Maps, as favorites can be shared across devices, and, critically, it allows for downloading offline map data from anywhere in the world. You just search for a place, click on the place name, and then select the three dots on the top right. "Download Offline Map" will be an option, and the data will then be stored locally on your phone for one year.

Waze's usefulness depends on what city has largely adopted it, but the tool can be a big help when bypassing traffic jams or local demonstrations.

TRACKING AND MAPPING APPS

The next most valuable navigation tools are backcountry-specification applications such as Gaia, onX, Hema Maps, Tracks4Africa, REVER, and others. Their greatest strength is access to topographical map layers, offline satellite images, and user-contributed routes and data points. The best maps have organizational-validated tracks, either done with 100 percent ground truthing by mapping professionals (like Hema Maps in Australia) or by aggregating user-contributed data to improve accuracy (Tracks4Africa). Additional features can include land designation and route types (e.g., 50-inch or motorcycle-only trails on onX). These apps should also include reliable tracking of routes for future sharing and reference of GPX (a text file with geographic information such as waypoints, tracks, and routes) or KML (Keyhole Markup Language) files.

SUPPORT APPLICATIONS

Support applications like iOverlander (a platform that shares camping, parking, and other information) are relevant for the traveler and will help solve that 2:00 a.m. need-a-campsite problem. But with great power comes great responsibility.

Try to avoid using these popular and overused campsites to distribute impact. And if you do stay at one, ensure that the campsite is a legal place to crash for the night, and do everything possible to clean up all trash (even trash left by those before you). These user-curated sharing apps are among the most significant developments in vehicle-based travel in the last decade, as they provide key insights into finding water, laundry, or say that specialized Vanagon Syncro mechanic.

GAIA GPS

The crucial deliverable of the Gaia app is reliability—a dead-on dependability of both tracking and offline maps. While it might seem surprising, recording a reliable track without crashing or producing erroneous data appears to be a challenge in the space. Yet Gaia seems to have figured it out. I have countless tracks, waypoints, and routes saved to the app, and they all sync flawlessly across devices and the desktop browser. For the remote and international traveler, it is often necessary to be able to upload track data as a breadcrumb or save a completed track as a GPX for future reference and sharing. I still remember getting hopelessly lost in a labyrinth of small streets in a Moroccan city, only to reverse my way out thanks to a reliable breadcrumb track. Bells and whistles are good, but a reliable map and track is the DNA of good navigation.

The Gaia app is feature-rich, but it (thankfully) does not look like it. The main screen is taken up almost entirely by the map, and a few small and recognizable buttons and pages are easily accessible. Along the top is a search function (which has improved markedly in recent versions) and full-screen, current location, add, and map layer buttons. The map layer button is where the magic happens, allowing adjustments to the map overlay and which base map renders on the screen. The layers are extensive but critically include USGS Topo, satellite, and several land-use overlays. International sources are primarily OpenStreetMap and satellite, which is more than sufficient and generally reliable. All of these maps can be saved for offline use, and there is even a 1900 historic topo layer that sent my explorer

vibes into the stratosphere. My complaints with the application are minimal, as recent updates have greatly improved stability. Apple CarPlay is available on Gaia but is rudimentary, and getting the full benefits of the app does require a $40 per year investment. My personal wish list includes a paid option to access the National Geographic Maps (like Baja) as a map layer.

ONX OFFROAD

For overland travel, knowing the land designation is critical, as trespassing is just as problematic as crossing state trust lands without a permit. onX Offroad uses a topo or satellite hybrid base map and overlays it with land designation and track data to present an up-to-date accessibility profile. State trust, Bureau of Land Management (BLM), National Forest System (NFS), and private lands are clearly defined by name and colored map tiles. However, it is important to note that these features are only usable in North America.

The app is modern, with clean icons and minimalist menus. The top of the screen is occupied by a drop-down menu on the left, which accesses account information, sharing, and version data. On the right is a search icon that has proven adequate in use but needs better filtering to improve efficiency (for example, a long list of churches was generated when searching for Valley of the Gods in Utah).

On the map, there is a toggle button for switching between a topo layer, satellite layer, and hybrid option. This is a quick and convenient feature that improves user efficiency. Below that is a locate button that quickly anchors the center of the map to your current location. At the base of the map are a few thoughtful touches, including a weather icon (which will expand to show a detailed weather forecast). Most notable is the brilliant and compact display of distance scale, current latitude/longitude, and elevation. The bottom menu accesses trail type, saving offline maps, my content (tracks, waypoints, and so on), map tools, and the tracker.

Specialized Tracking and Mapping Apps

In addition to the popular apps previously mentioned, there are a few more important offerings to cover that are region-specific or provide unique support for the overland traveler. Some of these require an annual fee or have restricted features in the free versions.

TRACKS4AFRICA (AFRICA ONLY)

Africa is a glorious continent requiring a good map. That prompted Tracks4Africa founders to start their mapping empire in 2003, providing paper maps, GPS data cards, and now mobile applications for the backcountry explorer. The amount of ground-truth data is expansive and represents nearly two decades of user-contributed tracks.

Their app has improved considerably in recent years and now provides a reliable tool for exploring trails and remote regions of the bushveld.

In use, the application is extremely rudimentary but is at least reliable and accurate. There is no tracking function, and each country or regional map must be purchased for a reasonable fee ranging from $3 to $13. Nearly the entire screen is dedicated to the map, with a top bar including an add map icon, a search bar, and a filtering function. The best feature is the results icon, which will display selected POIs on the map overlay, including attractions, parks, and campsites. There is no tracking function, but the app has everything you need.

REVER PRO

REVER was cofounded by Justin Bradshaw of Backcountry Discovery Routes (BDR) fame. Justin has traveled large swaths of the world by overland vehicle, which is reflected in the user experience. The base app has several useful features, but the value proposition dramatically improves with the (paid) REVER Pro version. Pro activates the LiveRIDE function, providing active ride updates via a link you can share, and active SMS updates that you can send to your desired contacts who receive notifications of your location (this uses cellular data).

The overall look and feel of the app are perhaps the most attractive in the segment, but the free version does hit you with ads and a fairly heavy push toward the Pro version. Essentially, the free version is a liability for most travelers, as you cannot export GPX data or download offline maps, so either pay for the Pro version or stay away. The app also emphasizes the community aspect, with a social media undertone of challenges, shared rides, friends' rides, and upcoming meet-ups. Tracking has been reliable, and the LiveRIDE feature and Butler Maps Backcountry Discovery Route tracks are worth the price of admission.

HEMA 4WD MAPS (AUSTRALIA ONLY)

When traveling in Australia, the only serious mapping tool is Hema Maps, and their best offering is their 4WD Maps app, which provides complete offline maps of the country. I have used it to cross Australia from coast to coast a few times, and though somewhat primitive as an application, you are buying the data, which is the most accurate and validated for this region of the world. The app includes 1.5 gigabytes of offline data, including dozens of detailed base maps.

These maps render precise overland track routes, campsites, watering holes, and significant POIs. The main screen has only a few icons along the bottom, including a maps menu, search function (effective), locate button, add waypoint, and toggle to the tracking/settings screen. Tracking has proven to be reliable. The detailed maps include trail names, distances between junctions, and anticipated difficulty, represented by line thickness and dashes. Campgrounds and other services are also shown. There are a few limitations, as the maps do not allow for turn-by-turn, and additional layers come at a fee. However, there is also nothing else like it for exploring the Land Down Under.

iOVERLANDER

Few apps have resulted in such rapid and broad adoption as iOverlander. The app provides a collection of user-contributed campsites, campgrounds, wild sites, and traveler services. It was started as a nonprofit by Sam Christiansen and Jessica Mans, and there are no costs associated with its use (although you can donate).

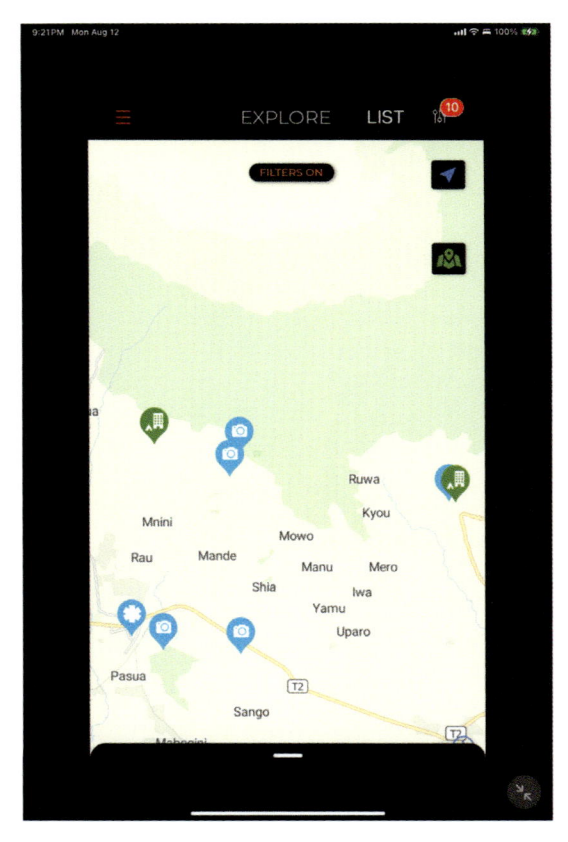

↑ **iOverlander** is the go-to resource for domestic and international travelers looking for informal campsites, fuel stations, POIs, and even police checkpoints. The recent updates also allow for offline maps.

The application is intentionally simple, and the main map screen is where all the magic happens. Its most powerful feature is the filtering menu, which only displays the service or campsite type you seek. I have used this to find wild camping areas throughout North America and Africa, although I rarely camp at the exact spot shown (with a few notable exceptions). Other useful features are the amenity icons, which indicate if cellular data is available, and so on. It also shows details on the contributor, including the date the site was last visited. This app remains one of the most useful tools for domestic and international travelers.

CAMPENDIUM

If you live on the road in North America, Campendium is another useful tool for finding a place to boondock, stealth camp, or resupply. The app is well curated and free but features ads and paid content. The data favors RVers and trailer campers but does filter for dispersed camping (camping outside of a designated campground).

I like several features of Campendium, mostly related to the user reviews of various sites and the cell coverage reports (for those who work remotely). Each entry provides photographs and additional information like vehicle size restrictions and amenities. The functionality feeds off the main map, with only a search bar along the top and a filter icon. The filters are effective, but I would like it to include a "cell coverage" selection in amenities. The map is easy to navigate, and the campsite or service icons, including water and dumpsites, are easy to distinguish when planning. Once an icon is selected, a detail window opens at the bottom of the map with more information, including user ranking, cost, and when it was added to the database. While not specifically for the overlander, it is free and serves as another data source for planning.

GOOGLE EARTH

While there may no longer be blank spots on the map, there are certainly places humans rarely, if ever, visit. This is where Google Earth shines, as it allows for detailed and efficient route planning using satellite data. This is particularly useful when crossing large dune fields or traveling in countries with poor base map data. Even on the phone (the desktop version is better for route planning), the app allows quick pin drops, distance measurements, and, most importantly, highly detailed satellite overlays. It's as close to ground truthing as you can get without boots on terra firma.

As an app, it is both interactive and dynamic and even allows for a wonderful surprise. There is a randomized POI icon called "Feeling Lucky" that flies you to an obscure and fascinating location on the planet (the last one I checked was Lake Rusanda in Serbia). To get the best from the app for route planning your next crossing of the Sahara, start with the Chrome version and build a travel project. It is far more powerful than described here, but it allows everything from route creation to importing images to displaying POIs. Then, it all syncs across your devices. In addition, it is worth checking out Google My Maps to create detailed route files, import and aggregate GPX tracks, and share these with other travelers.

The Edge of Gondwana

The wind from the Southern Ocean clawed against my skin, and the mist from the crashing waves of Cape Carnot speckled my sunglasses. I was standing on some of the oldest rock in Australia, with nothing between me and the coast of Antarctica. I stood in awe of my surroundings, humbled by the scale of the place, by the immensity and age of the continent behind me, and the reality that it was once connected at this very spot to Antarctica. During the Early Jurassic Period, the supercontinent of Gondwana began to tear apart, and Australia shifted north, creating the Great Australian Bight. This area is famous for its remoteness and the stark beauty of the world's largest limestone plain, the Nullarbor.

Any good adventure starts with a table full of maps and a team of willing (and equally daft) participants to embark on a journey. For this trip, Rob Bogheim, a great friend and arguably one of the most experienced overlanders in Australia, called me with a proposal: "Hey, mate! What do you think about following in the footsteps of John Eyre and Matthew Flinders and crossing the Bight?" My response was more of an autonomic yes than a considered agreement, but like most good answers, it came from the gut.

Captain Matthew Flinders (1774–1814) conducted three major expeditions to Terra Australis by his fortieth birthday, including the first coastal circumnavigation of the continent that he would ultimately name. He died at forty, having achieved more than I could ever envision in a full lifetime. Edward John Eyre lived to the ripe age of eighty-six.

He led several major expeditions, including the first land crossing of the Great Australian Bight with John Baxter and his longtime Aboriginal companion, Wylie. Eyre died in 1901, having explored much of Australia and having served as a lieutenant governor in New Zealand and as the governor of Jamaica.

Australia is a fascinating place to me, mainly because of my love for the world's great deserts and the happiness that comes from being able to drive for days along the beach, the nights a chorus of crashing waves. I have always been intrigued by the south coast of Australia and was fortunate in recent years to explore much of it, including Tasmania. With our objective of staying along the southern coast, the challenges came quickly and often, especially in the coastal dunes. Within an hour of entering the erg, one Land Cruiser had already departed terra firma in a dramatic display worthy of a trophy truck (with the trailer attached), and another had been stuck to the frame.

It took me over a month to drive from Brisbane to Perth through the continent's center and then along the Great Australian Bight to the west coast. Even with modern navigation tools from Hema Maps, GPS units, and satellite communicators, we still struggled to route-find at times. It was a humbling realization that explorers like Flinders and Eyre had accomplished the same feat with nothing but a compass and the stars. Completing the journey also reminded me of the joys that come from experiencing the unknown. As I stood at Point Malcolm, I considered where we had been and what was next. That is the contemplation of all who love to explore—remembering the last adventure and dreaming of the next horizon.

←

The southern coast of Australia
left me breathless; this pristine white beach crashing against the ocean and a cliff wall that disappeared into the horizon.

CHAPTER 8

TOOLS AND RECOVERY EQUIPMENT

Once you leave the pavement, finding a tow truck or mobile mechanic becomes a significant challenge, both logistically and financially. For this reason, overlanders should consider training in managing field repairs and stuck vehicle recoveries. These skills vary widely—depending on location, vehicle, and situation—and expecting most travelers to solve all possible calamities is unreasonable. Still, some basic knowledge and the right tools can be the foundation for diagnosing the problem or working over the phone (or satellite) with a mechanic back home. As discussed in Chapter 4, training in recovery assessment and rigging is an important investment that greatly improves your safety and success. This chapter will cover the basic recovery skills and recommended tools for the beginner overlander.

Before the Breakdown

As with most other scenarios, the planning that occurs ahead of time makes all the difference, and this is never more evident than with vehicle systems. Both motorcycles and 4WDs will benefit from preventative and predictive maintenance programs and daily and weekly travel inspections.

Preventative maintenance is achieved by following the manufacturer's recommended service intervals and taking the vehicle to the dealer or trusted mechanic for routine inspections. A good mechanic will tell you everything that is wrong or should be changed but also work with you on determining what needs to be repaired. Each vehicle has a recommended service schedule, including oil changes, fluid changes, filters, brakes, belts, and more. Sticking to those guidelines and keeping the vehicle serviced according to the guidelines is a good idea.

Predictive maintenance is an entirely different animal—in this case, you use crowd-sourced information (like the forums on https://expeditionportal.com) to help predict when the major systems may fail. With enough fidelity in the data, the traveler can confidently determine that the alternator should be changed before 120,000 miles or that the rear driveshaft should be rebuilt by 140,000 miles. Knowledge like this is powerful and helps you avoid known failure modes on the model you drive or ride.

One tip I learned early on was to use the tools I keep in my vehicle to perform the routine service and repairs on it. This helped me determine not only which tools were most often needed but also allowed me to remove some wrench and socket sizes that weren't necessarily for anything on my vehicle's model. This is particularly important

for adventure motorcycles, as space and payload are limited. Bring only the necessary tools. This extends to diagnostics as well. If your vehicle is acting up, try to diagnose the problem yourself before dropping it at the mechanic, or ask them to show you where the failure occurred and how they plan to fix it. Working through those problem-solving skills when the opportunity arises makes you more confident in the field.

New versus Old Vehicles

The debate of new overland vehicles versus tried-and-true stalwarts is as old as the wheel. There is an argument for both brand-new and older cars that are easy to work on. Regardless of the manufacturer, old vehicles will inherently require more repairs than newer ones, particularly when comparing the same model. For example, despite how reliable a 1994 Toyota Land Cruiser 80 Series is, it will never be as reliable as a 2024 Land Cruiser 300 Series. This is because wiring, seals, and systems degrade over time, even if the mileage remains low. In my multiple circumnavigations, I have always used a new or newer vehicle and have never experienced a single significant breakdown. For Expeditions 7 (mentioned in Chapter 2), we drove hundreds of thousands of kilometers without even a switch failing on the 70 Series Land Cruisers.

↑ **Few vehicles are as reliable as the new Toyota Land Cruiser 300 Series,** engineered to last a half-million miles of fieldwork.

On the other hand, the argument for older vehicles is also compelling. To start, older vehicles cost less to purchase and are less expensive to insure. If your older model falls off the ferry in Turkmenistan, the financial loss is (often) more manageable. Also, there is a certain pride that comes from maintaining and servicing an older vehicle, not to mention the ethical benefits of reusing, renewing, and recycling something meaningful. Older vehicles also keep your mechanical skills sharp, and they nearly guarantee the likelihood of adventure on the trip. Breakdowns always seem to occur in the least convenient locations, but the stories of meeting locals, overcoming challenges, and channeling your inner MacGyver are priceless.

Daily and Weekly Checklists

Your vehicle is your magic carpet to adventure, and it requires both mechanical sympathy and regular inspection and service to improve your chances of arriving at your destination. The goal of the following checklists is to provide measured and accessible suggestions that can be modified as desired. The weekly checks are best completed in a place with access to supplies and service support (like in a campground near a town or city). These checklists should be used after you leave for a trip and have completed all appropriate service, maintenance, and repair.

Daily Checks

- ☐ Visual inspection of the front of the vehicle.
- ☐ Open the hood and check the battery hold down, belts, engine oil, and engine coolant.
- ☐ Visual inspection of the engine bay, looking for chafing or loose components.
- ☐ Visual inspection of suspension components.
- ☐ Visual inspection of tires (look for cuts, chunking, and signs of low pressure).
- ☐ Visual walk-around of vehicle (look for loose trim, damage, or leaks).
- ☐ Communication and navigation check (radio, satellite beacon, and start track recording).
- ☐ Equipment is loaded and lashed safely.
- ☐ Wellness check with all fellow travelers and a driver's brief.

Weekly Checks

- ☐ Tool kit and jack inspection (serviceability, inventory, and accessibility).
- ☐ Front number plate (if fitted).
- ☐ Front bumper inspection (secure).
- ☐ Winch inspection (secure, power cables, and rope/cable).
- ☐ Lighting check (auxiliary lights, low/high beams, indicators, and hazards).
- ☐ Physical suspension check (look for leaking dampers, broken jounces, and loose bolts).
- ☐ Physical steering check (tie rod ends, damper, bolts, and watch while the wheel is turned).
- ☐ Transfer case and axle checks.
- ☐ Chassis inspection (look for cracks, inspect attachment points and cross members).
- ☐ Open the hood, check all fluids, belt tension, and condition of all hoses and the air filter.
- ☐ Inspect battery and cables, wiring and sensors.
- ☐ Inspect operation and condition of wipers; clean windshield.
- ☐ Inspect each tire, pressure check (tire pressure monitoring systems (TPMS) can fail) inside and outside tread face and sidewalls.
- ☐ Auxiliary power system checks (battery mounting, cables, charger, and solar).
- ☐ Water storage checks (leaks, levels, cleaning, and potability).
- ☐ Loading and lashing (drawer system inspection, tie downs, and straps).
- ☐ Recovery equipment checks (accessibility, serviceability, cleaning, and traction boards).
- ☐ First aid and ditch bag kits (accessibility, damaged or missing items, and expiration dates).
- ☐ Documentation (inventory, copies, and upload new documents to the cloud).
- ☐ Communication systems (cell, radio, satellite, and PLB).
- ☐ Navigation systems (map/compass, GPS, apps, download tracks, and updates).

Diagnostics and Bush Mechanics

An entire book could be dedicated to bush mechanics, but a few key principles apply to the 101 level. The most important first step when a vehicle breaks down is to ensure that the occupants are safe and that the vehicle is properly secured (off the road or trail, if possible) against rolling or sliding. The next steps are to slow down, think, listen, and observe. For example, do you remember the log that popped into the chassis a few miles back or the faint smell of electrical smoke? Taking a moment to assess the situation often helps pull the puzzle together and allows diagnosis of the failure. Often, it is safe to assume that the simplest explanation is the most likely one. For example, in all my years of driving Toyotas, it was nearly always true that the warning light on the dash was due to a loose negative battery cable, not an alternator that had failed. So, stop and think to yourself, "What is the simplest explanation for this breakdown?" If you have cell coverage or a satellite messenger, take a moment to call a friend with strong mechanical aptitude. They can often help diagnose the problem and may even be willing to drive out to help you fix it.

Once the root cause for the breakdown has been found, determine if you have the spare parts or tools required to fix it. If a spare is unavailable, can the existing unit be rebuilt in the field or bypassed altogether? Lay out a tarp (and change out of your nice shirt) before starting, as organization is important. Having a tarp under the repair area helps capture any fluids that may leak out and catch any tools (like that pesky 10-millimeter socket) that may have otherwise fallen into the mud or sand to be lost forever. Take your time, stay hydrated to keep sharp, and avoid working until dark unless safety dictates. Usually, most repair work can continue in the morning.

↑ **Getting stuck is all part of the adventure,** so use it to test your skills or develop new ones.

Understanding Equipment Rating and Load Matching

The process of vehicle recovery is one of the most complex and dangerous activities in overland travel, so it requires more vigilance than most. This starts with selecting the correct equipment for the vehicle, the curb weight, and the anticipated load. For example, if you are traveling with a vehicle much heavier than your own, you may need to purchase additional pulleys and rigging straps for safe bridling and connection. Once the loads are known, then you will start matching the minimum breaking strength and materials to the task at hand.

The greatest challenge with gauging your equipment's rating and then matching it properly to the anticipated load forces is the limited standardization of recovery equipment in the 4WD market. Standards for equipment ratings exist in the rigging industry, and some of those components are also used in vehicle recovery kits, but navigating the various terms is difficult. To help you, here are some of the key terms:

MINIMUM BREAKING STRENGTH (MBS)

Minimum breaking strength is arrived at by taking a sample set of a component and testing the units to failure (typically per American Society for Testing and Materials (ASTM) D4268). The sample that failed at the lowest strain will set the MBS. It is typical for straps and ropes to have a placard with their MBS on them, though straps may also be listed with "minimum breaking strain" or "never exceed" values.

WORKING LOAD LIMIT (WLL)

Working load limit is the maximum intended load for the component in normal service. This term was born from the rigging industry for overhead operations and is intentionally conservative, with some components having an MBS rating of *four or six times* the working load limit. For example, a 19-millimeter shackle with a WLL of 4.75 metric tons (10,471 pounds) and a safety factor 6x would have an MBS of 62,826 pounds.

Safety factors are established by the rigging industry, yet they apply to the overlander too. In most overhead crane operations, a shackle will need a 4:1 or 5:1 WLL to meet Occupational Safety and Health Administration (OSHA) standards, which would put a 4.75 metric ton shackle's breaking strength at a minimum of 41,884 pounds. In general, it is best to plan your recovery kit around an MBS of three to four times your actual curb weight (as measured on a scale) with full kit, fuel, and occupants.

LOAD MATCHING

It is important to make sure that all the components in your recovery kit are rated to the three to four times curb weight of your vehicle so that one underrated component does not create a weak link. The manufacturers of recovery kits often overlook load matching, especially when a pulley block is included. A pulley block provides additional mechanical advantage to the winch, doubling the potential load on the pulley and on every connection between the pulley and the anchor, including the tree strap, shackle, and so forth.

A recovery strap should be rated to three to four times the anticipated load. In a double-line winch pull scenario, the pulley block should have a MBS of two times the rating of the winch, and the tree strap and supplied shackles must also be able to operate safely at twice the winch's capacity. The same applies to winch extensions (typically used between the pulley block and anchor point), which should be selected with a MBS of two times the winch's capacity.

Recovery straps and ropes should be matched to the vehicle's curb weight to ensure proper stretch. For example, using a kinetic energy recovery rope (KERR) with an MBS of 30,000 pounds on a 3,200-pound Suzuki Samurai will result in insufficient stretch to ensure a proper dynamic recovery. Overrated equipment can also be heavy and more expensive than a kit designed for approximately three to four times your curb weight (you should err to the heavier side).

↑ **The new AEV recovery kits** are some of the best available, using high-quality components and listing minimum breaking strength and working load limits.

Straps and Ropes

Since the advent of synthetic materials for the marine industry, the overlander's recovery kits have improved for the better, now weighing less, being more durable, and far safer. The foundation of most of your recoveries will be a strap or a rope, often made from Dyneema, nylon, or polyester. In most cases dynamic straps and ropes will be made from nylon (for stretch). For static recovery straps and ropes (like for winching operations), they will most likely be made from Dyneema or polyester. The advent of new coatings has helped all material types resist sun and chemical damage, but all require a thorough inspection for rating and serviceability before use.

TOW STRAPS

A tow strap is not a recovery strap. A recovery strap is stronger and made for pulling a vehicle out of a tough spot, while a tow strap is made for towing a vehicle. It is important to avoid conducting a vehicle-to-vehicle recovery with a tow strap. Tow straps should only be used for flat towing of a disabled vehicle. A proper tow strap is usually constructed from polyester and has nominal stretch. This lack of stretch makes them a poor choice for vehicle-to-vehicle recovery scenarios. The tow strap will also adjust its length to accommodate the variation in distance between the tow vehicle and the vehicle being towed by using sewn-in bungees to prevent it from dragging on the trail or road.

RECOVERY STRAPS

A kinetic recovery strap or rope is used for vehicle-to-vehicle recoveries and some specialized driving during winching operations. Kinetic straps are constructed from woven nylon rope or webbing, allowing for stretch in the 20–35 percent range. The stretch helps to reduce the shock loading to connection points while also aiding in the kinetic energy developed during the stretching phase, much like how a rubber band can be stretched and shot through the air upon release.

STATIC WINCH LINES, ROPES, AND EXTENSION STRAPS

A static rope or strap is used for proper winch line and for rigging a winch extension. The most popular is a section of synthetic line typically made from Dyneema with thimbles on each end, but some companies produce polyester extension straps. The big advantage of the rope over the strap is that a winch line extension rope can run through a pulley block, while a strap cannot. The advantage of the strap is better wear and cutting resistance.

RIGGING STRAPS AND UTILITY ROPES

While rigging straps are often called tree straps, they can be used on nearly any anchoring point, which can include trees, rocks, and even the odd termite mound. A rigging strap is designed to go around the anchor tree to prevent damage to the bark and to protect the winch cable. This is also why most rigging straps are wide, which distributes the pressure on the bark. Rigging straps are used like climbing webbing, where the goal is to create a secure rigging anchor for the winch line or pulley to be connected. Rigging straps are constructed from synthetic materials like polyester or Dyneema. When used on a live tree, the primary function of the rigging strap is to protect the vulnerable bark and live outer layers, so the strap should be wide and soft.

Utility ropes have also become popular, combining a Dyneema core with a thick polyester sleeve, and sometimes even a third layer for abrasion and cut resistance. If the utility rope has

↑ **A rigging strap and a utility rope** often serve the same purpose, but the strap does a better job of protecting a tree because of the width.

enough diameter and cushion, they can be used as a tree protector too.

Additional Equipment

Beyond straps and ropes, some additional items should be considered, like a pulley block, proper shovel, utility straps, a transit cluster, and more. Each item comes at an expense to your wallet and your available payload, so it is important to monitor how much recovery gear you store in your vehicle.

WINCH RIGGING COMPONENTS

Winch rigging components include high-quality screw pin D shackles for connection points, soft shackles, and a pulley block for changing the direction of a pull or rigging a double-line pull. Also essential is a method of damping a loaded winch line with a weight (mass). In the event that your winch cable breaks under its load, the winch dampener will weigh down the line so that it is pulled toward the ground while also reducing the speed of the line.

SHOVEL

A shovel is one of the most useful tools for the overlander, performing humble duties during toilet breaks or coming to the rescue when the vehicle is mired to the frame in snow. A shovel

↑ **The shovel** is the foundation for most vehicle recoveries and is also useful around camp.

can also be critical in reducing the strain associated with recovery, as you can remove material from dragging on frame components, reduce the angle of exit from the hole the tires have dug, and so on. It is not recommended that you use a small folding shovel for recovery. You should buy a high-quality fiberglass or ash-handled spade shovel.

TRANSIT CLUSTER

The transit cluster is used in the transportation industry and allows for a secure connection to a vehicle without proper recovery points. The transit cluster connects to the transit lashing points of the frame or unibody.

Adventure Motorcycle Recoveries

Adventure motorcycles are not immune from needing some recovery gear. However, the contents are essentially three items:

1. A 50–70-foot section of 4-millimeter climbing accessory cord
2. 2 micro pulleys
3. A 15-foot section of 1-inch climbing webbing

If your adventure motorcycle becomes mired in mud or slides down a slope, having a small rigging kit can make the difference between wind in your hair (through the vents in your helmet) and a long walk.

Recently, using a compact Warn winch for adventure motorcycling has become more common. Admittedly, I was skeptical until I traveled

↑ **Bill Dragoo climbs Elephant Hill** in Canyonlands before rigging the Warn winch to pull several damaged bikes to the top.

the Utah Traverse with Sinuhe Xavier, Bill Dragoo (of the D.A.R.T. School), and a few friends. The route was technical for BMW R1200GSes, even with experienced riders. While traversing Elephant Hill in Canyonlands, we reached our limits and used Bill's winch to pull the remaining motorcycles up the slickrock ledges. In an extreme situation, carrying the winch makes sense, as other team members can help spread the equipment load across multiple bikes.

Overland Essentials: 4WD Recovery Gear, Equipment, and Tools Checklist

↑ **Having sufficient payload** and storage allows trucks like this AEV Bison to support expeditions into the Altar Desert of Mexico.

I have always found checklists helpful for packing and ensuring I don't forget that one critical item. Still, I also feel these lists create an unreasonable and expensive expectation of what is needed for travel. People have ridden around the world on a Vespa, so I suspect their list was much shorter. Please use this checklist as a helpful guide to determine what is most important and to help make sure you don't forget the locking lug nut key (I learned that one the hard way).

Basic Recovery Kit (with a Vehicle-Mounted Winch)

- ☐ 2 metal shackles
- ☐ 2 soft shackles
- ☐ 30-foot kinetic recovery strap or rope
- ☐ 10-foot utility rope or tree protector strap
- ☐ Pulley block
- ☐ Line damper
- ☐ Full-sized D- or T-handled spade shovel
- ☐ Leather gloves and safety glasses

Suggested Additions

- 20-foot utility rope
- 50–75-foot winch extension rope
- Pull-Pal ground anchor
- Second pulley block
- Transit cluster

Tools and Spares

- ☐ Tire repair kit
- ☐ 12-volt air compressor
- ☐ Long travel bottle jack

- ☐ Tire deflator and gauge
- ☐ Mechanics tool set
- ☐ 12-volt repair kit and spare fuses
- ☐ Spray lubricant
- ☐ Plastic funnel
- ☐ General hose repair kit
- ☐ J-B Weld SteelStik
- ☐ Fluids (brake, engine, and power steering)
- ☐ Spare accessory belt
- ☐ Engine oil filter
- ☐ Engine air filter
- ☐ Fuel filter
- ☐ 10- or 20-liter fuel can
- ☐ Super siphon hose
- ☐ Extra wheel studs and lug nuts
- ☐ OBD-II code reader
- ☐ Engine code printout
- ☐ Jumper cable (heavy duty)
- ☐ Emergency triangles

Support Equipment

- ☐ Two-way GMRS or HAM radios
- ☐ Combo lock
- ☐ 2 ratchet straps
- ☐ 40-foot cord (4 millimeters in diameter)
- ☐ GPS
- ☐ Satellite communicator
- ☐ Paper maps or gazetteer
- ☐ Country guidebooks
- ☐ Spare AA, AAA, and 9-volt batteries
- ☐ Compact inverter (100 watts)
- ☐ Compact foldable solar panel for emergency charging

Overland Essentials:
Motorcycle Equipment Checklist

One of the wonderful things about adventure motorcycle travel is the simplicity, eschewing the complexities and excesses of daily life. As a rider, you can only bring so much, and the more you travel, the more you will tend to leave behind. The less you take, the better the bike will handle, which is part of the fun.

While preparing this comprehensive rider, bike, and equipment list, I pored through my notes, paring it down to the essentials. It is important to address the critical pieces, starting with riding gear (protecting you from the environment and accidents), survival basics, tools, navigation, and communications. Although bringing the kitchen sink is tempting, I rarely cook food on motorcycle trips. Otherwise, local offerings are a

much better choice, allowing you to mingle with people and stretch your legs. If off the grid internationally for a few days, I am happy to eat meal bars or Meals, Ready-to-Eat (MREs). As a result, I bring only a few small items for food prep, which mostly involves making coffee.

As a departure from the 4WD checklists spread throughout the book, I have included the entire adventure motorcycle equipment list in this section, covering rider gear and where I store equipment in the various luggage positions. While traveling with a motorcycle, you should stash your wallet, passport, and spare cash in your base layers, not in your motorcycle jacket. If someone were to steal the coat off your back or the back of a chair, you would lose those important items.

↑ **Traveling off a motorcycle** is the definition of freedom, but you can still be comfortable enough to camp in the backcountry.

The Rider Gear

- ☐ Lightweight helmet with sun visor and Bluetooth communicator
- ☐ Sunglasses
- ☐ Aether Expedition Suit with D3O jacket and pant
- ☐ Garmin Montana with inReach and GPS maps
- ☐ Multitool
- ☐ Tire gauge
- ☐ Lighter
- ☐ Ear protection
- ☐ Sunscreen and lip balm
- ☐ Motorcycle or leather boots
- ☐ Leather gloves coated in beeswax
- ☐ Large wool or cashmere scarf (can also be used for first aid needs)

Waterproof Duffle

- ☐ Wool base layer
- ☐ Mid-layer hoodie
- ☐ Hard-shell jacket (can layer under moto gear)
- ☐ Travel pants (one pair)
- ☐ Travel shorts (one pair)
- ☐ Two wicking T-shirts
- ☐ Pearly's Possum and Sealskinz socks (3 pairs total)
- ☐ Synthetic underwear (3 pairs total)
- ☐ Wool collared shirt for border crossing or semi-formal dinners
- ☐ Wool beanie
- ☐ Dopp kit for toiletries
- ☐ Barefoot trail-running shoes (black)
- ☐ iPad Pro to serve as navigation tablet and computer
- ☐ International plug converter

Tank Bag

- ☐ USB-C charging block
- ☐ Charging and data cables
- ☐ 8-TB solid-state drive
- ☐ Mirrorless camera
- ☐ Compact prime lens
- ☐ 24–105-millimeter zoom lens
- ☐ Headlamp

↑ **Using lightweight backpacking gear,** you can fit all the equipment for remote overlanding off a motorcycle.

- ☐ Smartphone with mapping and travel apps preloaded
- ☐ Paper map and small compass

Pannier #1

- ☐ 1–2 person backpacking tent
- ☐ Backpacking pad
- ☐ Ultralight sleeping bag (add liner for comfort)
- ☐ Inflatable pillow (can be used as a splint)
- ☐ Tarp/poncho

Basic Tool Kit in Pannier #1

- Basic wrenches matched to the motorcycle
- Vise-Grip pliers
- Crescent wrench
- Multi-bit driver set with ratcheting grip
- Tire plugs or spare tube and hand pump
- Tire irons (if tubed)
- Hub wrench
- Duct tape
- Wire and zip ties
- Spare Rollercam strap
- Electrical wire pair (for jumping) and spare fuses
- QuikSteel metal repair
- Lithium jumper pack (also for phone charging)

Pannier #2

- ☐ NOLS Med Kit 3.0 with medications
- ☐ Israeli bandage
- ☐ Tourniquet
- ☐ QuikClot trauma gauze
- ☐ 4-liter MSR Dromedary bag for water storage (with shower or hydration hose)
- ☐ Grayl GeoPress water filter
- ☐ Ready-to-eat food or good-to-go meals (72-hour supply)
- ☐ Backpacking stove or Jetboil
- ☐ Backpacking pot/pan combo
- ☐ Ultralight bowl/cup/utensils
- ☐ Starbucks Via instant coffee or AeroPress

The Minefield

According to *Scientific American*, of the 212 deaths on Everest, 56 percent occurred during the descent. Call it Summit Fever or something else, but the toll of a long expedition often reveals itself in the second half of the effort. For us, that did not come until nearly the end of our crossing of the Greenland Ice Sheet, where easy travels high on the plateau and a pleasant stop at the Summit Station (the highest point in Greenland) gave us a false sense of security. We were days ahead of schedule and could nearly taste the pizza in Kangerlussuaq, but Greenland had one last challenge.

Emil and I had been watching the GPS track closely, weaving between glacial lakes hidden below a layer of ice and snow. The conditions were still good, but we knew a section of massive miss-melting was just ahead—as the Arctic has gotten warmer, the glaciers are not only moving and calving into the sea, but they are also starting to melt rapidly at the tops, causing rivers, valleys, and mountains of ice to form. We only made it a few hundred meters in before the first truck was stuck, and out came the winches and shovels. The snow was so deep in the valleys that even 44-inch tires at 2 pounds per square inch (psi) were not enough to get through.

While we contemplated a plan, the radio crackled to life, Kurt's voice yelling, "Stop, stop, stop—your trailer just fell in a crevasse!" Greg's truck had broken through a crevasse and barely exited with the rear tire, but the trailer was in it, held up only by the chassis and its connection to the Hilux. The impact was powerful, tearing the rear tire off the Toyota and breaking the frame, a 3-inch crack visible just aft of the coil spring. The crevasse was huge, more than wide enough to swallow a person, and we could not see the bottom. The conditions greatly complicated the recovery, as this was not the only crevasse there, and probes revealed that the entire area was littered with them. Despite this, the team was in action, a chorus of clanking carabiners and whirling tools. Everyone was roped to their vehicles, and not a single word was said as the initial attention was placed on reseating the tire on the bead and then welding the frame.

We all worked through the night, with Emil and I driving in each direction, searching for a path out of this minefield. At daybreak, with better light, we could finally see a line of ski tracks in the snow and deviate our course to follow their path. We continued to drive for hours, occasionally getting stuck, but then we could see the first of several bright orange tents next to a rocky outcropping. We had made it and became the first in history to drive the long axis of the Greenland Ice Sheet.

←
With the rear tire torn off the wheel and the trailer wedged into the crevasse, the team sprang into action, conducting repairs and rigging the recovery. Everyone was harnessed to a vehicle to prevent a fateful fall into the icy depths.

CHAPTER 9

CAMPING

While an overlanding trip does not necessarily require even one night of camping, most travelers enjoy an evening under the stars. Camping has numerous benefits, including access to more remote locations, reduced costs, and the sense of having a home on wheels. Those traveling with a 4WD can choose between a ground tent, roof tent, camper, or trailer. From a motorcycle, camping will be confined to a ground tent, bivvy, or hammock. In a pinch, I have even slept in my motorcycle gear with a tarp pulled over me.

Camping is one of the most popular choices for sleeping on the road and one of the most personal. Camping often carries the widest range of options and costs, from a $100 tent to a $1 million expedition camper. This chapter will cover the fundamentals of sleeping in the backcountry, including the decision process for selecting the best camping solution for you, your vehicle, and the conditions you may encounter. Each option has its strengths and weaknesses, which are covered in detail, and all framed within the emphasis that less will almost always be more.

Embrace the Idea of Less Is More

It is important to remember that "The overlander's gear will expand so as to fill the available space in the vehicle." While Cyril Northcote Parkinson's law originally intended to highlight a mathematical equation for describing the rate of expansion of bureaucracies ("Work expands so as to fill the time available for its completion"), it has since been related to many other applications, including my previous quip. Somehow, I can travel for months on a motorcycle with all of the "stuff" I need, but then take a similar trip with a camper and fill all the available space with even more "stuff." The same applies to campers and trailers, and it serves as an important reminder to buy the smallest camper that works for your needs, not the biggest.

Consider Your Shelter Options

The decision on what type of shelter you will use should start with a look at your budget and how often you plan to camp. If the goal is only to camp a few nights per month, then a lightweight and compact backpacking system or sleeping inside the vehicle will keep the costs low and minimize the impact on the payload. Sleeping inside the 4WD will almost always be the best compromise for the infrequent camper as it provides the best security. If the vehicle is too small or has too many occupants, an appropriately sized ground tent could also meet your needs.

ROOFTOP TENTS

For a compromise solution, many overlanders choose a rooftop tent (RTT), which comes in both soft-shell and hard-shell variants. Soft-shell RTTs will generally be lighter, take up less rack space, and be less expensive than a hard-shell. The downside of the soft-shell is setup complexity and often less long-term durability. The sweet spot for RTTs is a lightweight wedge-style hard shell that pops up using gas struts and can be angled into the wind. Roof tents can be easy to deploy and quite comfortable in mixed conditions, but they will put a lot of weight on the top of the vehicle. (More on RTTs later in this chapter.)

TRUCK CAMPERS AND TRAILERS

Over the past decade, truck campers and trailers have become popular, often allowing for full-time overlanding in even the most remote environments. Truck campers are frequently lighter, less expensive, and provide better maneuverability than a trailer while reducing toll road and ferry costs. Overland trailers have many advantages, like leaving them parked in camp and often reducing the payload impact on the tow vehicle. Trailers can also range widely in size and amenities. Lastly are expedition campers, which are fully integrated into the base chassis and are designed specifically for remote extended travel with large water tanks, massive battery capacity, and robust construction for abusive road conditions. (You can learn more about all these camping options later in this chapter.)

Good Sleep Is Critical

Before we delve into *where* you will sleep, it's important to take a few moments to talk about the importance of sleep while traveling. One of the pillars of healthy travel is restorative sleep, which helps combat the effects of jet lag, long days behind the wheel, and the general stressors of a nomadic existence. While some people can fall asleep immediately despite the conditions, many benefit from a thoughtful routine to improve slumber. The baseline is to employ a 6/4/2/1 routine of stopping caffeine 6 hours before bed, having your last meal 4 hours before sleep, then taking your last sips of water 2 hours before, followed by turning off all the screens 1 hour before lights out. In that last hour, talking with a travel companion or reading a printed book is magic for sleep.

With the baseline addressed, other tools around sleep hygiene include going to sleep earlier and waking up earlier to make the best use of available daylight and darkness. Those first few hours of daylight are ideal for making miles with reduced traffic and (usually) no drunk drivers on the road. On rare occasions, I will use earplugs if the location is exceedingly noisy, like when I was detained at the Djibouti border for four days with bright area lights and a constant stream of buses from Somalia. The extreme heat, light, noise, and stress all resulted in my lowest sleep scores in years. In situations like that, window blackouts, earplugs, white noise, and even a gentle sleep aid like melatonin can all make a difference. Poor sleep compounds and can result in drowsy driving, reduced motor skills, impaired decision-making, and even increased chances of illness. Good sleep makes everything better.

Sleeping Inside the Vehicle

← **Sleeping on the coast of Mozambique,** the cool wind keeps the bugs away and allows for a comfortable night in the back of the Grenadier.

The least expensive and most practical method for camping is inside of the vehicle, and coincidentally it is also the method I have employed for most of my continental crossings. From a functional perspective, the vehicle is one of the most secure, quiet, weatherproof, and insulated methods for camping, combined with the benefits of weight and cost reduction. With a simple flat load floor, the back of most 4WD wagons becomes a retreat from the environment beyond and still allows the occupants quick access to the driver's seat.

There are a few key considerations for sleeping inside the vehicle, starting with the number of occupants. In most cases, overlanders are traveling with one or two people and possibly a pet. Once it becomes a crowd, the inside becomes impractical and cramped. The vehicle must also be long enough, with the front seats tilted forward, to allow the tallest person to stretch out comfortably. Depending on the roof height, the platform height might need to be shorter to allow everyone to sit up for snacking or changing. For this, a high-roof vehicle like the Land Cruiser Troopy is ideal.

↑ **Over the course of three years,** I slept hundreds of nights in the back of this Land Cruiser, this particular photo captured in the sand dunes of Namibia.

The added benefit of the sleeping inside method is the forced minimalism it requires, with most of the tools, spares, and cooking equipment going under the sleeping platform and just a few soft bags lashed to the top of the deck. Once in camp, all that is needed is to toss the soft luggage in the passenger seat and go to sleep. I leave the bedrolls set up in my configurations to make everything easy. Additionally, with most of the items below the platform, the entire rig is less of a theft target as passersby can only see a few blankets and pillows through the windows.

For ventilation, I use Mombasa netting that is cut and sewn to the dimensions of the windows, and then I lower the windows as much as the weather and security allow. The conveniences of sleeping in your vehicle include map lights already in the ceiling, phone chargers, and even a sound system or heater for short periods (use caution idling the vehicle). On a cold morning, I start the car and let the interior heat up before putting on clothes and shoes—a traveler's little luxuries.

Ground Tents

While ground tents have become less popular for overlanders, they are one of the market's most flexible and lightweight options. Tents will also be the only sustainable camping solution for motorcycle travelers. For vehicle and motorcycle tents, buying units that use part of the vehicle for support and wind protection is possible. Still, it is usually best to have a ground tent that can be pitched anywhere, including on surfaces that do not allow for staking (like rock or a parking lot).

In our testing, we have found that ultralight backpacking tents do not hold up to months or

↑ **Ground tents** are just as popular for an overnight trip as they are for a polar expedition.

years of use or are exceedingly expensive if they can. For this reason, it is better to favor durability and a heavier-duty construction as key attributes. The material can still be polyester but should be thicker and be supported by larger diameter poles. Long-term overlanding exposes a tent to a wide range of conditions, wind speeds, and snow loading, so a strong freestanding style is preferred.

For our polar expeditions, we have used heavy wall freestanding tents capable of providing the entire team with an escape from the weather, and I have found that these features are also important for day-to-day camping. Because of the vehicle payload, bringing a tent with standing height and three- or four-season capability is feasible. On a motorcycle, you will likely be confined to the backpacking models to save weight and space.

One common mistake in buying a tent is skimping on ventilation, often to gain a four-season rating. While hard to find, there are three-plus or four-season tents that have sufficient ventilation, but you should favor ventilation over snow loading for most trips. This will likely result in an inner tent with massive, vented doors and a ceiling covered by a rain fly (a layer of water-resistant fabric that goes over the larger tent) with chimneys to help exhaust the hot air and improve the cooling breeze. Another feature to emphasize is a "bathtub" floor with tall enough sides to prevent water ingress, in case the campsite starts to have standing water.

It is common for tents to be damaged during overland travel, so take care during pitching, takedown, and storage. Even if the wind is light, ensure the tent is properly secured (even using a guy line to the vehicle or motorcycle) to prevent it from blowing away or blowing into something sharp. I learned this lesson the hard way, puncturing a hole in a rain fly of my new tent when it blew over into a sharp tree branch. When storing the tent in its stuff sack, make sure that other sharp or hard-edged equipment does not rub against it and wear a hole. I also caution against packing heavy canvas wall tents for overlanding as they are designed to be set up just a few times per season and can take hours to pitch.

→
While riding through the Andes in Peru, a compact ground tent was my choice off the motorcycle.

Soft-Shell Roof Tents

There are pros and cons to fitting an RTT to your vehicle. Despite this, RTTs are more popular than ever, often now on display in stores like REI and frequently seen mounted to the tops of Subarus. Also gone are the days when the only high-quality and expedition-grade RTTs were made in South Africa and Europe. But more importantly, we are finally seeing innovation and unique solutions for the wants of RTT buyers. The style, weight, quality, and setup now vary significantly from the original Brownchurch rack tents of fifty years ago—all the better for buyers in the twenty-first century.

Choosing a roof tent is no longer the easy process of deciding which canvas color you like best, as there are now over fifty different brands and hundreds of models. There are tents available for under $500 online, and other units that cost ten times that much, and everything in between. The quality gap has also narrowed considerably, with ruggedized units now being manufactured in Asia and discount models currently being produced in South Africa. Despite all this, several attributes are critical for long-term use and reliability.

Keep in mind that it is easy to exceed the roof load limits of most SUVs once an RTT and full-sized rack are affixed. Only a few vehicles have roof load ratings exceeding 200 pounds, yet we often see oversized tents mounted to full-length metal racks with fuel cans and Hi-Lift jacks—a precarious and dangerous situation. This means smaller, lighter tents may have to be selected and usually mounted to simple crossbars. Fortunately, some units weigh only 100 pounds, which will still allow you to use a proper aluminum rack. Total up the weight of the tent, rack, accessories, and any bedding to be sure your vehicle roof is not overloaded.

When researching an RTT, it is important to determine the real-world pitch and stow time, as some tents can take 15–20 minutes to set up if the annex and all poles are utilized. That is often not practical for how many overlanders travel. This process can demand significant time and effort each day to pitch or close a tent, which can be even worse if weather conditions are poor.

↑ **Soft-shell tents** are affordable and can be purchased in numerous sizes to accommodate any vehicle, like the smaller bed of this Chevrolet Colorado AEV Bison.

Pay extra attention to the cover, which can be a struggle on certain models if constructed too tight to pull over the bows or fitted with undersized or difficult-to-operate zippers.

One of the best arguments for buying a roof tent is for a good night's rest, so test the mattress at an overland event or read reviews and comments on comfort before purchasing. I have seen buyers need to install memory foam and even air mattresses to augment the poor support of the stock pad. Look for a 2-inch (50-millimeter) minimum thickness and preferably dual density. Also, thicker canvas walls reduce light ingress, allowing for the luxurious option of sleeping well after sunrise.

As with anything you count on in the backcountry, quality and durability are paramount, or you are better off not having it. For example, a cheap winch that doesn't work when you need it, or a roof tent that fails in the first heavy wind, is a liability. An $800 ground tent will be superior to an $800 RTT, so it is suggested to avoid bargain RTTs altogether. The devil is in the details—the best things to look at are zipper size, cover thickness, tent wall stitching, and waterproofing method.

Hard-Shell Roof Tents

If soft-shell roof tents are good, hard-shells are even better. The hard-shell models set up and stow more quickly, typically have thicker mattresses, and can endure more extreme weather. The hard-shell will be made from reinforced plastic, fiberglass, composite, or aluminum, resulting in long life and increased durability. If the model is wedge-style, the vehicle can be nosed into the wind to reduce buffeting and water ingress. But the hard-shell often comes at a price to both weight and wallet.

↑ **I prefer a wedge-style hard-shell tent** like this Eezi-Awn, as they can be positioned into the wind and perform much better under snow loads. They also set up in seconds.

↑ **The Autohome** is one of the first hard-shell tents and still one of the best with lighter weight and generous interior space.

When you roll into camp at the end of a long day or are trying to get on the road early in the morning, the last thing you want to do is spend 20 minutes fumbling with a tent, especially if the weather is bad. Hard-shells alleviate this issue with much faster setup and breakdown times. Instead of removing a dirty cover and folding the tent over, a hard-shell pops up on gas struts after releasing the latches, reducing setup time from minutes to seconds. Breakdown is just as easy and eliminates the worst part of soft-shell tent ownership: tucking fabric and installing the cover.

Another bonus to hard-shell tents is that they are more aerodynamic than soft-shells, resulting in less wind noise on the highway and better fuel economy on long drives. While soft-shell tent covers are replaceable, years in the sun will cause them to rot and fade. Hard-shells, however, are much more durable and can survive for decades when cared for properly. Often overlooked is the number of features hard-shell tents provide—things like built-in solar-powered fans to prevent condensation, built-in lights, and exterior racks for accessories like fly rods, standup paddleboards, or solar panels.

The fact that most hard-shell tents don't fold over gives them many advantages, like storing bedding and even pillows inside, but it also means their footprint is quite large compared to a traditional soft-shell tent. This might be a problem for people with the space constraints of a smaller vehicle or anyone who needs to run additional boxes or gear on their roof rack. The other potential downside of hard-shell tents is weight; some units we have tested exceed 200 pounds. For example, a Toyota 4Runner has a total roof load limit of 150 pounds, so it is easy to exceed roof ratings on an already tall vehicle.

Habitats and Wedge Campers

One of the fastest-growing segments for camping is the wedge camper and habitat market, providing lightweight and durable truck toppers with integrated pop-top sleeping modules. This allows the travelers to stand up inside and retreat from the weather. The interior is only the truck bed unless the owner elects to build a custom camping system, but the best features of these units are simplicity, lower costs, and a light weight.

The wedge camper shells are an excellent choice for light-duty pickups like the Toyota Tacoma and Tundra, allowing the fitment of a camper while remaining under GVWR. These campers will enable the use of the bed for trips to the hardware store or hauling mountain bikes, but it can be fully transformed into a home on the road by lashing down a few storage boxes for seats and a table insert for working and cooking. When the weather turns to rain and snow, there is still enough room to relax, prepare meals, change clothes, and sleep, even with two people. Some units like the AT Overland Equipment Habitat Truck Topper even cantilever open entirely to permit a cavernous space to sleep a family of four.

The style of wedge camper you select will be based on numerous factors, including weather, driving style, and interior buildout goals. For example, some models have "arctic pack" insulation accessories that can turn the camper into a four-season retreat. Others employ impressive origami to use hard sides that fold and collapse during stowing. All these features cost money and

↑ **Habitats like this AT Overland Equipment Truck Topper** are both lightweight and spacious, allowing for an entire family to sleep inside.

add weight, so choose wisely to ensure the camper stays under the vehicle payload and within the travel budget.

Durability and dust-proofing are the final two considerations for the wedge units, with models like the Go Fast Camper being some of the most lightweight, durable, and affordable. At the other end of the spectrum is the Alu-Cab ModCAP, which has a fully dust-sealed rear door, is built like a tank (and weighs over 500 pounds), and can even be optioned with a Dickinson propane fireplace. For most light-duty pickup owners, the wedge camper is just right.

←
Wedge campers can do it all and provide a compromise that works in nearly every condition.

Truck Campers

Pickup trucks are the jacks-of-all-trades, doing hard work during the week and adventuring on the weekends. Trucks also tend to have higher payloads and more storage space than wagons and can be paired with a truck camper. The advantages of the slide-in truck camper include the ability to move the unit to a newer vehicle, remove it between trips, and fit within the overall length of the pickup for better maneuverability over a trailer.

There are two major categories of truck campers: the hard-sided units and the lifting roof models. Both have distinct advantages, and neither is superior, so the decision comes down to either the lower profile and improved fuel economy of the lifting roof or the four-season comfort, quiet, and no setup of the hard-sided. Pricing and the general list of amenities are often comparable between the two styles. The lifting roof is usually preferred for international travel as the truck will likely still fit in a high-top shipping container. In contrast, the hard-sided camper must either be removed for containerizing or shipped using a roll-on/roll-off (RoRo) vessel.

Considerations for the hard-sided models should start with the construction method and insulation, with bonded composite panels being the preferred method. The panels will be several inches thick and filled with insulation to improve extreme weather performance and reduce outside noises. The panels are often bonded to reinforced metal corners or extrusions to give impact protection (think tree branches) and rigidity to the entire structure. These corners and extrusions should also be insulated or covered on the interior to reduce thermal bridging and the likelihood of condensation. Hard-sided campers will often have a high-output heater for winter camping, and it is becoming more common for them to have 12-volt air conditioners too.

↑ **Slide-in truck campers** can be surprisingly lightweight, comfortable, and affordable.

←
Pop-top campers like this compact Scout Yoho will fit smaller vehicles and allow access to tighter trails with trees.

The downsides to hard-sided models are few, but it is important to consider the camper's weight and the impact on the center of gravity when traveling off-highway. The suspension rate should be increased to keep the truck level, and the rear anti-sway bar and shocks may also need to be changed to control sway on the road and trail. For backcountry use, the most common issue is the overall height of the camper and the likelihood of contacting tree branches and even rock outcroppings. Check the height of the camper using a tape measure to the highest point (often a vent cover) and put a label with the height on the windshield for the driver to be reminded. As a clever hack, many camper owners will install an antenna to the front bumper that matches the height of the camper and works as a strong visual indicator if the tree branch or coffee shop drive-through is tall enough to drive under (another lesson I learned the hard way).

Lifting roof or pop-top slide-in campers are becoming increasingly popular, and there are more models than ever on the market. This includes aluminum-framed options with a skinned exterior and composite panel models with insulated tent sides. The pop-top is great for daily driving, off-highway use, better fuel economy, and lower overall height. The lifting roof models also (usually) have a lower center of gravity and much-improved clearance on tight trails with tree branches and rock overhangs. In the developing world, the lower height also reduces the chance of hitting overhead powerlines or exceeding height restrictions on bridges and ferries.

The greatest limitation with the lifting roof campers is in extreme weather, as a tent will never have the same insulation and sound-deadening properties as a hard-sided camper. There is also an increased chance of leaks, tears in the tent fabric, and lifting mechanism wear over long-term use. Other practical limitations include restrictions on roof loads, smaller entry doors, no overhead cabinets, and reduced heater/air conditioner performance. Despite these considerations, the pop-top camper will be one of the most effective camping solutions for long-term overlanders, striking the ideal balance between size, performance, maneuverability, and value.

Expedition Campers

Expedition campers are sometimes viewed as excessive or even a liability to use for remote overland travel. However, realities in the field have yet to prove this to be the case. In 2009, I drove to the Darién Gap in a small Jeep-based expedition camper called the EarthRoamer XV-JP, and it performed as I had hoped, allowing me to travel deep into the jungle. The same model took me safely across the Rubicon Trail and was the first RV to cross the infamous track. During the Panama trip, we also had a full-sized EarthRoamer XV-LT with us for the journey. While it was too large for some of the most isolated jungle tracks, it did drive every mile between Arizona and Panama City with minimal issues. Certainly, we needed to plan our route to avoid tight streets in colonial-era villages, and we kept a PVC pole handy to lift wires above the roofline, but we made it. Similar campers from Unicats to Bliss Mobils have been driven around the world and across nearly every continent. Expedition campers are exciting to consider as a home away from the mundane, a magic carpet with a kitchen and shower, whisking you off to the next horizon.

↑ **For many around-the-world travelers,** the Mercedes-Benz Unimog with a camper box is a reasonable compromise and still capable in remote conditions.

↑ **One of the most popular expedition campers is the EarthRoamer,** which has a proven reputation for quality and good customer service.

There are definite pros and cons that you should consider before purchasing an expedition camper. The most evident advantage is having an entire home on top of a durable and capable commercial 4WD. Most expedition campers will also have luxurious amenities like hot water showers, air conditioning, in-floor heating, thick mattresses, and even drop-down porches for viewing the megafauna in comfort. From a practical consideration, these campers also have large galleys for cooking, which can help support travelers with dietary restrictions. The large space and climate control can also support full-time remote work wherever you may be parked that day.

Having a home on wheels has some challenges, primarily size, weight, and cost. While expedition camper owners will valiantly defend their choice of vehicle, such a large camper is a constant liability and risk. There are well-documented incidents of historic walls and bridges being damaged beyond repair by large overland trucks. The vehicle also inherently limits cultural interactions with locals, as they will often be too intimidated to approach, or the occupants might be sequestered inside. These large vehicles will be limited to commercial trucking routes or more open terrain. The cost can also be a nonstarter, with expedition campers regularly exceeding $500,000 along with increased insurance, operating expenses, toll charges, ferry fees, and import bonds. In many countries, the driver will need a commercial driver's license. None of these negatives are intended to dissuade a purchase, but entering an investment like this with your eyes wide open is important.

Overland Trailers

We can all see the appeal of a fully stocked trailer in the garage, everything packed and organized, a faithful companion just waiting for Friday afternoon and a weekend of exploration. The benefits are clear, but there are dozens of trailer manufacturers and endless options to consider. What makes for the ultimate trailer? What performance attributes are critical and often overlooked? Trailer styles include compact and trail-worthy models with a roof tent mounted, traditional teardrop units, and fully self-contained travel trailers with all the comforts of home.

One of the ideal scenarios for buying an overland trailer is a large family or a vehicle with limited payload (but a higher tow rating). The only way to safely add payload is with a trailer, which shifts the total capacity from gross vehicle weight (GVW) to gross combined vehicle weight rating (GCVWR). Put a family of four in a two-door Jeep Wrangler, and all the usable space is gone. The best way to add storage volume is with a small trailer that has a lot of usable space. Look for products that eschew systems and gadgets in favor of an open container. These are easy to tow

↑ **A heavy-duty composite panel overland trailer** will provide comfort and durability, yet still work on many trails.

and give the same space as a truck bed to stow bags, supplies, and camping equipment.

A trailer is also better than an overloaded roof rack. Roof racks should be reserved for the lightest of loads, but unfortunately, it is the first place that travelers tend to stash heavy, bulky items. Generally, most vehicles have a roof load limit of 100–150 pounds, while most trailers can easily transport many times that (within the limits of the vehicle's tow rating). This also lowers the load, which makes everything easier to access. In our testing, we found the highway fuel mileage impact of a trailer to be nearly identical to that of a roof rack with boxes.

We all lead busy lives, so having a full-stocked bug-out trailer has universal appeal. It can be parked in the garage with all the gear properly organized and ready for service. Even late on a Friday night, the unit can be easily connected, and after a stop at the store to stock food and drinks, it is off to the campsite. This eliminates all of the packing and organizing required with a daily driver and also helps reduce the number of camping-specific modifications that have to be done to the tow vehicle. It's also a perfect solution for leased SUVs or vehicles that serve multiple roles in the family.

The advantages of an overland trailer are many, but they can also come at a surprising cost once optioned appropriately. There are even trailers with just a fabric tent that will cost more than a new tow vehicle. By nature, a trailer also brings complexity, adding another axle (or two), more

bearings, additional tires, suspension, a chassis, and many other systems. Trailers often have less robust components than the tow vehicle and less suspension travel, translating to increased abuse to the entire unit and its stored contents on rough terrain. They also lengthen daily checks and service time in the field and require unique spare parts.

Any warning about trailer towing would be complete only with mention of backing up and parking. Even the most experienced drivers can struggle on technical terrain with a trailer, where backing up any distance can be difficult or even impossible. If tight trails and long shelf roads are typical for you, a trailer might pose a risk worth considering. In my travels, there were several instances where backing up quickly was paramount— a charging elephant is the first example that comes to mind.

Due to the popularity of overland trailers, there are many sizes, styles, and prices to choose from, but it is always important to focus on durability and serviceability first. How long has that trailer manufacturer been in business? Do they have a good warranty reputation? Was the unit designed to be serviced and repaired in the field? Based on my testing, selecting a trailer specifically designed for off-road use is best, and it will be constructed from either a heavy-duty aluminum frame or a bonded composite assembly. In general, it is not recommended to tow a trailer that does not provide some material comfort beyond what can be found with just the vehicle and roof tent.

←

A teardrop trailer can meet the needs of many weekend travelers and perform well in all four seasons.

Camping in the Cederberg of South Africa

The Cederberg Mountains rise above the bushveld of the west cape of South Africa, peaks extending up to 2,000 meters above the tumultuous seas to the south. Before starting my crossing of Africa, I wanted to test my Grenadier in the mountains, including the challenging terrain and the remote camping outpost of Bakkrans. This boondoggle was the highlight of Southern Africa, as fortuitously, my travel companion Joe Fleming was able to contact Ozzy Yerlikaya who suggested we drive to his newly constructed eco-lodge and camping area at the end of a 14-mile, low-range track deep in leopard country. The Bakkrans Private Wilderness Concession showcases 100,000 years of human history and is located within a World Heritage Site that houses the Cape Floral Region and the Cape Leopard Trust. (The Cape leopard is geographically distinguished from the African leopard and is extremely rare, with an estimated 35 remaining in the Eastern Cape.)

Getting an early start, we lowered the tire pressure and pressed toward Wupperthal, which ended up being one of the finest overland routes I have driven in South Africa. We climbed steadily into the bushveld, only passing a few motorcycles on our traverse along Hoek se Berg Pass, the entire escarpment a canvas of yellow and purple wildflowers interrupted by red rocks and green brush. It was a complete surprise, yet we had been gifted our journey at peak bloom.

The trail continued with a steep 4WD low-range climb out of Wupperthal, culminating in a slow meander through towering red rock spires, sandy washes, and cedar-lined slopes. It was undeveloped and nearly uninhabited, save for the single village of Eselbank. We were late and making slow progress with the unexpected rains and washouts. Eventually, we arrived at Keurbosfontein, a historic farm with a homestead that is nearly 200 years old. It is run by Justin Bonello, a famous South African author, chef, filmmaker, and traveler. Justin has turned the farm into an incredible cooking and exploration retreat,

↑ **We entered the Cederberg** during the wildflower bloom, our route covered in a sea of color.

and it serves as the last outpost before climbing up the Matjiesrivier Nature Reserve escarpment to Bakkrans.

I would place this rustic and remote accommodation in my top five in all my travels. The combination of a long overland track, challenging low-range obstacles, the leopards, aboriginal rock art, and views make it a deeply meaningful experience. The sheepherders originally used the stone huts, but they have been outfitted with hot water showers and solar lighting. There is a dining and kitchen hut, complete with massive fireplaces and long, rough-hewn tables for eating and conversation. At one point, I noticed a mouse and mentioned it to Ozzy, with his reply being, "They are our friends and are free to come and go as we do." With limited power, our music came from an original phonograph, projecting the sounds of the 1920s big bands playing through the pavilion horn. The sun dipped lower as we enjoyed a drink and watched the remaining rays cast through the dangling *naẓar* meant to keep the evil eyes of the Cederberg at bay.

CHAPTER 10

COOKING AND CAMP EQUIPMENT

With the growing popularity of overlanding and camping, there have never been more options to curate a comfortable campsite, including everything and the kitchen sink. Today, compact hot water showers, espresso makers, and even two-stroke gas margarita blenders exist. The challenge isn't having enough options; it is having far too many. You should bring less gear so the experience becomes about nature, not the equipment. However, there are a few items that can improve the experience—and there is nothing wrong with starting the day with a cappuccino.

This chapter will focus on selecting the fundamental cooking supplies, including water storage, stove options, and cookware. Should you cook with gas, liquid fuel, or over the open fire? This chapter will review all of these options and even the emergence of induction cooktops. With your food preparation addressed, you'll then review 12-volt refrigerators, awnings, camp furniture, and traveler bathing.

Cooking Supplies

From my experience, it is tempting to overpack for cooking, so you should start with the basics and build from there. For example, on a motorcycle few supplies can be packed along, so limit what you bring to water, water filtering, a backpacking stove, and a small kitchen set. The kitchen set will have a pot/pan, bowl, mug, fork, knife, and spoon. The knife serves double duty as a folding paring knife, and some models also have a wine bottle opener in the handle. Add salt, pepper, spices, and coffee and the entire kit will all fit in a small Cordura zippered sack. These are the basics, but they can serve as a starting point to slowly add other items in a 4WD or camper. (See the packing list later in this chapter.)

↑ **The entirety of my motorcycle kitchen kit** fits in a small canvas pouch.

↑ **Larry Brady** serves hot coffee on a cold fall morning in the High Sierras.

STOVES

The stove is the foundation of any culinary campsite, and the selection process begins with the fuel source. The best choices for international travel are butane (fuel canister) and induction (electric). These choices are superior because of both their availability and their safety. It is common for international travelers to consider a multi-fuel stove (one that can burn a variety of fuels such as white gas, kerosene, unleaded auto fuel, and diesel), but those are prone to causing fires and require regular cleaning and service. The advantage of multi-fuel is that you can burn unleaded in a pinch, although most users end up using white gas, which is also difficult to source in remote areas. However, the most common stove worldwide is the classic butane model, and I have seen canisters in almost every rural market on every continent. It is recommended to buy the stove and fuel locally as they can be had for less than $20—if you like two burners, buy two!

Induction stoves are becoming more popular and provide numerous advantages. It is common for newer vehicles to have built-in inverters or for travelers to have portable power packs for running Starlink and charging laptops and cameras. The inverter should have a minimum continuous run wattage of 1,800 at 120 volts (or about 2,500 watts at 220 volts if using an EU spec inverter). Induction stoves use a lot of power while running, but even boiling water only takes a few minutes at max output (using about 15-amp hours of battery). Longer cooking processes are usually run at lower settings to prevent food burning, so overall power consumption is manageable. If you run the vehicle during cooking, the alternator will help make up the amperage difference. Induction cooktops are easy to find internationally, are safe in confined spaces, and are easy to clean. Portable units will be less than $100 and take up no more space than a standard camp stove.

For North American and European travel, propane stoves are common and have the benefit of bulk fuel (which can also be used for heating or for a portable firepit), inexpensive refills, and good burner performance. The stoves vary from compact to four burners and everything in be-

↑ **After being detained for three days,** we made our last two ramen cups at the border of Djibouti and Ethiopia using our trusty $20 butane stove.

tween. It is good to compare British thermal unit (BTU) output and wind protection when looking at propane stoves and grills, along with overall durability. Also, examine how the burner knobs are constructed and protected, as unprotected plastic knobs will likely fail early on a trip.

The final category of stoves is the ultra-compact backpacking units that normally burn a Lindal B188 valve multi-fuel gas cylinder. It is best to find one that uses a blend of propane and isobutane for better performance at high elevation and colder temperatures. This type of stove will be most popular for adventure motorcycles due to its compact size, light weight, and ability to nest the canister inside a small pot and pan set. I have also used these stoves in smaller vehicles or when my travels are concentrated in North America and the European Union. It is also possible to purchase a Lindal valve to butane canister adapter to improve fuel options when farther afield.

POTS AND PANS

Pots and pans will often be the biggest compromise in the camp kitchen, as material and thickness significantly influence how evenly heat is distributed across the unit. Most backpacking pans perform poorly in this area, so you should look for sets tailored more for car camping with thicker aluminum and reinforced handles. Along with cooking performance, you should note how the units nest together and how they are packed and protected. Quality brands will have a storage bag, and I put dishwashing pads between each layer to manage rattles. For most campers, a 10–12-inch pan and a pot that nests inside that diameter is the best compromise. Ideally, a strainer and the handles will fit inside the pot, and the lid will be secured.

It is difficult to talk camp cooking without talking cast iron, and because it cooks superior to other metals, I would never judge anyone who lugs around a cast iron or aluminum deep-dished pan, but they are heavy and can wreak havoc if not secured properly.

TABLEWARE

For tableware, picking the right shape and materials makes a difference. Unfortunately, many camp sets are made from plastic, which is difficult to clean properly (particularly after wear and knife cuts). Stainless steel is a preferred material for plates, bowls, forks, and spoons. A folding knife is best for your knife choice and can serve multiple purposes depending on the sizes you select. Cups also benefit from being multipurpose, serving as double-walled coffee cups in the morning and wine glasses in the evening. The cups should also have lids because nothing can make an overlander (okay, me) cry faster than a spilled mocha. Other utensils and even entire cutlery sets from several manufacturers can be combined into well-organized kits. Packaging at least one additional place setting is also a good idea, as you never know when a guest will be invited or an item will go missing.

Support equipment includes a collapsible sink, biodegradable soap, quick-dry towels, and an antibacterial-style scrubber. A solid hack is to use wet wipes to perform the initial cleaning on items, followed by the hot water and soap in the sink.

WATER STORAGE

Water is one of the most important items you bring into the backcountry, so there are a few important best practices for storage and usage. Water is also heavy at 8.34 pounds per gallon, so even 20 gallons weighs 166 pounds plus the container. At a minimum, you will want 2 gallons of water per person per day of remote camping to address all basic drinking, cooking, cleaning, and hygiene needs. As a result, overlanders should focus on conserving water and distributing the liquid across several containers, as low down and as close to the vehicle's centerline as possible. Smaller containers reduce the chance of losing all your water in one mishap and allow the weight to be placed strategically.

↑ **A 20-liter water can** with integrated filter is a convenient way to store potable and non-potable water. It is also possible to fit a shower attachment and pressurize the can for bathing.

You'll find that 10–20-liter water canisters and 10-liter bladders (like the classic MSR Dromedary bag) work well to store the required volume, and I find that the bladders store well in the rear footwells of a wagon. The canister should accommodate a filter (or filter the water before filling the container). It is important to clearly label potable and non-potable containers to reduce your group's chance of getting sick. I like a filter that uses a combination of mechanical filtration and an ultraviolet LED. Bring along bleach (eight drops of 6 percent bleach per gallon) or water filtration tablets as a backup.

REFRIGERATION

When camping, you also need a way to store food and keep perishables cold. This can be solved (like on a motorcycle) by not bringing any food that requires a refrigerator or cooler. However, most backcountry overland campers prefer having fresh food and cold drinks along. Depending on how items are stored, most vegetables will last a few days without refrigeration, and unwashed and never refrigerated eggs can go several days to a week, depending on the climate. A nice combination is a soft-sided cooler for storing dry goods and tuber vegetables, rice, cereal, and bread, complemented by a smaller 12-volt refrigerator.

One of the luxuries of overlanding is the 12-volt fridge/freezer, filled to the brim with cold drinks, coffee creamers, chocolate, fresh fruit, and your favorite protein. The ability to make ice in a dual-zone refrigerator will bring a smile to any campfire gathering. While many consider the refrigerator a necessary addition, it comes at a high purchase price, power consumption, and weight. For that reason, it is recommended that you

↑ **A fridge/freezer unit** like the National Luna will last for decades of overland use and is designed for maximum insulation and power efficiency.

purchase a smaller refrigerator than estimated. A 25-liter fridge for one to two travelers, a 40-liter unit for two to four people, and a 50-liter model for larger families. Space can be saved by storing shelf-stable milk and drinks until you need them and only keeping important items (like chocolate) in the refrigerator.

Avoiding Food Illnesses

Food illness can be a serious stressor for some travelers, and food allergies are challenging to communicate and manage in foreign lands. Fortunately, there are some effective strategies for staying healthier on the road, starting with how you eat locally purchased food. For this, the mantra of "piping hot, peeled, or packaged" needs to rule the day. If you peel an orange, the chance of getting sick is minimal, as is opening a protein bar purchased in the last city. The other option is to frequent restaurants that are busy and serve dishes that are piping hot. If you are worried about foodborne illnesses, skip the salad and enjoy the curry that is still boiling in the dish.

The other option is having calorie-dense packaged foods in your vehicle. While tubes of Pringles are not a healthy choice, a tub of protein powder and several boxes of shelf-stable milk (or alternative) are. I have found protein powder in nearly every country I have traveled to, and it doesn't take up much space and gives dozens of servings. By substituting one meal daily with known food options, the chances of getting sick drop accordingly. Another option is powdered vitamin drinks with sufficient dosing (like magnesium, zinc, and vitamin D) to support the immune system and good sleep. It can be a good break from sugary canned drinks and help keep you healthy for future adventures.

Basic Camp Equipment

Who doesn't love a "Taj Macamp," complete with wooden and canvas chairs, an expansive awning, table linens, and a crackling fire? A campsite can be as elaborate and comfortable as you choose, and some overlanders enjoy all the setup and luxury available. On the opposite side of the same coin is the motorcycle traveler, for whom one pannier becomes the chair and the other the table, with perhaps a tree or tarp for some shade. Both approaches are rewarding in their own rights and complete with their own pros and cons. For basic camp equipment, the goal is to focus on shade, seating, a toilet, and fire.

SHADE

When camping, your priority should be shade and shelter, as any trip long enough will result in a sodden campsite or sunburned skin. This is where an awning can prove invaluable and make the campsite even more inviting. There are permanent and bag awnings, both of which have distinct advantages. The permanent awning is typically mounted to the vehicle's rack or side of the camper to allow for ease of use and quick deployment. The most common awning sizes unroll to form a simple 90-degree covering or can unfurl into a 180-degree or even 270-degree coverage. A 90-degree awning will meet the needs of most campsites, cost less, and take less time to deploy. However, a 270-degree awning shines when it can swing around the rear of the vehicle and provide sun and rain protection over the back of a camper or wagon with a rear entry door or pull-out drawer kitchen.

The other type of awning is a bag-style, which is transportable between vehicles and stores to be about the size of a backpacking tent. These awnings can have aluminum bows that help with rain shedding (and reduce flapping). The tensioned cross poles allow the awning to be strapped to a rack or suction-cupped to the vehicle's side. They are often supported on the outside edge by a rafter

↑ **South Africans know how to camp** and produce some of the most durable gear on the market. The Eezi-Awn DragonFly 180 awning provides expansive shade in the bushveld.

pole and one or two adjustable upright poles. Sometimes, bag awnings eschew upright poles entirely, becoming a domed enclosure on the side of the vehicle (great for buggy conditions).

SEATING

Having a comfortable place to sit at the end of a long day is nice. Fortunately, there are chairs for every need, body type, and budget. If the chair is only used for relaxing, a more reclined sling-style unit is often best, but it can be awkward when eating at a table. The seating position is personal; some campers will want a more upright chair for eating and working. Despite the shape, the chair should be sturdy and stable, so the occupant doesn't tumble out of it on a slope. Chairs are a common failure item when traveling because the quality varies too widely, and they need to support a human-sized load on uneven terrain for months or years of use. Look for a robust structure with strong connection points and reinforced stitching. The chair should set up quickly and store easily in the vehicle, or it will rarely be used.

↑ **Dr. Bryon Bass** waits patiently in the heat of the Danakil Desert for our documents to arrive, his situation made slightly more comfortable with a Melvill & Moon camp chair.

TABLES

The camp table can take many forms, with some mounting to the vehicle or dropping down from a rear swingout door. Other tables are simple folding plastic units, while others require minutes to set up. If the vehicle has a rack, some tables slide under the slats and set up in seconds. Stability should be a priority for a table, followed by ease of setup. The size should also reflect the size of the party. With the theme of multiuse, I prefer a metal top table that can be sturdy enough to be used as a workbench should repairs to equipment or the vehicle be required.

CAMPFIRE

A crackling campfire is a quintessential camping accessory but must be taken seriously in the backcountry. Building a fire in an existing rock fire ring is generally acceptable, but it is discouraged for you to make new ones. Fire restrictions are also common, often reducing s'mores production

↑ **A firepit on the coast of Baja** catches the ashes and provides a warming glow to the star-filled sky.

to a propane firepit. If open flames are permitted and safe, it is still good form to use a portable fireplace that can trap ash and often provide a grilling surface too. As travelers, we are responsible for fire safety, which includes ensuring that an unattended fire is completely out and cool before departing. As Smokey the Bear says, "If it is too hot to touch, it is too hot to leave."

TOILETS AND BATHING

Some often overlooked camp equipment is a toilet and a bathing method. Certainly, it is acceptable to relieve oneself in nature if done properly, and if there are no facilities nearby. Toilet paper should be packed out (we have all seen the campsites littered with TP), and bodily waste should be buried or packed out. If you are traveling on a motorcycle options are limited, but in some vehicles, it is possible to bring the toilet with you and depart with the waste for proper disposal. Inside a camper, there will often be numerous options for a toilet, including porta potties, bagged systems, and composting toilets. These can also be used in conjunction with a tented privy and provide the benefit of privacy and removing all waste from the campsite. For longer-term travel, the composting toilet can be the best choice and last for weeks or even a month of regular use, with urine stored separately for ease of disposal.

Bathing can be done in many ways, from hot water showers to large wet wipes or even a simple sponge bath. It is good to have a few large body wipes available in addition to a shower solution, as you can clean up inside the vehicle or tent in populated areas. Otherwise, a simple gravity or pressurized shower works magic at the end of a hot or dusty day. With care, water use is minimal but ensures good hygiene while on the road. The same privy used for the toilet can also be used for bathing, and some enclosures can be permanently affixed to the rack for ease of setup. A pressurized shower is best as it cleans more effectively and uses less water. Adding hot water from a pot on the stove can make the experience more luxurious.

4WD Camping and Cooking Equipment Packing List

There is real anxiety in packing for a trip, in trying to remember every possible item you might need and finding a place to store everything. The expenses and payload can really add up. About ten years ago, I had a revelation of sorts, which is that I don't need much at all. In Chapter 3, I discussed the ABCs, which can serve as a foundation, but even more elemental are the things I call the "travel trinity," which is a passport (identification), a debit or credit card (universal problem solver), and a smartphone.

If you have your passport, a way to buy services, and a means of communication, it is possible to travel with just the clothes you boarded the plane with. Rolf Potts demonstrated this concept perfectly in his No Baggage Challenge. Rolf spent six weeks flying and driving 30,000 miles around the world with only the clothing and personal effects on his back. While the challenge may appear more asceticism than travel, the exercise proved that less is more, as he could focus entirely on his experiences in the moment. In the lens of overlanding, this is a gentle reminder that your vehicle isn't perfect when you have added the last possible piece of kit but rather when you have removed the last one. Here is some recommended equipment for cooking and camping:

BASIC COOKING EQUIPMENT

- ☐ Stove
- ☐ Cooking fuel
- ☐ Fire blanket
- ☐ Pot and pan set (with lid, handle, and case)
- ☐ Tableware set (deep-dished plates and bowls)
- ☐ Mug set (double-walled with lid)
- ☐ Utensil set (forks and spoons)
- ☐ Folding knife set (paring and steak knives)
- ☐ Kitchen tool set (whisk, spatula, ladle, and cutting board)
- ☐ Can and wine bottle openers
- ☐ Salt and pepper mills (refillable)
- ☐ Spice kit
- ☐ Cooking spray
- ☐ Cooking oil
- ☐ Coffee kit
- ☐ Collapsible wash basin
- ☐ Quick dry kitchen towels
- ☐ Antimicrobial dish scrubber
- ☐ Biodegradable soap
- ☐ Reusable grocery bags
- ☐ Zip-top bags
- ☐ Aluminum foil
- ☐ Water storage
- ☐ Water filtering (mechanical, UV, and chemical)
- ☐ Dry goods storage
- ☐ 72 hours of shelf-stable backup food
- ☐ Refrigerator and/or cooler

BASIC CAMPING EQUIPMENT

- ☐ Shelter (ground tent, rooftop tent, inside the vehicle, and so on)
- ☐ Sleeping pad
- ☐ Sleeping pillow
- ☐ Sleeping bag or insulated quilt
- ☐ Wool blanket
- ☐ Camp chair
- ☐ Camp table
- ☐ Awning
- ☐ Heavy-duty stakes
- ☐ Lighter (with backup lighter and matches)
- ☐ LED flashlight
- ☐ Hygiene kit (shower, body wipes, towel, tissues, and biodegradable soaps)
- ☐ Waste kit (shovel, toilet paper, and zip-top bags)
- ☐ Portable toilet and privy (if space and budget allow)
- ☐ Small hand whisk broom
- ☐ Trash bags
- ☐ Hand axe
- ☐ Firepit kit (varies by condition and local regulations)
- ☐ Laundry line with clothespins
- ☐ Bleach

Camping in the Serengeti

I prefer camping inside the vehicle for most of my journeys, and my recent journey through the Serengeti of Tanzania was no different. Despite the social media appeal of an elaborate campsite, there is a simplicity and security that comes from crawling into a sleeping bag surrounded by a metal cage. We had driven all day through the Serengeti, meandering along tracks teeming with wildlife. Over an hour had passed watching a parade of elephants, complete with calves pulling branches off trees the size of my arm. The next trail took us along Turner Springs to a bloat of hippos, their ears announcing our arrival with a flurry of wiggles and spraying water. Before we knew it, the light of day was fading, and it is never good to be driving around lion country at night.

Fortunately, we had good maps of the area and a capable vehicle to navigate the challenging and remote terrain. Our camp for the evening was just a dot on the map, a "Special Campsite," as the park officials called it, a level spot under an acacia tree in the middle of the bush. We finally made our way to the main gravel road before finding the turnoff to the camp, its only identifier being a small stone painted with the number six.

We drove for several kilometers before the road turned to a two-track, the grass high and the hillsides dotted with wildlife. Rounding a bend, we both gasped, a sea of wildebeest and zebra stretching to the horizon. Our pace slowed to a crawl as we waited for the migration to part, allowing us to gently meander through their ranks. There were more animals than we could count. Zebra dazzled in every direction and interspersed with a confusion of wildebeest. Having been to Africa more than a dozen times, this was as close to legend as my imagination could bear.

Off in the distance, I could see a lone acacia tree punctuating the skyline, a beacon of what would become our home for the night. There was no sign of humankind in any direction save for us and the track we drove in on. This campsite was special indeed, as there was no fence, no signs, no toilets, and no guards. We were truly alone amongst the megafauna, and just as we pulled to a stop, the clouds opened up in a downpour Toto would be proud of.

As the rain pelted the Grenadier, I reminded myself why I configured the vehicle the way I did. Setting up camp didn't require getting out of the car, so within a few minutes, we had bags moved into the front seats and a plate of cheese and crackers prepared to watch the show. I could not have imagined setting up a roof tent in those conditions, soaked to the bone and constantly looking over my shoulder for what might be lurking or slithering through the tall grass. Instead, we listened to the rain patter against the roof rack and watched the sun dance through the clouds to the horizon. Darkness finally descended, and I made one last pass of the flashlight around the vehicle, hundreds of eyes illuminated by the beam. We just laughed, and I felt overwhelmed by the wonder of camping under a lone acacia tree in the Serengeti.

←

Camping under a lone acacia tree in the middle of the Serengeti during the great migration was a memory for a lifetime.

PART 3

THE OVERLAND VEHICLE

Vehicle-based travel has been undertaken with any mode of transportation imaginable, from EVs to tuk-tuks to London double-decker buses and everything in between. While many options are possible, most overlanders use a 4WD truck, SUV, or an adventure motorcycle. This choice is based on those platforms' inherent durability and performance in a wide range of weather and road conditions.

Choosing a 4WD starts with understanding why the pinnacle vehicles are so exceptional and learning the balance between reliability, durability, capability, and capacity. Fortunately, there are still models sold around the world that embrace those attributes while also appealing to the needs of a wide range of drivers. Most pinnacle overland vehicles can be driven daily and taken around the world with equal ease.

Once your vehicle is selected, there are some core principles you should follow to modify the platform to best suit your needs. Some travelers choose to haul a heavy camper, while others love the challenge of the most remote and difficult routes. Understanding how traction, suspension, storage, and electrical systems all work will inform which modifications are most important and which can be skipped to save money and weight.

←

The Grenadier that transported me across Africa continued on for my crossing in Europe, including this stunning overland route through the mountains of Albania.

CHAPTER 11

BASIC VEHICLE SELECTION

One of the most enjoyable parts of overlanding is the connection you develop with the vehicle. The 4WD or adventure motorcycle becomes your backpack on wheels and the magic carpet to adventure, allowing you to explore efficiently while also incorporating your own equipment and customizations.

This chapter will review the modes of transportation which include cycling, motorcycles, 2WD cars, 4WDs, and large commercial platforms. For most travelers, a durable and reliable 4WD or adventure motorcycle will provide the best compromise between purchase price, off-highway performance, payload, and durability. If your travels will be confined to your home country, then options expand based on service and your available dealer network. In most cases, you are better off starting with the vehicle you already own and determine if it meets your needs without a large expense. You should only buy something different if the terrain or payload requirements demand the upgrade.

Choosing Your Class of Vehicle

<- **Few modes of travel are as pure as cycling across a continent.** While driving the Silk Road in a Suzuki Jimny we encountered this cyclist heading the opposite direction. It was humbling.

It is said that walking is the purest form of travel, followed by cycling, then a motorcycle, a 2WD or 4WD vehicle, and lastly a camper. The reason for these rankings is entirely related to connection to the land. While walking, everything slows down; you notice every detail, and you depend entirely on local communities to access water, food, and shelter. A bicycle is nearly the same, but the pace picks up significantly. The downsides to these two methods are that seeing a country takes a long time, and pace becomes the limiting factor. The motorcycle is the sweet spot on the continuum, making the traveler more approachable and connected yet still able to travel at any desired pace. The right motorcycle can access nearly any road, carry camping and personal effects, and still access remote areas. The limitation of the motorcycle is how remote you can get, as fuel range is limited, and only so much food and water can be carried. Payload becomes the limiting factor.

Next you should consider the drivetrain. Around-the-world trips have been completed in 2WD cars, including vintage cars, London taxis, and even Rolls Royce Phantoms. The reason to use a 2WD will typically be restricted to cost or nostalgia. For example, a traveler might set off around the world in a vintage Porsche or their father's diesel Mercedes-Benz E-W123 sedan. The argument could even be made that those are better choices than the typical Land Cruiser, as the connection to the trip can be deeper and the challenge more intense. 2WD vehicles usually have a better fuel economy and can blend in more seamlessly with the local populations. And don't underestimate where a 2WD vehicle can go—I have been humbled many times by a Toyota Corolla that passes me on a mountain switchback while I am lumbering along in a large 4WD in low range. Capability becomes the limiting factor of a 2WD.

A 4WD with low-range gearing is often selected for durability, capability, and capacity. A 4WD usually has a robust body-on-frame construction with at least one beam axle for load carrying and consistent ground clearance. This configuration is also associated with more robust duty cycles where the vehicle is engineered to operate with heavy loads in challenging road conditions. The Toyota Land Cruiser 70 Series, for example, is specifically designed for remote and rugged driving, and as a result, survives hundreds of thousands of kilometers in the care of overlanders. This durability also supports increased payload for hauling equipment, water, and fuel into the remote corners of the globe. The 4WD is the most common overland platform because it is the most appropriate for the job. Cost becomes the limiting factor.

Truck, SUV, or Van

Once the class of vehicle has been selected, it is time for you to decide between an SUV (wagon), pickup, or van configuration. Neither is a superior choice as the decision is highly personal. The SUV benefits from having all occupants and equipment stored within the vehicle's security and climate control (for example, the fridge won't have to work as hard and most equipment will be spared months of dust and sun exposure). These wagons are often more comfortable for occupants, have more sound insulation, and have better overall ride quality. The downside to a wagon is

↑ **There are few vehicles** as suitable for carrying a load than a full-sized diesel pickup. The GMC Sierra AT4X AEV is one of the most capable and comfortable options on the market.

the difficulty of fitting a camper (there are options from Alu-Cab and Ursa Minor), so most users employ a rooftop tent, ground tent, or sleep inside the vehicle. The use of a roof tent will be limited by the roof load capacity set by the manufacturer.

In North America, the pickup truck is ubiquitous, with the Ford F-Series being the most popular new vehicle sold in the United States at over 750,000 units for model year 2023. The reason for this is a combination of comfort and utility. Modern pickups can include all the luxuries of a sedan, including massaging seats, but that luxury comes at a cost both on the purchase price and the reduced payload. Fortunately, most manufacturers have contractor-grade trucks with fewer amenities, more capacity, and a lower purchase price. For example, a two-door Hilux purchased in South Africa will have a payload of 1,800 pounds, a turbo-diesel engine, a six-speed manual transmission, and only cost $37,000. Pickups are the jacks-of-all-trades, allowing for the fitment of a camper, a habitat,

or even a couple of motorcycles in the bed. The compromise is typically occupant comfort and equipment security (if stored in the bed).

The final option is the enclosed van, which has rapidly grown in popularity for its ability to balance comfort, capacity, and capability. Over the past decade, AWD and even 4WD models have become available with low range, a locking center differential, and traction control. The aftermarket has responded further by engineering suspension systems, winch mounts, skid plates, and even robust 4WD conversions with three differential locks like the Iglhaut Allrad. A van strikes a balance between the comfort and security of a wagon and the capacity of a pickup. While the vans may seem too large for international travel, they are often ideal, as most delivery and contractor services in the rest of the world are conducted using vans like the Mercedes-Benz Sprinter and Ford Transit. The compromise is international shipping, as most vans will not fit in a container.

←
Vans like this Mercedes Sprinter Iglhaut Allrad have become increasingly popular for travel due to the ideal compromise between payload, size, and the ability to easily convert them into a camper.

Key Attributes of an Overland 4WD

A traditional overland vehicle will be a wagon or pickup with a body-on-frame configuration and robust payload. At the top of this mountain are the pinnacle overland vehicles, which include the Toyota Land Cruiser, Toyota Hilux, Nissan GU Patrol, INEOS Grenadier, and Land Rover Classic Defender. These vehicles are often easy choices for overlanding as they are specifically designed for international and developing-world non-governmental organization (NGO), commercial, and governmental uses. There are many other vehicles well-suited to remote overland travel and each can be evaluated against your needs and the key attributes of capacity, capability, durability, and reliability. Other buyers may also consider important factors like comfort or cost.

The following criteria comprise the most critical attributes of any overland platform, including motorcycles. Driver comfort is also important to reduce fatigue and is determined by the overall noise, vibration, and harshness (NVH) experienced by the occupants.

- **Capacity:** the vehicle's ability to carry weight as measured by payload specifications and interior storage volume in the load area of the bed or aft of the front seats.
- **Reliability:** the vehicle's ability to operate without engine, electrical, or support system failures due to component malfunction or other quality errors.
- **Durability:** the vehicle's ability to travel for extended periods (years or decades) over rugged terrain while fully loaded without chassis or driveline failure.
- **Capability:** the vehicle's ability to traverse rocky, muddy, and cross-axle terrain, including deep water crossings, severe side slopes, and hill climbs and descents.

The Challenge of Ultra-Low Sulfur Diesel (ULSD) in Vehicle Selection

Instigating a serious blow to international travel, modern diesel engines often include features like diesel exhaust fluid (DEF) and diesel particulate filters (DPFs), which are not designed to operate on fuel with a sulfur content higher than 50 parts per million (ppm). In recent years, emissions requirements have necessitated ultra-low sulfur diesel, and this has made it challenging to use North American and some European diesel trucks sold after 2012 for international travel. Most developing countries have fuel with around 500 ppm sulfur content, with some developing-world outliers being as high as 2,000 ppm or more.

There are a few methods for resolving this issue: Purchase an older base vehicle built before 2012 (without DEF), buy a camper that uses a gasoline power plant, or investigate the possibility of removing restrictive systems using several kits on the market. It is imperative to note that emissions systems cannot be deleted or defeated. At the same time, the vehicle is still being operated in the United States, and making modifications can void the warranty or create other reliability or compliance problems. (Note: The owner should perform all due diligence regarding the legality and international compliance before modifying any emissions system.)

Top Overland Vehicles

The best overland vehicles are constantly morphing with consumer interests and regulatory pressures, but there has never been a better time to choose your next adventure machine. With the growing popularity of overlanding, original equipment manufacturers (OEMs) have doubled down on suitable models, and in the case of INEOS, an entirely new car company has been created to support vehicle-dependent travel. Choosing the best vehicle for you is a highly personal decision based on your budget and travel needs. It is also important to acknowledge that new cars are often prohibitively expensive, so used options or even the vehicle you currently own might be preferred. The following lists are in alphabetical order by manufacturer.

SUVS

In most of the world, these high-clearance wagons are called sport utility vehicles (SUVs), representing the most common choice for overlanders and commuters alike. They are spacious and comfortable while providing a degree of utility for hauling and towing. Capability is relatively easy to find in this segment, but payload still tends to be elusive in the higher trim levels.

- **INEOS Grenadier.** The Grenadier was designed in the UK, engineered at Magna in Austria, and manufactured in a Mercedes-Benz factory in France. The Grenadier combines an impressive payload of 1,800 pounds (816 kilograms) with available triple differential locks, large-diameter tires, and long-travel suspension.
- **Jeep Wrangler Rubicon.** The Jeep is the original factory 4WD SUV and all other brands came after its 1942 debut. The Jeep Wrangler Rubicon is more suited for overlanding than ever with the new full-floating rear axle and 6,250 pounds (2,835 kilograms) GVWR package. This provides a payload of over 1,300 pounds (590 kilograms) and the most capable technical terrain 4WD available today.

↑ **The Toyota Land Cruiser 250** is being sold globally, which improves access to repair parts and service. The vehicle also represents a good value given the pedigree and capability.

- **Lexus GX, Toyota Land Cruiser Prado, and 4Runner.** The Toyota 250 platform provides exceptional rigidity and durability with lighter weight. Capability is above average, but payload can dip below 1,000 pounds (450 kilograms) in some configurations.
- **Suzuki Jimny.** The Suzuki Jimny is not available in the US but is affordable and ubiquitous, so it is easy to rent one on your next flight or buy and register it in another country. The Jimny is available in three-door and five-door configurations and benefits from solid axles and coil springs. It can be purchased as a diesel or petrol and is still available with a manual transmission, but its capability is average, and the payload is a challenging 770 pounds (350 kilograms).
- **Toyota Land Cruiser.** If overlanding had a king, it would be the Land Cruisers 70 and 300 Series. While they are all below average in both comfort and capability, they are without peer on durability, reliability, and payload.

TRUCKS

Starting with the Ford Model T pickup in 1925, the popularity of trucks has been universal, providing more utility for less money than an SUV or a van. If you are considering a pickup, the payload should be your primary objective, followed by durability and capability. Most travelers will consider a mid-sized pickup (like the Hilux or Ford Ranger) as they will be more suitable for driving internationally, fitting in a container, and finding service. However, nothing beats a full-sized American pickup if a large camper is the goal.

- **Chevrolet Colorado/GMC Canyon.** The partnership with American Expedition Vehicles (AEV) has provided genuine overland upgrades to the Colorado and Canyon. For example, the AEV edition of the Chevy ZR2 Bison and GMC Canyon AT4X comes with factory 35-inch tires, a Multimatic suspension, robust skid plates, locking differentials, and an optional winch. If capability is the goal, nothing else on the market is even close, but payload is limited.
- **Ford Ranger.** The humble Ranger has become one of the bestselling pickups globally. The reason for this is three-fold, starting with payload. Few mid-sized pickups in North America can match the 1,711-pound (776-kilogram) payload. The Ford Ranger is also an impressive value in any market. Lastly, the Ranger is available in variants from mild to wild. You can buy an XL with a rear locker all the way up to the impressive Ranger Raptor (which has a 1,400-pound payload).
- **Ford F-350.** The Ford F-350 can be configured in three different cab configurations and have a payload of up to 5,000 pounds (2,260 kilograms). It is available with a Powerstroke diesel or the durable 7.3-liter petrol version (when low-sulfur diesel isn't available). The Ford has a broad range of options, including the affordable XL off-road package or the Tremor package with front limited slip and integrated Warn winch. Ford also benefits from the largest international dealer network of any domestic truck.
- **INEOS Grenadier Quartermaster.** The Quartermaster is a unique platform that combines the engineering and capability of the Grenadier wagon with a longer wheelbase and truck box. The transmission is the well-regarded ZF eight-speed paired with a gear-driven two-speed transfer case. The vehicle can have front and rear locking differentials, dual batteries, and a factory-hidden winch. The payload is an impressive 1,800 pounds (816 kilograms), striking a balance between capability, capacity, and comfort.

- **Nissan Frontier/Navara.** The Frontier or Navara is available in 190 countries and represents an important confluence of reliability and value. The Frontier can cost 20 percent less than a similar Toyota while offering a 310 horsepower V6. The Nissan pickups are honest and reliable alternatives that will provide most travelers with decades of service. The Frontier king cab configuration can see a payload of 1,505 pounds (682 kilograms), and the regular cab Navara can haul an impressive 3,000 pounds (1,360 kilograms).
- **Ram 2500 HD.** The Ram is included here because of the optional AEV Prospector package. The Prospector can be configured with either 37-inch tires or as an XL with 40-inch tires. Additional modifications include a modular steel front bumper with winch, skid plates, snorkel, molded fender flares, model-specific suspension systems, and full integration with factory computers and safety systems.
- **Toyota Hilux/Tacoma.** While the two Toyota mid-sized trucks look similar, it is best to view the difference as the Hilux being a commercial application and the Tacoma being a consumer application. Numerous 4WD Hilux models have a metric ton capacity, while the Tacoma's run about 1,200 pounds (544 kilograms). Both are supremely reliable and durable, with global service and aftermarket support.

VANS

The van is the perfect compromise between a truck and wagon, providing inside sleeping with a pass-through and significant payload. AWD vans are quickly becoming the option for full-time overlanders, and the aftermarket has noticed. Consider these options a blank slate for whatever home on wheels you envision.

- **Ford Transit AWD.** The Transit is manufactured in Turkey, Uruguay, and the US and can be specified with numerous powerplants, wheelbases, and roof heights. As of 2020, the AWD model was released, and more recently, the trail package, which sports 3 inches more tire clearance and a 3-inch wider track. Some AWD models can be specified with an impressive 4,900-pound (2,222-kilogram) payload.
- **Mercedes-Benz Sprinter 2500 AWD Diesel.** If anything is responsible for #vanlife, it is the Sprinter van. The Sprinter has a few noteworthy attributes, including a high-output diesel with AWD and a nine-speed transmission. Unfortunately, recent models have eliminated the low-range gearset, but the AWD will work for 90 percent of an overlander's needs, and a winch can help solve the rest. Fuel economy is noteworthy at 23 miles per gallon (mpg) average, giving a range of nearly 500 miles with the stock tank. Payload is 3,781 pounds (1,715 kilograms).

← **The Ford Transit** is available in AWD for improved dirt performance, while still providing class-leading payload. A commercial van like this can be purchased for a reasonable price.

Key Attributes of an Adventure Motorcycle

← **With a competent rider,** even a larger motorcycle like the BMW GS can be operated in technical terrain.

When considering a motorcycle for adventure travel, there are attributes that improve performance, safety, and durability. Due to their simplicity, most motorcycles are reliable, but they can vary widely in capability and durability. For this reason, it is helpful to consider a motorcycle with the following features.

- **200-mile minimum cruising range:** Traveling in developing countries or on remote tracks requires a sufficient fuel range. A 200-mile improved road range and 150-mile dirt trail range is a good starting point.
- **19-inch minimum front wheel diameter:** The front wheel of a motorcycle is not driven, it is free rolling. As a result, leverage and the ability to roll over a rock, ledge, or pothole are important. Consider a 21-inch front wheel in technical terrain.

- **3,000-mile minimum service interval:** Changing your oil every 1,000 miles isn't practical on a long trip.
- **Ability to run on 85 octane fuel:** Many parts of the world still have fuel served from crusty drums and plastic containers. Finding premium fuel can sometimes be challenging. The bike needs to be able to run on low-octane fuel, if even for a few tanks.
- **7.5-inch suspension travel (minimum):** Suspension travel helps cushion the bike and occupants from impact and assists in maintaining traction and control in the dirt. Look for 8 inches or more for any prolonged dirt use.
- **300-watt power supply (minimum):** Travel often includes gadgets like GPS units and important comfort items like heated vests. If traveling in cold conditions, consider 500 watts at a minimum for heated gear.

- **Frame designed for luggage fitment:** A proper adventure motorcycle is intended to support equipment loads. As a result, the frame needs to be strong enough to handle panniers, water, dry bags, and other equipment.

- **Ergonomics that allow for standing riding position:** Riding on corrugated roads, sand, mud, and remote trails requires a standing position for visibility and control. A cramped cockpit or low bars makes standing impossible for extended periods.

Top Adventure Motorcycles

Few possessions express the owner's character like a motorcycle; the machine is like an extension of limb and emotion. For this reason, motorcycles are highly personal. However, some adventure models are better suited to travel than others by having larger fuel tanks and provisions for luggage. Any one of the following bikes will take you around the world—and back. The motorcycles are listed in alphabetical order by the manufacturer.

- **Aprilia Tuareg 660.** The Tuareg combines Italian design with a lightweight 80-horsepower twin and pairs it with 9.4 inches (240 millimeters) of suspension travel. The model weighs 412 pounds and includes a 21-inch front wheel and 18-inch rear. Despite being a smaller bike, it is still comfortable on the highway and has a 4.8-gallon tank for sufficient range. The 660 is well suited to technical terrain.

- **BMW R 1300 GS Adventure.** The GS Adventure strikes the impossible balance between touring comfort, fuel range, and off-highway performance. It weighs 593 pounds but still has a long-travel suspension and a 19-inch front wheel for better sand and dirt capability. The motorcycle has class-leading comfort for long distances and can be configured to support both the rider and pillion for long-term travel.

- **Ducati DesertX.** The Ducati DesertX is an off-road capable and travel-optimized model with a 21-inch front wheel, 110 horsepower, and 9 inches of suspension travel. There is even an auxiliary fuel tank that fits in the rear subframe

and provides an additional 2.1 gallons. The DesertX strikes the balance between performance and comfort, while only weighing 492 pounds.

- **Honda Africa Twin Adventure Sports.** Honda motorcycles hold the hilltop for reliability, and this translates into the capable and durable Africa Twin, now available in an Adventure Sports variant with a larger 6.6-gallon fuel tank and 19-inch front wheel. The standard model has a 21-inch front wheel and longer suspension travel, but it also carries a taller seat height and less range. The Africa Twin also has a unique dual-clutch transmission, which functions like an automatic and the adventure model weighs 535 pounds.

- **Honda XL750 Transalp.** The Honda Transalp is a historically significant model for travel with the newest models having nearly 8 inches of suspension travel in the front, a 21-inch front wheel, an efficient 755cc parallel-twin engine, and a 460-pound wet weight. With the 4.5-gallon fuel tank and 56 mpg fuel economy, the range is a comfortable 250 miles. The XL750 is also known for supreme reliability and durability, reasonable dirt performance, and a 32.6-inch seat height.

- **Kawasaki KLR 650.** This affordable, minimalist adventure bike combines a 21-inch front wheel with 8 inches of suspension travel and a 6.1-gallon fuel tank. This 490-pound bike is reasonably comfortable and capable yet known for superior reliability.

↑ **The new Ducati DesertX Rally** is one of the most capable mid-weight adventure motorcycles sold today, yet it can still be optioned with eight gallons of fuel for long-distance touring.

- **KTM 890 Adventure R.** Overlanders ride KTMs because they want the best suspension, the most horsepower, and the lightest weight. The KTM 890 weighs only 432 pounds (dry) and boasts a 5.3-gallon fuel tank. The 21-inch front and 18-inch rear wheels provide good technical terrain performance, but the 34.6-inch seat height makes the model difficult for shorter riders. The KTM pushes the limits of capability.
- **Suzuki V-Strom 800DE Adventure.** The V-Strom 800DE starts with a 21-inch front wheel, multiple skid plates and crash bars, factory luggage, and a 5.3-gallon fuel tank. Suzukis are famous for their reliable and smooth engines, which continue with the 776cc parallel-twin engine. Additional features of this 507-pound model include off-road traction control and anti-lock braking system (ABS), and a notable 8.7 inches of suspension travel.
- **Triumph Tiger 900 Rally Pro.** For overlanding, the mid-weight 900 Rally Pro provides 106 horsepower and a 5.3-gallon fuel tank. The 9.4 inches of front suspension travel improves technical terrain performance, but the 503-pound bike is still safe and comfortable with advanced ABS and even cruise control and a heated seat.
- **Yamaha Ténéré 700.** There are many great motorcycles in this weight class (the Ténéré weighs 452 pounds), but few have the chuck-it-off-a-cliff reputation of a Yamaha. This model also benefits from ultra simplicity, with no traction control, cruise control, or other refinements. It has a new three-mode ABS system, an important safety system. The 680cc engine is a smooth-running twin with 72 horsepower and approximately 50 mpg. The 4.2-gallon tank provides just enough range to meet our distance requirements. Suspension travel is a respectable 8.3 inches in the front and 7.9 inches in the rear.

Crossing the Altar

Almost any adventure is worthwhile, but what makes a particular trip so special? For me, it begins with a unique idea or a location with some rare or unusual attribute. In the case of the Gran Desierto de Altar, it is the largest dune system and the only active erg region in North America, a feature that spans north and east of the Colorado River Delta. The sand in the dunes and sediment in the delta has come from the Colorado River, and the Grand Canyon it carved over eons. This area is significant to the overland traveler for many reasons, including the remoteness, technical challenge, research and skills required for route finding, and its international location. This is not a place to drive into without a plan.

One of the other elements of a successful journey is selecting the right vehicle and equipment for the adventure. This is not to say that most overland trips require some highly specialized machine and a dozen Pelican cases filled with exotic gear. Still, some environments do necessitate a level of capability and reliability. In the case of the Altar, the dunes are big, easily taxing the available flotation and performance of the average SUV or pickup. Even when we crossed the ergs in 2012, the Land Rovers were often stuck, and the learning curve was steep for the less experienced drivers. For this trip, we used Jeep Wranglers and a Chevrolet Colorado Bison with extensive modifications, larger tires, and higher horsepower motors. The results were night and day, without a single 4WD requiring a winch or strap. This allowed for more time in camp and a more relaxed pace, although it did remove some of the fun of testing the limits of smaller tires and underpowered Rover V8s.

In contrast, the Jeeps and Chevrolet for this trip were equipped with significantly taller and wider tires, the smallest being a 35-inch Interco on the Colorado Bison. The Wranglers sported tires as large as 37 inches and benefited from higher horsepower V6s and 8-speed transmissions. The Wrangler JK Outpost enjoyed the bark of a Hemi V8. As a result, the drivers were able to climb taller dune faces with shorter runups and even correct for a poor line choice or loss of momentum with a press of the accelerator. The suspensions were also significantly modified, with taller springs and custom-tuned shock absorbers.

The other surprise from the trip was taking a self-contained camper along for the crossing, the Outpost II. This machine is the brainchild of Dave Harriton from AEV. Dave is a longtime friend who wanted to see if a "house" on wheels could make the crossing. In the end, what made the Outpost II work was the attention to detail, from the use of lightweight composites and minimalist design to the fitment of a 5.7-liter Hemi and 37-inch tires to help propel the camper through the dunes. Dave slept in total comfort, sealed off from the blowing sands.

Each trip is special, but there is something so rewarding about the hard-won adventures that impart the most vivid memories. Experiences like this help inform which vehicles and equipment work the best for your needs while also showing how little is required to have an adventure of a lifetime.

→

Dave Harriton's custom Jeep camper crosses the empty expanse of the Altar dunes.

CHAPTER 12

BASIC VEHICLE PREPARATION

The oldest dunes in the world are in the Namib Desert, a sea of sand that covers three countries and stretches 1,200 miles from the edge of the Kalahari in the south to the Moçâmedes Desert in Angola. It is home to the Skeleton Coast, one of the most difficult coastlines in the world to access, separated from southern Africa's Great Escarpment by up to 100 miles of massive dunes. Crossing the erg requires a well-prepared vehicle. However, it rewards the traveler with abandoned diamond mines, stretches of crimson sand filled with rubies and garnets, and over 1,000 shipwrecks.

Having a properly prepared vehicle is nearly as important as being a well-prepared and trained traveler. This starts by selecting the *correct* vehicle for the job, not the one with the best brochure or celebrity endorsement. The right vehicle works like the proper tool and makes everything easier and less stressful. However, even the best stock vehicles can require unique preparations and modifications to support your unique travel or terrain requirements. This chapter delves into the ten commandments of overland modifications followed by a deep dive into the categories of suspension, tires, storage, and traction. As always, only invest in the necessary changes to aid with reliability and reduce the overall vehicle investment.

Categories of Vehicle Preparations

While the vast majority of overland travel can be accomplished in a reliable 4WD or even a durable car, there are many top destinations that require special preparation to reduce risk or improve success. Vehicle preparation falls into two categories, travel-specific modifications and terrain-specific modifications.

Travel-specific vehicle preparations include minor modifications, terrain-specific tires, adjustments to spring rates, electrical systems, and storage solutions. It is always best to limit these kinds of changes to only the ones you need and save the rest of the money for travel.

The second category of terrain-specific vehicle modifications covers significant overland vehicle modifications to support high-latitude snow travel or when crossing extreme terrain, including deep mud, river fording, large rocks, or when driving in remote and unknown track conditions. As the modifications become more specialized, the vehicle will be less suitable for road use and may even be illegal in many countries. As the changes become more complicated, they will also require specific knowledge of repairs, atypical tools, and custom components that will be difficult to source. These types of changes should be avoided unless necessary to traverse the overland route or achieve the expedition objective.

The Ten Commandments of Modifying an Overland Vehicle

Antoine de Saint-Exupéry said it best: "Perfection is achieved, not when there is nothing more to add, but when there is nothing left to take away." The same is true for your overland vehicles, where complexity and weight will likely reduce reliability and serviceability. Modifications can often look impressive, like car jewelry, but detract from the experience and budget. Here are the top ten rules you should keep in mind when modifying your vehicle:

COMPLEXITY IS THE ENEMY

Keep the vehicle as simple and reliable as possible, thus minimizing the number of systems and variables that can fail in the field. Adapt only as required for the vehicle to perform in the environments and conditions expected in your route.

Consider the engineering performed by the OEM manufacturer and how all the factory systems interrelate. Most failures you will see to 4WDs are aftermarket modifications; and of those, electrical and engine system modifications are the most prone to failure.

WEIGHT IS ALSO THE ENEMY

Keep the vehicle as light as possible, removing heavy items that provide limited value, are purely aesthetic, or are never used. The goal should be to stay under 90 percent of GVWR, which will ensure the best performance in technical terrain, particularly snow and sand. "Stuff" is always a reflection of lack of experience and training. The more experienced, well-traveled, and well-trained the traveler, the less stuff they carry, and the fewer modifications they need.

ENSURE PEAK SUSPENSION PERFORMANCE

The suspension system, geometry, and handling with a load are a reflection of proper design. The vehicle must perform just as well on pavement as on dirt. A suspension serves several critical roles, including emergency handling (think avoiding a deer or child that runs into the road), load carrying, and technical terrain performance. The suspension should also be robust, with quality shocks and durable components. Properly configured, a modern vehicle should be able to manage technical obstacles and also exhibit predictable and safe handling during high-speed dynamic inputs. Tune your suspension to your travel load, including the spring rates, lengths, compression, and rebound valving.

KEEP THE ENGINE STOCK

This is the most common mistake with vehicle preparation: dozens of little modifications to the engine, including changes to the engine control unit (ECU), headers, cold air intakes, aftermarket turbochargers, and so on. These all seem like a great idea until you need to repair one of those items in the middle of the Gobi Desert or find a replacement belt in Uganda. Certainly, there are proven or even mandatory upgrades that address known failures of the factory components, but otherwise, leave the engine mods alone. If the environment you are traveling in demands a certain amount of power (like sand), then consider purchasing the best vehicle and powertrain to begin with.

ISOLATE AND MINIMIZE ALL ELECTRICAL MODIFICATIONS

Electronics are the bane of all travelers, taking more time and requiring more "fiddling" than any other system. The reality is that most modern overlanders use and often need electronics to enhance their experience, including digital cameras, GPS units, and tablets to navigate and record their journey. However, miles of wiring, fuses, and connections are some of the most common failures. As a result, all "house" electrical systems (house

↑ **Reliable, robust vehicles** with minimal modifications rule the day and will exceed expectations in nearly all conditions when combined with driver training and experience.

↑ **Nearly everything I have learned about minimalist overlanding** has come from travel on a motorcycle. All of the gear I needed for months on the road fits in a few bags. Less is more.

↑ **While a mild all-terrain tire** may not satisfy the aggressive look many people want, they work properly for overland travel in mixed terrain and all desert environments. As a driver, there is the added benefit of increased fuel economy and lower driver fatigue.

systems describe camper and aftermarket electrical loads) are completely isolated from the factory harness, and a dual-battery system, portable power system, or low voltage disconnect should be used to protect starting voltage. Spend the time or money necessary to ensure the wiring is 100 percent correct, including quality components, weather-tight connections, and proper fusing.

USE HIGH-QUALITY TIRES WITH AN APPROPRIATE TREAD PATTERN

Tires are the most common failure item on a vehicle as they are always in contact with the terrain. Because they are the only interface between the vehicle and the surface, tires are also a critical performance and safety consideration. Install a high-quality radial tire (for most vehicles) in a tread pattern most appropriate to the primary trip conditions. For example, an all-terrain (AT) is the most effective choice if your travel is concentrated in the desert. Buy a tire with a load rating above your GVWR and look for manufacturers with heavy-duty sidewall construction. Due to the critical nature of tire selection, it is covered in more detail later in this chapter.

AVOID ROOF LOADS

This is one of the most common mistakes of the new overlander: packing everything on the roof. There is nothing wrong with a lightweight roof rack, but having a roof tent, spare tire, and six jerry cans on your roof is extremely dangerous. These types of loads create a litany of problems, including dangerous handling due to the raised center of gravity (COG), poor technical terrain performance, reduced fuel economy, and potential roof damage. Loads must be as low as possible and as close to the centerline of the vehicle (fore/aft) as possible. If you find that all your gear needs to be on the roof, you might have the wrong vehicle to meet your needs. For most vehicles, the maximum roof load should be less than 120 pounds—I prefer less than 70 pounds, or ideally, a completely empty roof rack.

DON'T FORGET SELF-RECOVERY

Often overlooked, proper training and equipment for self-recovery are critical. Self-recovery equipment and the skills to use it are more important than any other modification and should be your first consideration when leaving the beaten path. The reason for this is simple: Everyone gets stuck, even with the best possible vehicle and most experienced driver. There will always be mud too deep, or a rock too large, or sand too soft. A winch can provide control and mechanical advantage that no 4WD modification can match. If your route includes remote, off-highway (off-road) travel, consider a high-quality winch rated to 1.5 times the GVWR, a ground anchor, a comprehensive recovery kit with pulleys, line extensions, and related connections. We have also found traction boards essential for extreme conditions and now carry at least four. Mounting a winch often includes installing a quality bumper, which can also protect the vehicle from an animal strike, low-speed accident, and so on.

SECURE THE LOAD

Take the time to secure all loose items in the cab, ensuring that proper lashing points are installed throughout the vehicle. Even a big bump or ledge on the trail can cause items to shift forward in the cab, impacting passengers or, worse, the driver as they are attempting to clear an obstacle. In the case of a rollover, those items can kill or seriously injure occupants. Install load mats and ratchet straps to keep items from sliding and bouncing. Watch items that can roll forward along the floor

↑ **This Jeep military-spec J8 Wrangler** is designed for a full metric ton of payload. We kept it at stock height and only added a winch and rack from the stock specification. It served as our training platform for years with the US Special Forces.

into the driver's footwell and secure small items in a properly sized center console. Drawer systems can be quite convenient and also improve loading and lashing but be careful with their weight.

QUALITY AND DESIGN OVER QUANTITY

Contrary to what you may see on the Internet, it is not the truck that defines you, but your experiences. Experiences can be enhanced by thoughtful design and a quality product, but you can also easily end a trip with a broken aftermarket spring that saved you a few dollars when substituting for the proven brand. If price is a factor, then consider leaving the vehicle stock. You are far better off modifying your vehicle with slow and deliberate purpose than just checking off the list of things you think you "need." A properly maintained and unmodified Land Cruiser can easily drive around the world and take on some seriously remote and rugged terrain along the way. So, make modifications only as necessary, and save all that money for gas, a good camera, and that 20-foot container shipment to Cape Town.

The Fundamentals of Tire Performance

From a romantic viewpoint, overland travel is a series of endless remote dirt roads. However, in reality, long pavement and graded gravel sections separate you from those majestic backcountry photo opportunities. For example, a trek to Nordkapp, Norway (the northernmost point on a continent accessible by road), will be nearly all pavement, but odds are good that it will be a snowy, icy, or wet surface. If your goal is to cross the BR-319 road across the Amazon in Brazil, the conditions may be entirely muddy.

Your tires must be durable, reliable, and work well when everything goes sideways. Deciding on the best tire for your overland travel is multifaceted and complex, with aesthetics often close to the bottom of the consideration set. A puncture is typically a minor inconvenience, but rounding a corner at speed and hitting the ice with the wrong tire could be a trip-ending event. Performance influences safety, so you want to take tire selection seriously. Installing larger tires reduces driveline reliability and even vehicle payload limits. Before specific tread patterns are suggested, here is a 101 class on the basic attributes of tire performance.

ADHESION

Adhesion is realized during the period of contact between the tread and the tractive surface. It is most relevant on dry surfaces and diminishes rapidly once moisture (as frozen or liquid water) is introduced. A tire's rubber compound, a cocktail of natural and synthetic rubber, carbon black, silica, sulfur, and other agents, greatly influences adhesion. For example, when driving on slickrock in Moab, how well a tire "sticks" to the terrain is a property of adhesion. The same applies on the road, where effective adhesion improves grip while cornering, braking, and accelerating. With road racing tires, such as those used in Formula 1 racing, the focus is maximizing the tire-to-track

adhesion and micro keying (explained later). Tire manufacturers have worked hard perfecting their rubber-carbon-silica formulas, and most currently utilize a proprietary compound to optimize for a combination of tread wear, wet surfaces, and dry surfaces.

DEFORMATION

How a tire's carcass and tread lugs deform provides several notable traction and flotation benefits. Deformation allows the tire to fold around and conform to obstacles such as rocks, ledges,

↑ **This image clearly shows the carcass deformation** at low pressures on this Hankook Dynapro XT hybrid tire.

ruts, and roots. This increases the contact area, allowing maximum adhesion and mechanical keying, critical for traction on irregular surfaces. As you might expect, deformation is one of the key benefits of reducing a tire's air pressure. Tread lug deformation, influenced by rubber compound (hardness) and tread block design, is also important. As the tread encounters an irregular surface, such as a rock, it can deflect, shift, and partially interlock with the obstacle's edges.

However, deformation comes at a cost. A too flexible carcass may not support a heavy payload properly, which can cause the tire to overheat and possibly fail. It may also be less resistant to punctures. Too soft or compliant lugs can tear or deflect completely under the input torque. In short, you want a durable tire that is also compliant in rough terrain. Some manufacturers employ Kevlar in their carcass plies to improve deformation and durability.

MECHANICAL KEYING

There are two forms of mechanical keying: micro and macro. Macro keying is the interface between the lugs and a tractive surface. The tread blocks interlock with irregularities in the terrain, which aids the vehicle in climbing the obstacle. It can be best compared to a rock climber ascending a cliff wall by interlocking her fingers with small cracks in the surface. Micro keying is the deflection of the rubber itself and is equally important. The rubber can receive an impression on the micro level from irregularities in the surface. The rubber's "softness," typically measured with a durometer, directly influences micro keying. As with deformation, a soft rubber compound may come with compromises. If the rubber is too soft, lugs may tear, the tread face may smear away, and the tread life is reduced.

SIPING

Sipes are thin slits in the face of the tread lugs. They provide additional biting edges on the contact patch, significantly improving wet surface and snow/ice traction. The effectiveness of these

hairline cuts should not be undervalued, as they affect mechanical keying (see previous section) and increase traction on other surfaces. However, siping can impart compromises, including accelerated wear and rubber tearing. Siping has pros and cons, but usually the trade-offs are worth it if you anticipate wet or icy surfaces.

TREAD DESIGN

Tread design significantly influences traction and mud clearing, with components including lug void space, lug shoulder shape, siping, and lug integrity. Void space in the tread primarily assists in evacuating mud, snow, and water, allowing the lug face to present a clean, biting surface to the medium on the next revolution. The shape of the lug and void space contribute to how the tire maintains traction in mud and snow. Interrupted void channels improve slope-holding (lateral slip) for a cambered sidehill and down/uphill (longitudinal slip) in mud and snow but reduce the effectiveness of water evacuation. Look for a shoulder lug with a beveled profile to minimize stone retention and improve lug integrity.

ALL-TERRAIN TREAD PATTERN

All-terrain (AT) tire development has gone through a renaissance in recent years, with improved tread design and advanced rubber compounds resulting in significant improvements. As a result, it is possible for AT tires to not only look great but also to perform effectively on- and off-pavement. Premium AT tires will strike the balance between road safety, wet condition grip, mud clearance, fuel economy, and carcass durability. The AT tire is tasked with a near-impossible job, but many options get close. While the AT tire endeavors to strike a compromise in performance, the one thing you cannot sacrifice is durability and puncture resistance. For a standard 4WD, find an AT with a three-ply sidewall and shoulder lugs to help reduce punctures. The AT tire will be the best choice for overlanders who spend most of their time driving on paved or gravel roads.

MUD-TERRAIN TREAD PATTERN

Mud-terrain (MT) tires do look cool, but they also serve an important role for travelers who explore tracks in the rainy season or are on longer routes, such as the west coast of Africa. As a general consideration, MT tires should be considered once regional or seasonal rainfall exceeds 60 inches (150 centimeters) per year. Unfortunately, MTs only perform well for mud and technical rock crawling, so they should be avoided if those are not regular requirements. The downsides are numerous, including poor fuel economy, driver fatigue (due to noise, vibration, and road wander), reduced braking performance, and poor grip on all pavement conditions. In sand, MT tires are a poor choice for all but high-horsepower applications due to the reduced total tread face surface area. The MT tire will be the best choice for overlanders traveling in tropical or equatorial regions.

HYBRID TREAD PATTERN

Hybrid tires have entered the scene like a gift from the overland gods. It started with the Goodyear Wrangler DuraTrac in 2009 and has expanded to offerings from nearly every major manufacturer. The hybrid tire is a third option positioned between the all-terrain compromises of the AT and the extreme terrain performance of the MT—and should be combined with significant improvement to vehicle traction systems (including locking differentials available from most OEMs). The hybrid will not be as smooth and efficient as the AT but will have heavy siping and an AT-style centerline tread pattern. The shoulder lugs will look more like an MT but have smaller voids, often including stone and mud evacuation bars between the lugs. The hybrid tire is best for transcontinental overlanders who plan remote off-pavement routes.

CHOOSING A TIRE DIAMETER

Big tires look awesome and they provide significant benefits in extreme terrain. Unfortunately, the more the tire size is increased from stock, the greater the impact on vehicle reliability, efficiency, safety, payload, and center of gravity. As a result, a few metrics will help you strike a balance. If the goal is maximum off-highway performance, you will want the rim diameter to be 16 or 17 inches and the tire diameter to be twice the rim diameter. This optimizes for flotation and ground clearance. Ideally, the tire diameter will remain similar to your model's largest factory fitment, but some conditions demand larger tires. For this, it is not recommended to exceed a 10 percent increase in either diameter or width. Conservative estimates from industry engineer Dave Harriton with American Expedition Vehicles recommend that available payload be reduced by the same percentage as the tire diameter increases. For most overlanders, the optimal tire height will be equal to the largest factory option available, or if extensive backcountry travel is planned, try a diameter increase of no more than 5–10 percent.

CHOOSING THE TIRE WIDTH

It is a common misconception that flotation comes from a tire being wide, but 80 percent of the increased tire footprint comes from the carcass gaining length, not width. As a result, you will want to favor slightly taller tires and keep the width the same as the factory fitment. As an example, a 255/80 R17 tire would be more appropriate for overlanding than a 305/65 R17, even though they have approximately the same diameter. The narrower tire will have less rolling and wind resistance, weigh less, have fewer punctures, and compress into the wheel well more effectively. There are limitations to how narrow you should go, too, as the sheer forces can exceed lug integrity and adhesion, resulting in rubber chunking or smearing (there is a reason why dragsters have wide tires due to adhesion). The optimal width for most overland applications is when the tire width is approximately 30 percent of the tire height.

Traction Aids

With quality tires installed, you will want to option or modify the vehicle with appropriate traction aids. The most common and simple type of differential is called "open," which allows differences in inner and outer wheel speeds to accommodate turns while also reducing wheel hop and handling instability. However, once the terrain becomes uneven or there is sufficient variation in surface traction between the tires, the open differential can allow the two tires to spin at different speeds (including the possibility of one tire not spinning at all). This is best demonstrated when a vehicle becomes cross-axled in a ditch, and one front and one rear wheel spin freely. Older vehicles and some aftermarket traction aids are *limited-slip differentials*, which use either discs or

helical gears to improve tractive performance, often with mixed results. A limited-slip differential is not generally optimal for tractive performance.

BRAKE TRACTION CONTROL

The most common traction aid is called brake traction control (BTC), where a combination of wheel speed sensors, a four-channel braking system, and a computer work in concert to modulate a spinning wheel and sometimes even reduce engine torque through throttle modulation. In recent years, these systems have become increasingly effective, working in conjunction with drive modes and numerous sensors to optimize performance in varied terrain. For example, in a rock mode, the system will work to control individual wheelspin quickly, often within an eighth of a tire rotation. The benefits of TC over a mechanical locker include better steering control and improved line holding. Because the system relies entirely on the brakes to control the spinning wheel, longitudinal tractive force is lost to both friction and drivetrain resistance, and many TC systems also reduce engine torque through throttle modulation. For overlanding, a multimode traction control system will be the most effective.

SELECTABLE LOCKING DIFFERENTIAL

The driver-selectable locking differential is at the top of the traction performance list. With the touch of a button, these differentials will mechanically lock to provide equal wheel speed to both tires on the same axle. In technical terrain, the driver can preemptively engage the locker(s) to improve the chances of climbing the hill, rock, or ledge. The most capable factory overland vehicles will be equipped with a rear and front locker, and in the case of a full-time 4WD, often a center differential lock (CDL) too. Lockers provide the most control of any traction aid, allowing the driver to turn it off and on at will, depending on conditions. Most vehicles with driver-selectable lockers will also have traction control when unlocked, giving the best of both worlds. If you can only install a selectable locking differential on one axle, it should be fitted to the rear one, as the majority of the tractive performance shifts rearward with gravity during a climb. If your vehicle does not have a locker, installing one from an aftermarket company may be possible.

↑ **A suspension upgrade** does not need to be complex or expensive to work well. We installed a simple Australian kit from Old Man Emu on our project Land Cruiser. The springs were 50 millimeters longer and the rate increased by 150 pounds in the front and 200 pounds in the rear.

Suspension Systems

For most overland vehicles, the suspension system can benefit the most from aftermarket improvement. That does not mean fancy remote reservoirs or external bypass coilovers but rather a thoughtful approach to optimizing spring rates, suspension geometry, jounce control, and shock valving. Overland vehicles are not trophy trucks, and forest service roads have a 25-mile-per-hour (mph) speed limit. So, a race-inspired suspension is generally not recommended due to the extreme cost, reduced reliability, and difficulty sourcing replacement parts in the developing world.

Changes to suspension should start with matching the spring rate to the travel payload. The role of the spring rate is to support the load, and the rate should never be used solely for an increase in ride height. Even if a vehicle is under GVWR, it still might sag too much in the rear, so an increase in spring rate will bring the 4WD back to optimal ride height and better control the payload as the suspension cycles. The role of spring length (or pack arc and thickness in the case of leaf springs) is to set the desired ride height. The ride height may be taller than stock, providing additional chassis and body clearance on the trail. While tempting, increasing the spring rate does not translate to increased GVWR for the vehicle, as excess payload can result in increased stopping distances, component failures, or regulatory issues with local law enforcement.

Damping performance can also be improved by matching the shock valving to the spring rates and payload, and any heat-related shock fade can be reduced by increasing the fluid volume. Expensive shocks are tempting, but most overland travelers never encounter cycle speeds and prolonged speeds that would justify a shock like this. Load control can also be improved by replacing the factory rubber jounces with a taller, more progressive unit that helps to decelerate the load as it cycles, thus reducing hard bottoming. For most overlanders, a quality monotube or twin tube shock absorber with load-appropriate valving and rock protection for the shaft is all that is needed.

Bumpers, Skid Plates, and Self-Recovery

With traction, ground clearance, and suspension addressed, you will want to consider protecting the vehicle from trail damage, animal strikes, and vehicle accidents. This will be done by confirming that the factory skid plates are up to the task and replacing them if underrated or absent. If your payload allows and your travel conditions require it, consider installing robust bumpers to protect the vehicle and allow the fitment of a winch.

BUMPERS

To save weight and cost, most new 4WDs are equipped with plastic bumpers and minimal skid plating to protect the engine, transmission, and fuel tank. If your payload allows, a front bumper with a bull bar can be a worthwhile investment. The bumper can help protect the radiator and occupants in the unfortunate event of an animal strike or even a minor fender bender. If your travel plans include remote backcountry tracks, a quality bumper will often have provision for a 12-volt self-recovery winch and driving lights. A quality aftermarket rear bumper will provide departure angle protection, robust GVWR-rated recovery points, and even the provision of a swingout tire carrier if the spare no longer fits in the stock location.

SKID PLATES AND ROCKER PANELS

The next priority should be to fit a steel or aluminum skid plate if your engine oil pan, transmission pan, or fuel tank is unprotected. Additional protection becomes a balancing act between budget, available payload, and the ability to mitigate trail damage. For longer-wheelbase vehicles, rocker panel protection is often considered and can serve as a step to aid access to the interior and roof rack.

SELF-RECOVERY

If your plans include solo-vehicle travel in remote or technical terrain, a method of self-recovery should be considered. Equipment can be as simple as a shovel and set of traction boards or as extensive as a front-mounted winch, pulleys, extensions, and ground anchors. If your travels are typically remote and as a solo vehicle, a winch is the self-recovery tool of choice. I have also used

winches to help farmers or to move downed trees and rocks on the road. The winch is a safety device, so it should only be purchased from quality brands and installed on a properly rated mount. The winch solenoid should be sealed against dust and water, and it is recommended that the winch have a wired remote, even if a wireless unit is supplied. The winch's rated pulling capacity should be approximately 1.5 times the actual curb weight of the vehicle. In most cases, you should purchase a winch with a synthetic line as it is 80 percent lighter and also safer than steel cable.

Electrical Systems

It is common for overlanders to need auxiliary power while camping to charge computers, run lights, or power a Starlink. It is not recommended that those loads be powered by the vehicle's battery, which should only be reserved for starting and vehicle systems. Camp or house system loads should be powered by an auxiliary battery and supported by a solar charge controller and photovoltaic (PV) panel. Even a decade ago, an overland electrical system was complex, heavy, and expensive, but now they can fit nearly any budget and vehicle.

An overland electrical system falls into two categories: portable power stations (PPS) and integrated house systems. Unfortunately, the term "house" creates some confusion, but it refers to the camping or camper power requirements, which should be isolated from the starting battery. For most overlanders, a PPS is the easiest and least complex option, where the battery, outlets, inverter, and solar charge controller reside in an easy to carry or tied down case. There are small PPS that will charge devices and a few camp lights, as well as large models with 100-amp hour lithium batteries that will run an entire camper with a refrigerator and induction cooktop. An integrated solar charge controller and a high-amperage 12-volt charging port are important features so the unit can be topped off from the alternator while driving. The portability provides the added benefit of using the PPS during a power outage or moving it from vehicle to vehicle. However, it is also heavy and must be secured properly should an accident occur.

An integrated house electrical system may be the best choice for more complex vehicle builds or in campers and trailers. These systems are broken down into four parts: the auxiliary batteries, battery management system with display, inverter, and fuse block. Additionally, these systems can include a solar charge controller and solar panels to provide off-the-grid power for days or weeks. These house systems have the advantage of flexibility and serviceability while also being capable of scaling to meet nearly any power demand. It is rare that systems like this are needed in an SUV, but they are ideal for trucks with campers, trailers, and expedition vehicles. It is recommended that a qualified mechanic install these systems and that detailed labeling and color coding of all wires be completed. The installer should also work with you to provide training and a detailed schematic of the harness and components. Any time electrical systems are modified, there is the chance of fire, so proper fusing and cut/chafe protection must be employed.

Motorcycle Accessories

Fortunately, adventure motorcycles require few modifications for overland travel, and most manufacturers have packages that include everything from skid plates to off-road tires to key-matched luggage. If most of your motorcycle traveling will be on improved roads, then a quality set of easily removable hard panniers is optimal. Hard panniers help to protect against theft and can also work as a chair or small table while camping. Including a hard top case, it also provides secure storage for your helmet and a backrest for your pillion rider. Additional considerations for a road-biased adventure bike include an adjustable windshield and premium, longer-wearing AT tires.

Once the route gets more technical, there are other priorities for preparing an adventure motorcycle, starting with the tires. On the front wheel, you will want an off-road tire with taller, well-supported lugs and enough sidewall coverage to support turning forces and line holding in ruts and mud. The lugs should also be interrupted across the tread face to improve lateral grip on side slopes. Because the rear tire wears more quickly than the front, you will want to fit a mild all-terrain to improve tread life and economy while reducing vibration. Once the annual rainfall exceeds 60 inches (150 centimeters) per year, you will want to install a dirt-biased rear tire with large lugs and an open pattern to help evacuate mud on the driving wheel.

Additional overland modifications should include a primary skid plate protecting the oil pan and filter. Crash bars will also be important if the radiator is unprotected or the replacement plastics are particularly expensive or vulnerable. Consider installing wider foot pegs with better grip for use in technical terrain. The wider pegs improve leverage and allow you to more efficiently counterbalance the bike at slow speeds through rocks and ruts. The final consideration is to switch out to soft luggage if the terrain is challenging. Durable soft luggage will endure more drops and not trap your leg if you dab a foot through a difficult section. Just like with a 4WD, it is tempting to load up a motorcycle with every piece of farkle (functional sparkle) available, but if the correct bike is purchased for the intended route, it rarely needs anything more than some good tires, luggage, and a full tank of gas.

↑ **This lightly modified Yamaha Ténéré** includes a stronger skid plate, off-road tires, luggage, and lighting. It is ready to ride around the world.

Driving the Silk Road in a Suzuki

At times, it is better to go and figure out the details later. This was never more true than during my 2010 crossing of the Silk Road from Spain to Mongolia via Central Asia and the 'stans. The trip was prompted by my good friend Charles Nordstrom, who wanted to take a few months off and participate in an adventure rally. As a result, our time for planning was limited to eight weeks, including buying a vehicle in Europe and arranging a half-dozen entry visas.

One of the limitations of the rally was engine size, so I quickly settled on a 1.3-liter gasoline-powered Suzuki Jimny. It was available as a left-hand drive in the UK and easily registered using the home address of a friend. Then there was the challenge of modifications and equipment to support 14,000 kilometers of driving through twenty-two countries on two continents.

The idea of being underprepared and traveling such long distances in a small, used, underpowered 4WD with minimal equipment seemed intimidating. Still, it ended up being one of the best journeys in all my travels. We had everything we needed for less money than a mid-weight adventure motorcycle. We both flew to Europe with backpacks and a duffle bag of camping equipment, and I bought the rest at the Brico Dépôt in France. This included a tool kit for 45 euros and two 20-liter fuel cans. My friend Patrice Ryder, who lives in Provence, handled the Jimny modifications, including an Old Man Emu suspension, a few skid plates, and a set of fog lights. Charlie wanted the stereo upgraded, so I swapped that out on a castle lawn in Czechia.

The vehicle started feeling small for two adults but quickly grew into our adventure mobile. All our equipment easily fit in the car without needing a roof rack, and we were still able to haul tents, cooking equipment, tools, recovery gear, and enough fuel for 700 kilometers. The exercise had the added benefit of us blending in entirely with the local populations; the Jimny was sold in all those countries and used regularly on the remote tracks of Tajikistan, Kyrgyzstan, and Mongolia.

Up to this point, I had always assumed that a Land Cruiser was the best choice for travel, but by the time I arrived in Ulaanbaatar two months later, I had learned that the vehicle mattered little. By using a small, unassuming, and inexpensive 4WD, the trip became entirely about the journey, and the Jimny never once complained or showed signs of wear. The Suzuki never broke down and averaged nearly 30 mpg. When the trip was over, we donated the car to charity, albeit with a touch of sadness to see it go. It is all about the journey, and sometimes it takes an honest little machine to help us see that.

↑ **Our trusty Suzuki Jimny** transported us from Spain to Mongolia through the Silk Road, including this section of the Wakhan Corridor between Tajikistan and Afghanistan.

CHAPTER 13

FUNDAMENTALS OF DRIVING, RIDING, AND RECOVERY

Unlike most travelers, the overlander sees everything between points A and Z, the landscape, villages, and cities unfolding as you pilot your vehicle along the journey. Driving is one of the great joys of overland travel, challenging the operator to employ mechanical sympathy to ensure that the vehicle not only survives the day but years of service. This is no easy task, and it starts from a position of humility and a student's mindset. While driving and recovery are best taught with hands-on instruction in the field, it is still possible to impart fundamentals and complex concepts within the pages of a book.

The foundation for good driving starts before you sit in the driver's seat or swing a leg over the motorcycle. It begins with a daily inspection of the vehicle, much like a pilot would preflight their aircraft. This chapter will review driver ergonomics, marshaling, and terrain-specific driving techniques. Additional details will cover getting unstuck and the process for safe assessment and recovery methods.

Driver Position and Ergonomics

Starting from the driver's seat, your priority is to reduce clutter, loose wires, and unsecured objects. The primary threat is a water bottle or similar object tumbling into the footwell and jamming under the brake or gas pedals. Organize accessories and electronics so they do not impede vehicle operation or distract the driver, which also applies to things on the dash and gadgets blocking the view forward. You should use the center console and various mounts that secure radio mics, cameras, and displays. It is also important to secure and inventory quick-access items like the ditch bag, first aid kit, and document case, which can be accomplished by securing the bag with the seat belt and running the webbing through the handles to keep it in place—still easy to grab and go.

The driver position should be close enough to the steering wheel that all essential controls are accessible but not so close that your range of motion is reduced or you are within 10 inches of the airbag. In most vehicles with sufficient seat and wheel adjustment, start with your back against the seat and your shoulders in a relaxed position. With your arm extended but shoulders in place, your wrist should rest on the noon position at the top of the wheel. This distance will allow your arms to have a natural bend once the hands are placed at 9 and 3 o'clock. This position optimizes leverage and control while minimizing the chance of injury during airbag deployment. The distance can be adjusted by sliding the seat or, if available, the steering column.

The wheel and seat adjustments also accommodate the pedal position, which should be a comfortable distance away, allow full pedal travel, and the legs at a natural and comfortable bend.

The height of the seat and wheel also strikes a balance between seeing the trail obstacles ahead and ergonomics. On a 4WD, the top of the wheel should not be higher than your shoulders. This optimal seat and wheel position may be impossible on some classic overland vehicles. In general, it is best to have the seat back in a more upright position than reclined, to optimize visibility, although comfort varies by person.

For positioning the feet, the goal is to exercise left-foot braking on an automatic transmission vehicle whenever possible, principally when traversing technical terrain. (It is also possible to left-foot brake or even heel and toe on a manual transmission vehicle, but that falls outside of the scope of this volume.) Left-foot braking is used for three primary reasons, beginning with faster reaction times.

- If the driver is only right-foot braking, there is a delay in lifting the throttle, moving the foot to the brake, and then engaging whatever braking application is needed to control the vehicle; in technical terrain like rocks or even during a panic stop on the road, that can be moments too long.
- The second reason for left-foot braking is to improve modulation of the throttle and brake while allowing simultaneous modulation. A good example is lightly applying the brake to keep the vehicle from rolling backward while steadily depressing the throttle to climb a ledge.
- The final reason for left-foot braking is to place the driveline under increased tension by getting the torque converter close to the stall speed and increasing available torque off idle. This tension extends to the suspension, too, by helping to control weight transfer, minimizing head toss, and decreasing the amount of wheel hop.

Once you get comfortable modulating the left foot on the brake, your passengers will immediately notice the improvement in ride comfort and how smooth you have become. Not everyone feels comfortable with left-foot braking, and some pavement-biased vehicles will not operate properly if both pedals are depressed at the same time, so it is good to test it out on a small obstacle first.

Storage and Lashing

When overlanding, there tends to be a lot of gear, bags, and cases along for the ride. It is the responsibility of the driver to properly secure the load to prevent injury during an accident, evasive maneuver, or even an unexpected speed bump. The team's well-being also improves when everything is accessible and well-organized.

STORAGE

The first step is to load the heaviest items as low in the vehicle and as close to the midline of the wheelbase as possible. On a wagon or four-door pickup, this is usually in the footwell of the second row of passenger seats. If there are no rear passengers, this is the place to lash tool rolls, compressors, and recovery kits. The back seat floor is also ideal for installing a footwell water tank or mounting the portable power station. If one or both rear seats are removed, this is also a good location to mount a 12-volt refrigerator, accessible from the front seats. Otherwise, the rear seats can store camera gear, clothing, and personal effects. These soft bags or luggage can be lashed using a combination of the seat belts through the handles and additional straps.

The next layer of storage is either a drawer system or a load platform in the rear storage area of the wagon or pickup bed. The platform can also consist of a layer of hard-sided storage boxes. The equipment layout remains the same as the previous methods, with the heaviest or rarely needed items being positioned down low and farther forward. Positioned closer to the rear door or tailgate should be your cooking equipment and dry food

←
For my recent Africa crossing, I installed a simple load floor built from aluminum. Front Runner boxes slide underneath and the 25-liter Dometic fridge easily lashes to the top. For a year and a half of travel, I only added a few duffle bags beyond what is shown here.

storage, as those items are accessed regularly and are relatively lightweight. On top of the platform layer should be the ground tent, bedding, chairs, table, and other camping items, all secured with a net or straps.

The last place you want to put weight is on the roof, but there is an argument for installing a lightweight and unloaded roof rack. The rack serves as reserve capacity should you need to collect firewood, help transport unexpected passengers, or buy that vintage armoire in La Paz. Depending on the trip, the roof rack can also be the most appropriate location to store extra fuel, so long as the load does not exceed the dynamic roof capacity. While the roof seems like a great place to mount a rack, roof tent, fuel, awning, and table, only some vehicles are designed to carry that load. For most overlanders, the roof should only have an empty rack or possibly a lightweight roof tent on crossbars.

LASHING

Securing equipment inside the vehicle, in the bed of a pickup, or on a roof rack is similar, but there are some subtleties. Lashing starts with ensuring that your tiedown point is rated to the intended load and is accessible for ease of use. Only a ratcheting strap with nominal stretch should be considered for heavy or hard-sided items, and the strap's WLL should exceed the weight of the unmounted items within the strap's compression. Straps should not be crossed over the load, so use enough straps to cover the equipment. Any time a handle or strap is available on a box or bag, run the ratchet strap webbing through the handle to help contain the item should the load shift (this is particularly important on a roof rack). Bungee cords are not recommended for most loads, although they can be appropriate to maintain compression tension on lightweight items like sleeping bags or pillows. On motorcycles, wide cam straps should be used to secure duffles to the panniers or racks. It is particularly important to secure the excess tail of the strap to prevent it from becoming caught in the spinning chain or wheels.

Obstacle Assessment

When encountering a technical challenge in the backcountry, stopping the vehicle and assessing on foot is common. With overlanding, we are often solo, remote, or in a different country, so your risk tolerance will be lower than that of a recreation four-wheeler. Surveying the terrain allows the driver (and marshal if present) to determine the best driving line, speed, gear selection, and traction aid for improved success. Getting out of the vehicle provides a complete view of the start of the crux of the obstacle, and the safest exit to position the vehicle for the trail ahead. This is a great time to communicate and determine the sequence of actions required. If there is deep water and you cannot see the path and depth, it is recommended that you wade through the crossing to check for large rocks or deep holes. If the cross-ing does not look safe on foot, it is most likely unsafe to cross with a standard 4WD or adventure motorcycle. An on-foot assessment may be unsafe in regions with crocodiles or other predators.

The obstacle assessment is also the right time for the marshal to change into appropriate footwear (as travelers, the passenger might be in flip flops) with appropriate tread on the sole. It is also suggested that long pants be worn, sunscreen applied, and work gloves, a hat, and glasses rated for eye protection be worn. Avoid wearing dark clothing at night and secure long hair to keep it from getting caught. This is also the time to grab two-way radios if appropriate or even set up the camera. While tempting, avoid filming and marshaling at the same time (use a tripod).

Marshaling

When driving in technical terrain, negotiating tight confines, or when backing up, it is common to use a marshal (also called a spotter) to reduce the chance of damage and help guide the driver through the optimal line. This process requires practice, good communication, and trust, as the marshal will almost always have a more complete view of the surroundings. Once a marshal is established, everyone else, including the driver, defers to their instructions. If there is a concern or suggestion from a bystander or the driver, the vehicle should be stopped, and the comment should be directed to the marshal for discussion. The marshal takes responsibility for the safety of the scene and all parties, including themselves. As a result, the marshal should avoid walking backward or placing themselves in the fall line of the vehicle should it lose control or roll. Plan so that you can stop the vehicle between obstacles and relocate safely.

MARSHALING HAND SIGNALS AND VOICE COMMANDS

Unfortunately, there is not an established standard for marshaling hand signals. The hand signals that are mentioned in this section follow as close to the aircraft, military, and commercial standards as possible. These are the hand signals I was taught as a US Air Force firetruck driver. Other signals can be as effective but should be reviewed with the driver and marshal before driving over the obstacle. Voice commands should be clear and at an appropriate volume to ensure the message is received. A combination of visual and audio instructions ensures greater understanding and faster implementation. Voice commands can be complemented with words of encouragement and reassurance, particularly if the driver is inexperienced or anxious.

ALL STOP

The marshal announces "all stop" while crossing their forearms above their head into an X while also making a fist with both hands, palms facing the driver. "All stop" is used as an emergency command to instruct the driver to stop driving and winching if being conducted simultaneously.

STOP DRIVING

The marshal announces "stop" while extending both arms toward the driver and closing both hands into fists, palms facing downward. The arms should be far enough apart to maintain a view of the vehicle and for the driver to see your face. Shaking the fists communicates a sense of urgency.

DRIVE FORWARD

The marshal announces "drive forward" while elevating the elbows to chest height and moving the upright hands forward and backward, hands open, palms facing the marshal. Sometimes, only one hand may signal a drive forward, while the other arm may communicate a steering instruction or other feedback. Moving the hands back and forth faster while providing the verbal command of "faster" will help the driver understand that additional momentum is required.

TURN PASSENGER OR DRIVER

The marshal announces "turn driver" or "turn passenger" while fully extending their arm horizontally in the direction of the desired input. The hand is open, palm facing the driver. The verbal command of "driver side" or "passenger side" is used to eliminate the confusion of a mirrored perspective (when facing the driver, their right is your left), no matter the position of the spotter. This is why starboard and port commands instead of left or right are used on ships.

SLOW DOWN

The marshal announces "slow down" while extending their arms forward, hands open, and palms facing downward. The hands and forearms are then moved up and down in alignment while repeating "slow down".

GO BACK

The marshal announces "go back" while elevating the elbows to chest height and moving the upright hands forward and backward, hands open, palms facing the driver. Sometimes, only one hand may signal the driver to reverse, while the other arm may communicate steering instructions or other feedback. This is commonly used to back a vehicle off an obstacle slightly or to reposition the vehicle for a different driving line. For reversing, the marshal will reposition to the rear of the vehicle.

Tips for Driving in Rocks and Ruts

Driving in rocks is one of the most challenging and rewarding terrains to traverse, but it also comes with the greatest risk to the vehicle. Slow and steady rules the day and helps to minimize damage and maximize the precision in which you overcome each obstacle.

1. **Know your vehicle.** Spend the time learning where low-hanging or unprotected components are on the undercarriage and memorizing the position of the differentials. Practice with cones to familiarize yourself with where the corners of the bumpers are in reference to the driver.

2. **Slow and steady wins the race.** Driving in rocks presents numerous hazards to the vehicle, but it rarely requires momentum. As a result, take your time and use a marshal to help prevent damage to the drivetrain and body.

3. **Lower the tire pressure to improve adhesion, deformation, and mechanical keying.** As a guideline, match the tire pressure (in psi) to the diameter of the wheel. With a 17-inch wheel, the tires should be lowered to 17 psi for most standard 4WDs.

4. **Engage low range and lock the center differential before entering rocky terrain.** Select rock mode and engage the rear locking differential if available and the conditions are challenging.

5. **For larger rocks that cannot be avoided, drive the tire over the rock as opposed to risking underbody damage.** In general, you want the tires high on the rocks to keep the undercarriage elevated.

6. **Watch the sidewalls.** As the tires climb and deform around the rocks, the sidewalls are particularly vulnerable to puncture, so the

←
The Land Rover Defender slowly descends Van Zyl's Pass in northern Namibia.

marshal should watch the path of each tire to ensure that the rock is encountering the tread face if possible.

7. **Approach ledges and ruts at an angle to help prevent grounding of bumpers or undercarriage.** The wheelbase and severity of the ledge will determine the angle of approach, but caution must be taken on severe slopes to prevent rollover. Approaching the ledge at an angle also presents one tire at a time to the obstacle, making it easier to cross.

8. **Avoid spinning tires and wheel hop on rocks and ledges.** A spinning tire can suddenly gain traction under high longitudinal torque, which can result in axle or driveline failure.

9. **Stack rocks or use recovery boards to address clearance or traction issues.** If the trail is used recreationally, return the obstacle to the condition you found it.

Tips for Driving in Sand and Dunes

Driving on sand and in the dunes is like a roller-coaster ride for overlanders and will have the most smiles per mile of any terrain. The key to sand driving is staying in the flow and maintaining steady momentum while being as fluid and smooth with each input as possible.

↑ **The Namib Desert** extends beyond the horizon toward the treacherous Skeleton Coast.

1. **Safety is the driver's responsibility,** so fit a flag if required (or even if not), and do not drive blindly over a dune crest. Look out for other users, which may include pedestrians or livestock.
2. **Drive with your headlights on** in the sand and dunes to increase safety.
3. **Lower your tire pressure.** Lower tire pressure is the greatest contributor to driving success in the sand and dunes for a standard overland vehicle.
4. **Select sand mode.** Most overland vehicles will perform best in low range and with only the center differential lock engaged. Select sand mode if available, and vehicle stability control may need to be turned off if it does not deactivate automatically in low range.
5. **Use an AT tire.** In sand with a standard (i.e., lower horsepower) vehicle, an AT tire with a modest tread pattern will perform best, as it provides increased footprint regularity for flotation and limited disruption of the surface silica structure.
6. **Check the temperature.** The cooler the temperature, the more compacted and nested the silica will become, increasing flotation and the sand's sheer strength. Hot sand expands the air between the silica, reducing load bearing.
7. **Check the moisture content.** The higher the moisture content of the sand, the better the flotation. The silica structure is partially supported and bound through surface tension by the water.
8. **Avoid midday driving.** Driving dunes in the midday sun is the most challenging time, as the surface will lack shadowing to aid route finding.
9. **Travel with the wind.** It will always be easier to traverse dunes by traveling with the wind. Windward slopes will have compacted sand and be more gently sloped, while the leeward (also known as the slip-face) slope will have poor load-bearing and be twice as steep on average.
10. **Back off the throttle.** Momentum is important when climbing a dune with a loaded overland vehicle. Still, it is important to gently back off the throttle as you approach the crest to prevent jumping the vehicle and to allow for a visual assessment of the route forward.
11. **Wash off the chassis.** When driving in sand on the beach, wash the chassis off as soon as possible to avoid corrosion.
12. **Use traction boards.** Traction boards are the easiest method of self-recovery. Consider bringing four if the route is remote or the vehicle is heavily laden.

Tips for Driving in Mud and Snow

Driving in mud is a combination of line selection and momentum, providing serious challenge to any heavily loaded overland vehicle. Mud driving can be fun, but mysteries lurk just below the surface that can include bottomless depths or large rocks and stumps. Similar to mud, snow driving requires flotation but benefits the most from the chess match of gentle throttle, light steering inputs, and fighting the urge to power out of problems.

1. **Air down the tires for flotation in mud and snow.** The tire will be much larger than stock for deep snow or glacier travel, and pressures will be reduced to single digits.
2. **Select a tire with an open lug pattern,** with a mud-terrain the most effective and a hybrid tire being the best compromise between mud and snow.
3. **Use caution when entering an unknown mud hole.** Check the depth on foot by using a long stick. The recce will also reveal if rocks or logs are hidden under the surface.

← **The Ford Maverick Tremor** is a joy to drive in mud and snow, the combination of light weight and effective 4WD system providing an impressive value.

4. **Bring self-recovery equipment.** In technical mud and snow conditions, bring traction boards, a recovery kit, and a winch if your budget and payload allow.

5. **Engage low range and lock the center differential if available.** If the vehicle is equipped with a selectable terrain feature, choose mud and ruts for both conditions. A rear locker may need to be engaged for muddy climbs or deep ruts.

6. **Use wheel spin in mud and clay.** In thick mud and clay, wheel spin is important to evacuate the material and prevent buildup or loss of grip. Wheel spin should be modulated on and off every few seconds to balance clearing the tire and maintaining line holding and control.

7. **Don't use wheel spin in snow.** In deep snow, wheel spin is rarely an advantage. The goal is to stay on top of the firmer top layer and limit digging in. At times, forward progress can be maintained by rotating the tire as slowly as possible.

8. **Compact ruts when needed.** When driving in snow, if you break through the top layer of snow, gently drive the vehicle in reverse a foot or so to compact the rut, then drive forward with just enough momentum for the tire to climb back up on the crust.

9. **Watch for snow drifts.** If there are no tracks in the snow ahead of you, look out for deep drifts that have blown onto the track and will be much more difficult to traverse.

10. **Stay in ruts.** In most cases, staying in the ruts is safer and more effective. Gently rock the steering wheel back and forth a quarter turn to help the tires grip against the walls of the rut.

11. **Clean the vehicle.** It is important to clean the vehicle thoroughly after traversing a muddy track. Mud can trap water and corrosives on the chassis, and the heavy mud can cause tires to be out of balance and add hundreds of pounds to the chassis and wheel wells.

It's important to note that in some areas, driving on muddy roads can leave long-term damage, with deep ruts that can take years to repair. The wetter the climate, the more resilient a muddy track will be. During heavy rain in the desert, be prepared to stay put until the road dries out. In Australia, there is a fine of $1,000 per tire if you drive on a track that was closed due to weather.

Tips for Driving on Gravel and Corrugated Roads

The reality of long-distance overland travel will include hundreds or thousands of miles of gravel roads. These improved surfaces help to improve transit times but come with increased risks of accident and rollover. Vigilance is critical and speed needs to be tempered to ensure proper control and stopping distances.

Corrugations are formed by axle wrap, wheel hop, and sidewall deflection. Over time, these motions slowly displace the gravel, stones, and sand, causing an indentation and subsequent mound. You cannot eliminate the extreme vibrations from the grooves, but you can lessen them by reducing your tire pressure and increasing your speed with-

↑ **On a long gravel road,** few vehicles perform as well as a half-ton full-sized truck with a good suspension system. Just air down the tires and go.

in legal and safety limits. The optimal speed over the corrugations depends on your tire pressure, diameter, suspension configuration, and wheelbase.

1. **Lower your tire pressure but monitor it.** Lower tire pressures improve braking performance and reduce harshness on corrugations. Caution is required with low pressures and high speeds, as heat can build in the carcass of the tire causing delamination or a blowout. Start by lowering the pressure by 30 percent and assess the tire temp with the back of your hand. The tire can be warm but never hot to the touch.
2. **Plan your stopping distances.** Braking performance is reduced significantly on gravel and over corrugations, so plan on as much as twice the stopping distance. This is due to both the reduced traction and the ABS engagement. You can improve stopping performance by modulating the brake pressure at the traction threshold.
3. **Watch your speed on gravel.** While driving at high speeds on gravel roads is tempting, many agencies have speed limits as low as 25 mph.

4. **Be cautious with turns on gravel.** Gravel and corrugations reduce turning grip, which can result in understeer. Applying too much throttle in a corner can result in an oversteer for rear-wheel drive or 4WD vehicles.
5. **Convoy travel requires extra precautions.** If traveling in a convoy, allow enough space for the dust to clear before proceeding. Use extreme caution when passing.
6. **Let the shocks cool.** Corrugations are one of the most abusive conditions for an overland vehicle, with the shocks taking most of the load.
7. **Take it slow.** Avoid abrupt steering, throttle, or braking inputs.
8. **Be safe when passing.** When passing oncoming vehicles, slow down and move toward the shoulder of the road to reduce the chance of a broken windshield.
9. **Limited sight means limited speed.** Speed should be even more conservative with a limited sight distance. When you can't see around the corner, slow way down. You never know who is coming the other way.

Fundamentals of Vehicle Recovery

Getting unstuck is a learned skill but is one of the most rewarding when executed properly. Approach recovery with a student's mindset and learn as much as possible through reading, watching, and quality instruction. When you feel the vehicle getting stuck, back off and prevent the problem from becoming bigger than it already is. Then take a moment and stop, assess, and form a safe recovery plan.

1. **Get training.** Training is the most important investment in vehicle recovery. Schedule a training course with an instructor, your local 4WD club, or at an overland event.

2. **Stop before you're stuck.** Stop accelerating as soon as the vehicle slows significantly or stops making progress. Getting unstuck is far easier when the vehicle is not buried to the chassis.
3. **Rock the vehicle.** In many scenarios, gently rocking the vehicle and steering the front wheels back and forth will aid the self-recovery.
4. **Pause.** Once stuck, take a moment to assess the situation and determine the safest and most appropriate next steps. Take as much time as needed to think and communicate clearly.

5. **Communication is key.** Communicate the plan clearly to others in the group. Establish the chain of command by assigning driving and marshaling duties to limit distractions and confusion.

6. **Move others out of danger.** Move all non-essential personnel outside the hazard zone. The hazard zone is determined by estimating a large circle around each connection point. The radius of the circle is set by the length of the strap, rope, or winch line (with any extensions).

7. **Get ready.** Unload the tools you need to do the job and inspect the equipment for damage and proper load ratings. Inspection is even more important if using someone else's gear.

8. **Safety first.** Don gloves and protective eyewear before rigging, digging, or recovering the vehicle. Secure loose clothing and long hair.

9. **Lower tire pressure.** If you haven't done so, lower the tire pressures to increase flotation and improve traction. Start with a pressure equal to the wheel diameter or half of the vehicle manufacturer's recommended tire pressure (whichever is greater). Even lower pressures may be required on soft surfaces or during emergencies.

10. **Dig!** Reduce the recovery load and resistance by digging out in front of the tires and removing material against the chassis.

11. **Slow and easy wins the race.** Few recovery scenarios require excessive speed or wheelspin, so go easy on the throttle and take your time with rigging and resetting.

12. **Try traction boards.** Traction boards are safe and effective recovery devices, particularly in sand, snow, and mud. Use low wheelspin until mounted on the traction board (preventing damage to the tire and board), then add throttle to use the board's length to gain momentum.

13. **Watch your ratings.** For vehicle-to-vehicle and winching recoveries, ensure the connection points are rated to the pull.

14. **Practice.** Remember that getting stuck and unstuck are all part of the joys of overland travel. Practice regularly to keep skills fresh and to work as a team.

Fundamentals of Adventure Riding

Riding an adventure motorcycle is about as much fun as a person can have overlanding. The combination of simplicity, maneuverability, power, and handling is hard to beat, but there are ways to improve the rider's capabilities on the road and in the dirt.

FITNESS

Conditioning is often overlooked before traveling on a motorcycle, but the rider needs a baseline of cardiovascular fitness and skeletal muscle strength to operate a loaded motorcycle properly. The best approach is a combination of steady-state cardio (also known as Zone 2 cardio) several days per week along with two sessions of high-intensity interval training. Strength training should focus on weighted squatting and lunging movements and upper body pushing and pulling movements like pull-ups and push-ups. The constant movement and counterbalancing on the motorcycle also benefit from regular core and lower back exercises. Last is grip strength, as most riders' hands and forearms give out before anything else in technical terrain.

BALANCE

Riding an adventure bike on the dirt requires excellent balance and counterbalancing. Spend time working on these skills in a dirt lot with a course of cones. Make progressively tighter turns at slower and slower speeds. Slide the bike to a stop and then balance it in the stationary position

↑ **On a lightweight adventure motorcycle** like the Tuareg, it is easy to feel ready for the Dakar Rally.

for as long as possible. Learn to rotate the motorcycle through a tight turn using the rear brake or throttle. Once you get good at all these, move the course to the side of a hill and start again. Work on your balance while standing on the pegs and seated, alternating between the two.

MODULATION

Acceleration and braking effectiveness is achieved through modulation of the throttle and the brake levers. Being able to accelerate smoothly will reduce tire wear and maintain traction. Fine control between the throttle and clutch will allow you to ride slower in technical terrain without stalling the motor or spinning the rear tire. It is a dance of the controls right at the limits of traction. Practice braking on the dirt to find the threshold that provides the shortest stopping distance but does not engage the ABS. Equally, accelerate as quickly as

possible without the rear tire spinning or traction control intervening. As a rider, you also need to be able to modulate your speed, reducing it smoothly before negotiating a pile of boulders or feeding momentum when you hit deep sand.

ASSESSMENT

We ride with our heads up and on a swivel for a reason, constantly scanning the trail ahead for obstacles and the optimal line while also checking our periphery for hazards or distracted drivers. Part of what makes a great adventure rider is their ability to rapidly and perpetually assess the world around them. When moving through technical terrain, that review process considers the bike's capabilities, the available traction, the rut's depth, or the rock's diameter. Your ability to assess quickly and accurately will improve with practice and exposure to a wide variety of conditions.

The Joys of Getting Stuck

I remember the first time I got stuck. The details are somewhat murky due to the decades that have transpired since, but the whole event started with me driving down Highway 101 to a pullout just east of Woodland Hills, California. Back then, a little Jeep trail departed the highway and disappeared into a jungle. Well, my active imagination wanted it to be a jungle, inspired by reading an article on the Camel Trophy earlier that week (that article ultimately put me on the path to creating *Overland Journal*). I was determined to bash through the bush like explorers of old, and the sound of semis and Harley-Davidsons on the nearby road served as the soundtrack. Before I share too much of what happened, this story requires a bit of context, mostly my complete lack of experience with anything off-pavement or anything else for that matter. I was nineteen years old and had traded in my faithful 1984 Honda Accord for a 1989 Isuzu Amigo. The salesman at the corner dealership in Van Nuys convinced me that 2WD was just as good as 4WD because it had big tires—as used car salesmen do. He even had me drive it over an abandoned railroad track to prove his point, and even that was a challenge because I had no idea how to drive a manual transmission.

Back to my Camel Trophy cosplay story, I blasted through an impressive mud pit at about Mach 3 and continued through the foothills until I came to a locked gate. No problem, I thought, reversing my course to start my expedition back to the interstate. All was good until the mud hole presented itself anew. Sure, I could drive around, but would a Land Rover Team America hopeful skirt such a gem? Selecting first gear, I attacked the mud repeatedly in a spirited series of intentional forays. And then I said the fateful words "just one more time" before everything came to a tire-spinning, engine-revving, desperate stop. Forward? Nope. Back? Nope. And being an adult for all but a year,

↑ **Nothing like getting stuck in Antarctica** to amp up the fun of overcoming obstacles.

I had nothing useful in the vehicle: no shovel, no traction boards, nothing—except for the window curtains that the boss from my entry-level salesman job had just entrusted me to get dry-cleaned.

I engaged my inner MacGyver (this was 1992, after all) and shoved, pushed, and otherwise packed those heavy drapes under my rear tires. Feeling confident, I entered my cockpit and channeled the green oval gods. Slowly taking up the clutch—no, dumping the clutch—the mighty Amigo lurched forward about 2 inches and spun furiously, pulling the curtains around the tires and through the mud. Now, I was good and truly stuck, and my utter incompetence precluded me from trying anything useful like airing down, using the floor mats, or even digging with my hands. Thus began the walk of shame up to the highway and the convenient Caltrans call box, glowing like a yellow sentinel. I could, of course, have called my dad, but what kid ever does that? Instead, I phoned a friend who had a Jeep, and he would be my savior. Some days, I think I have learned a lot since that fateful night, but I am pretty sure my next stuck story is waiting just around the bend.

PART 4

The Overland Journey

Do you have that one place on the globe that you have always wanted to visit? The best overland journeys comprise at least one of the following ingredients:

1. **Discovery:** A place with a deeply personal connection or sense of wonder.
2. **Connection:** A person you love and respect travels with you.
3. **Challenge:** The journey presents you with a significant challenge that tests your limits, and you find the strength to overcome the odds.

If you are lucky, the journey might include all three. The first two ingredients can have provenance during the planning process, but the third is made entirely of randomness and serendipity. But, for any magic to happen, it requires you to eventually stop the planning, cease the "somedays," cast off the bowlines, and go. There is no harm in enjoying the planning process, equipment selection, and vehicle preparation, but none of those can deliver the ingredients of traveling well. This final part endeavors to help you do just that, starting with researching a destination, communicating with other travelers, creating a team, assembling supplies, gathering the required permits and documents, and even the murky subject of sponsorship.

←
Jack Quinlan surveys the route forward through the Altar Desert.

CHAPTER 14

ROUTE SELECTION, LOGISTICS, AND FINANCIALS

While planning and logistics can often feel like a chore, they serve two important roles in the mind of travelers: First, they reduce anxiety, both real and imagined, and second, they provide the opportunity to set expectations and build excitement for you and your travel companions. Certainly, significant journeys can be undertaken with little or no plan, and that can also be charming in its own right, but even just the basics might save you from a few days detained at a border post.

Finding a great campsite can feel like a reward or a mini discovery that would have made our hunter and gatherer ancestors proud. Engaging in the ancient arts of wayfinding, fire starting, and gathering food in wild places is important, even if it is just a handful of pine nuts or some blackberries. It is also understandable that financial considerations may be at the forefront of your mind as you look toward longer trips. It is easy to see travel influencers on social media living exotic overland adventures and wonder how they can afford it or how you can do the same. Overlanding does not need to be expensive, but there are ways to monetize the journey or work while exploring.

Discovering Your Overland Route Plan

The destination may be a point on the map, but the flora, fauna, history, food, and local cultures are what give the journey a sense of place. The overland route plan is used to create a one-pager of trip-specific details that will be stored electronically, in printed form, and shared with your travel companions and emergency contacts. To create the one-pager and to help provide a framework for the journey, an overland route plan should cover the following:

- **How much time do you have?** Most travelers have a set amount of time available for their journey, so it is important to define the number of days and compare that constraint against the actual time travelers are taking on average to complete the route. Including a time buffer for unexpected challenges or serendipity is also important. It is recommended to plan one flex day for each week of travel and make sure that the first and last days of the trip are not too ambitious and include flexibility as well.

- **Is the trip region- or route-based?** In general, overland trips fall into the category of a route or a region. For region-specific trips, the goal is to drive to an area and use it as a base camp to experience the place. A good example is driving a remote route to a beautiful lake and then spending a week camping, fishing, paddle boarding, and hiking around the destination. Another example would be the Isle of Skye in Scotland, where you can camp along the way and visit various historic sites, villages, and green lanes. Route-specific trips center around an overland track, such as the White Rim Trail in Utah or the Canning Stock Route in Australia. For planning purposes, region-specific research will focus on points of interest, while route-specific trips will focus on GPS tracks, resupply points, campsites along the way, permits, and purchasing the relevant trail maps and guidebooks.

- **What are the maximum number of days between resupply points?** Before you can provision for water, food, and fuel, it will be important to determine the number of days and miles between resupply points. This will inform how many liters of water and fuel must be carried by the vehicle and the subsequent impact on the available payload (see the calculations later in this chapter). As the payload is finite, it might require taking less support equipment or planning a detour to reprovision. For routes that exceed your range and payload, it may be necessary to coordinate a fuel drop, which is common on the Canning Stock Route or high latitude expeditions in Antarctica and Greenland. Your ability to carry key supplies will determine how far you can travel and how long you can be remote. Fuel and water will always be the greatest constraint for an adventure motorcyclist.

- **Does the route require permits, health considerations, or specialty equipment?** While many planning details can be left to chance, the devil is always in the trip interrupters, like permits, visas, vaccines, and specialty equipment. The trip planning process must include thorough research on those constraints and a checklist for getting them completed. Some permits need to be applied for a year in

advance, and vaccines like yellow fever are subject to shortages. Does the route require specialty equipment to comply with local regulations or to ensure a successful journey? Specialty equipment requirements can include tire chains, country-specific vehicle placarding, and road safety items like warning triangles or safety vests. Finding mosquito netting is surprisingly difficult in equatorial Africa, as is antimalarial prophylaxis, but if you contract malaria, nearly every pharmacy and clinic will have the artemisinin-based combination therapy (ACT) treatment available on the shelf.

- **What resources are available along the route, and what are their contact details?** The planning process should include reviewing the websites for the agencies along your route, which may include the Forest Service, semi-autonomous native territories, state trust land agencies, Bureau of Land Management, and others. These websites will provide important information on road closures, events, permit requirements, entry fees, cultural considerations, and more. For example, all state trust lands in Arizona require a permit paid for before entry.
- **What are the unique points of interest along the route?** It is helpful to make a list of all the POIs in the area you are visiting. This is best accomplished using guidebooks and directly asking other travelers about their favorite spots. If you have enough lead time, reading adventure stories or historic accounts of the area can be surprisingly insightful. There are forums and groups that will be helpful, but that usually comes with a dose of vitriol. Once these sources have been exhausted, a web search can fill in the remaining gaps.

DETERMINING YOUR TRAVEL PACE

Knowing your pacing and applying it to trip planning is important. A pacing baseline will also help you pick travel companions and pair with other groups that have similar goals. The best way to estimate pace is to look at the GPS track from your last few trips. What was your average total driving time for each day (total moving time on the GPS)? If you drive four hours on average each day (not including stops), you can estimate how much distance you can cover once you input the speed limits and trail conditions for your planned route. I reviewed the GPS logs from my continental crossings and was able to estimate my average speeds in the following conditions. I am an efficient driver, but I am careful not to speed or abuse the vehicle, so my averages (which are rounded to the nearest 5 mph/kph) are a good starting point.

1. Developed World Primary Road (Freeway): 60 mph (100 kph)
2. Developed World Secondary Road (Highway): 45 mph (70 kph)
3. Developing World Primary Road (New Pavement): 40 mph (60 kph)
4. Developing World Primary Road (Broken Pavement): 30 mph (50 kph)
5. Maintained Dirt Road: 25 mph (40 kph)
6. Unmaintained Dirt Road: 20 mph (30 kph)
7. Dirt Two-Track Trail: 15 mph (24 kph)

Once you know your average speeds (or use mine) for these conditions, multiply the average speed by your average hours driven per day. It is not critical to be precise as it is hard to know what all the conditions will be, but if you are mostly on the trail for the day and you tend to drive for four hours a day, then your anticipated miles covered should be 60 ($4 \times 15 = 60$ miles). Those distances will help you plan campsites, accommodations, and provisioning, including fuel stops.

→

The surface
and line of sight determine your travel pace.

THE TRIP ONE-PAGER

Now that you have all of the planning information, it is time to summarize it on your trip one-pager. This document is best created and stored online for easy access and sharing with your travel companions and emergency contacts. Print off a few copies and stick one in your ditch bag and the other in the map case. If the trip is longer than a few weeks, prepare a one-pager at the end of each week for the following seven days. The document should include:

1. Name of the trip (even a nickname can be fun)
2. Emergency contact numbers with country code (important for satellite phone calls)
   a. Your personal emergency contact person's name and number
   b. Your evacuation insurance emergency contact number
   c. 911 or equivalent in the country you are visiting
   d. Your Department of State emergency line number
3. A trip summary by day, with each day including the following:
   a. Date and day of the week
   b. Estimated travel distance
   c. Provisioning waypoint if known (often includes a fuel stop)
   d. Point of interest waypoint and hours of operation
   e. Campsite or accommodation waypoint and address (important if someone gets lost)
4. Non-emergency contact numbers for local resources
5. Short list of helpful phrases and cultural considerations

Water, Food, and Fuel Planning

During an overland journey there are three primary consumables: water, food, and fuel. Water is the most important of the three but is often overlooked or improperly stored. This section will review methods of keeping water potable and ensuring that you don't put all your supplies in one basket. Food planning is similar, and there are many tricks and tips for keeping healthy food fresh while on your journey. The final calculations pertain to fuel planning and storage.

WATER

Water is the most important provision to plan for and should be protected from loss or pathogens. You never want all of your water in one container, and any water introduced to bulk storage should be from a known source, filtered, or treated. On a motorcycle, you should have water in two containers. Some riders prefer to have one of those bladders in their backpack. Although motorcyclists will use minimal water for cooking, cleaning, and hygiene, they still need 1 liter of water for every two hours of backcountry riding or 4 liters per day when road riding. In extreme conditions and warm weather, water consumption can reach 1 liter per hour and should be gauged against a urine color chart (i.e., pale yellow = okay, dark yellow = bad). As a result, motorcyclists should plan on having 6 liters of water for each day between resupply along with 2 liters of emergency water in a separate container and a means of boiling, filtering, or treating in the field.

For overlanders in a car or 4WD that plan to camp and cook in the field, they should plan on 8 liters per person per day between resupply, plus an additional 6 liters per person of emergency supply stored in a separate container. It is important to carry water in several containers should a leak occur and also have a method of boiling, filtering, and treating available. Given the critical nature of water, I recommend carrying it in several 10–20-liter containers or bladders.

FOOD

When planning meals, you will want to pack enough food for each day of remote travel, plus maintain three days of emergency dry storage meals. Even though most people can survive for days or weeks without food, travelers are generally happier and physically stronger in a fed state. When shopping for food, you are balancing palatability, ease of preparation, nutrition, and foodborne pathogens. Each group is different, so choose what you like to eat, but if you are concerned about the food supply at the local outdoor market, consider only buying items that can fall into the three Ps: peeled, packaged, or piping hot. It might seem trite to have prepper food in the vehicle, but I have tapped into my reserves more times than I care to admit. Sometimes, stores are closed, or you decide to spend another few days on the beach, or get detained at the Djibouti border for four days. Backpacking meals or even ramen can be found in every country.

FUEL

Fuel planning will be based on your trip one-pager, where you can total your anticipated miles between resupply and then calculate it as follows:

1. Divide the estimated miles between resupply by your average fuel economy, giving you the total fuel baseline in gallons.
2. If the majority of the miles will be on dirt roads and tracks, apply a 1.5 terrain multiplier to the baseline.
3. If the majority of the miles will be in sand or sand dunes, apply a 1.75 terrain multiplier to the baseline.
4. The final calculation is your emergency multiplier, which will be an additional 1.25 for established routes. For expeditions, you will have an emergency multiplier of 1.5.

↑ **Sinuhe cooks breakfast in camp,** setting the team up for a great day of travel.

For example, if you are planning to drive your 4Runner 172 miles between Escalante, Utah, and Page, Arizona, through the Grand Staircase-Escalante National Monument, your calculation would be 172 miles divided by 18.2 mpg = 9.45. 9.45 gallons multiplied by a terrain multiplier of 1.5 = 14.18 gallons. As the route is established and well-traveled, you will want an emergency

multiplier of 1.25 for a total of 17.73 gallons on board between resupplies. The emergency multiplier takes into consideration mechanical issues or the requirement to detour or even backtrack to your starting point.

When traveling in unknown areas or internationally, it is important to resupply often, as it helps keep your fuel tank full and isolates the risk of contamination to smaller volumes. I generally start looking for fuel when my tank reaches the halfway point. If the fuel source is questionable, use a filter funnel and bring along spare fuel filters.

Planning Resources, Books, and Communities

Information is easier to find than ever, which is both efficient and cautionary. The following list only includes sources where the content has been validated via ground-truthing or the company leadership has extensive and recent international overlanding experience.

MAPS AND GUIDEBOOKS

There are numerous quality resources and guidebooks to help plan your journey. The following volumes will serve as a cornerstone, but additional books specific to the region should be studied in advance of your journey. Travelers like Dan Grec and Graeme Bell have excellent regional books that are filled with important logistics information, but also excellent stories of adventure.

- *Kiss, Bow, or Shake Hands* by Terri Morrison and Wayne Conaway
- *The Royal Geographical Society Expedition Handbook* edited by Shane Winser
- *Oxford Handbook of Expedition and Wilderness Medicine* by Chris Johnson, Sarah R. Anderson, Jon Dallimore, Chris Imray, Shane Winser, James Moore, and David Warrell
- *Sahara Overland* by Chris Scott (Northern Africa)
- *Vehicle-dependent Expedition Guide* by Tom Sheppard (out of print)
- Hema Maps (various guides and maps for Australia)
- Tracks4Africa (various guides and maps for Africa)
- onX Maps (website and smartphone app with trail guides)
- National Geographic Adventure Maps (worldwide)

- Benchmark Maps Baja California Road & Recreation Atlas
- Benchmark Maps Road & Recreation Atlas (by US state)
- FunTreks Backroads & 4-Wheel-Drive Trails series (various western US states)

OVERLAND COMMUNITIES AND GROUPS

Even the solo traveler needs a community to support them and provide up-to-date information on the trails and routes they plan to traverse. These communities will contain thousands or even millions of posts about vehicle preparation, trip reports, and logistics discussions. At the same time, it is important to filter the comments based on the experience and recency of the poster's insights.

- Wikioverland.org: http://wikioverland.org (border and visa information by country)
- Expedition Portal: https://expeditionportal.com (global and North America)
- Expedition Overland: www.xoverland.com (global video adventures and guides)
- Adventure Rider: www.advrider.com/f (global for adventure motorcycles)
- 4x4Community Africa: www.4x4community.co.za/forum
- ExploreOZ: www.exploroz.com/forum
- iOverlander: https://ioverlander.com (global map with up-to-date information)

Additional groups can also be found on Reddit, Facebook, and other social platforms.

GOVERNMENT AND NGO RESOURCES

The cornerstone of good information is to utilize respected government sites or established NGOs like The Explorers Club or The Royal Geographical Society. The counterpoint is that most government sites will err on the extreme side of conservative, which may dissuade even seasoned travelers from visiting a country.

- Australian Department of Foreign Affairs and Trade: www.dfat.gov.au
- United Kingdom Foreign, Commonwealth & Development Office: www.gov.uk
- United States Department of State: https://travel.state.gov
- Royal Geographical Society: www.rgs.org
- The Explorers Club: www.explorers.org

Sponsorship and Influencers

Who doesn't like getting paid to travel or getting discounted or free gear? If sponsorships are on your radar or the idea of being an influencer piques your interest, how do you go from "please pay for my vacation" to a well-respected marketing professional?

Sponsorship is a business contract in which products or funding are provided in exchange for marketing exposure, product development deliverables, and media collateral (images, editorial, video, and so on). Just like any service, a professional and experienced approach will always yield the greatest return. The quality of design reflected in your website and materials, accuracy and clarity of your proposal, and demonstrated success will all improve your odds of gaining support.

Only a handful of sponsored overland travelers and influencers make a living wage. Even with the benefits of YouTube, Patreon, and social media, achieving a living wage is an extremely difficult balance. What is common is that thousands of influencers only make a little extra gas money or get a few free lights or tires. There is nothing wrong with that, but I suspect they all planned on it being their next career. Sponsorship is hard, and being an influencer is even harder, so most people are better off finding a remote work job or saving for the trip and then doing it on their own terms.

How much is your time worth? If you spend 200 hours and get a free bumper and a knockoff winch, was your time well spent? Likely not. Determine the value of your time, and don't pursue sponsorship if this is a single trip or a passing interest: No one benefits, and your trip shifts from the adventure of a lifetime to another job. Put a value to your time and keep track of the return on that investment. What often works is a combination of sponsorship, remote work (even as a photographer), and content production for magazines and websites.

Tips for Working from the Road

For the first time in history, large segments of the knowledge and creative workforce can conduct their career from the road. With tools like Starlink and 5G, it is possible to upload large files or conduct video conference calls. Here are some tips for working from the road.

- Talk to your current employer about options for remote work.
- It is important to be clear that you are remote working while traveling.
- Schedule time in your day for uninterrupted work.
- Shut off all notifications and remove social media from your phone.
- Work longer hours when you are stationary or feel inspired.
- Reserve calls for driving windows to gain efficiency.
- Check email during driving breaks to improve response times.
- Let your coworkers know that your connectivity may be interrupted.
- For critical calls or deadlines, ensure you have redundant methods of connectivity (like Starlink and a mobile hotspot).
- Take regular breaks to step outside of the camper and refresh in nature (you earned it).
- Work on proactive communication while you are connected to reduce unplanned communications.
- Set clear communication hours and boundaries with your employer and yourself.
- Prioritize good sleep, which will improve focus and creativity.

The Cradle of Adventure

Kenya stretched out before us. We moved slowly and deliberately along a rogue track through the rugged and sparsely vegetated area near Sogwass Mountain in northern Uganda. We were not convinced that this rarely used smugglers' route was even passable, let alone legal for access to the border—then we got caught. The tribal militia met us with crooked smiles and blank stares; two men unslung their HK G3 rifles, coming to the low ready. Walking toward the Mercedes G-Wagon, the leader's grin broadened, his eyes shielded by mirrored aviators and a baseball cap emblazoned with "Disobey" above the bill. Bryon Bass and I continued to take stock of the approaching party, a mix of camouflage and traditional cloaks, some even gripping wooden staffs and bows and arrows.

Fortunately, Stanley Illman's experience shined. He casually stepped from the Mercedes with his wild white hair, shorts, Izod shirt, and dusty Crocs over sockless feet. A big smile led the way, and he bellowed a "hello" to our hosts. They didn't smile but were taken off guard by what looked to be an overlanding Einstein; rifles were lowered, and the tension began to ease. A leader emerged, and a brief but heated conversation ensued. They began moving toward Bryon and me a few minutes later, where we were still held short of the village. We removed our aviators almost simultaneously and did our best to display the same disarming smiles. They were not amused and asked us a few questions, obviously verifying the story of Stanley and the others. One thing was clear: We were going to the police station.

With a few instructions and a stern warning that the police would be waiting for us, they radioed ahead, and we drove the few miles to the enclave of Oropoi. Just finding the building was difficult as it was tucked in a nondescript courtyard, with a few stray dogs lounging in the shade. When we rolled in, a few officers emerged from a fractured doorway in various states of dress and uniform. They were not happy to see us either, their annoyance more evident than anger. An officer took our passports

↑ **We filled up the Mercedes G-Wagon tanks** with a manual pump in northern Uganda. Fuel quality is a constant consideration.

and inspected our visas, recording the details of our documents and border infractions in a broken and tattered logbook. Without a word to us, he told Stanley, Franz, and Alex to leave—but he had further plans for Bryon and me.

They wanted to search our vehicle and started with Bryon's small, innocuous gray bag in the passenger footwell. Out spilled every manner of paraphernalia, from a compass to paracord. This raised the official's eyebrows, and with a stiff open hand, he motioned to the pile and said, "What is this?" Improvising, I grabbed the most touristy item, a spork, and replied, "For camping." He was far from convinced and demanded to know our mission, so I responded, "We are just tourists." "You are supposed to disclose your mission," he growled, clearly still agitated by what he was convinced were two American operatives. I remained silent. Frustrated, he shoved our passports back toward us and waved at us to leave. While loading up, he took several images with his cell phone. Again he grumbled, "You are supposed to disclose . . . " as the Mercedes diesel clattered to life. Onward.

CHAPTER 15

YOUR FIRST
INTERNATIONAL
OVERLAND JOURNEY

The use of a passport is 600 years old, initiated during the reign of Henry V of England; the documents included detailed descriptions of the carrier and allowed freedom of movement and commerce. In 1920, the League of Nations agreed on the basic format and construct of the modern passport, with detailed descriptions giving way to photographs and a standardized design.

There are few experiences as exciting as handing your passport to an official at a border, your heart filled with anticipation and maybe a bit of anxiety. International overlanding is not better than exploring your home country, but it is certainly different. This chapter will cover international travel concerns such as documents and permits for you and your vehicle, special medical considerations, border crossing, and possibly even driving on the other side of the road. Once that passport is stamped, a whole new adventure begins.

Vehicle Documentation and Regulations

In general, the more developed the country, the more they are concerned with people getting in illegally, and the more undeveloped the country, the more concerned they are with a vehicle not leaving legally. As a result, developing countries will take exceptional care in ensuring the vehicle you drive is not sold on the black market. Entry with a vehicle will be controlled with a wide range of temporary vehicle importation systems or a Carnet de Passage to control an illegal sale. Some temporary importation permits (TIPs) are brilliantly simple, using a stamp in your passport with a few lines of description related to the vehicle, most typically the vehicle identification number (VIN), license plate, make, model, and color. You cannot leave the country until customs has cleared the stamp, most often with another stamp on top of the first one.

Some countries are particularly detailed and will record all manner of information on the vehicle and inspect the car with equal care. If you have nothing to hide, this is almost always resolved with patience and time. In almost all countries, the document they are most interested in seeing is the original title, which should include a matching VIN and description, along with some validation of you as the owner. This gets more complex if your company or someone else owns the vehicle, requiring a letter of authorization on letterhead with the requisite signatures and the stamp of a notary. Ensure that the letter is executed within the same calendar year as you are traveling (in Panama and Mexico in particular).

The Carnet de Passage is a temporary importation document that financially bonds the vehicle

← The Carnet de Passage is the passport for the vehicle, allowing it to be temporarily imported easily. The kind customs official at the Uganda border made the process painless.

while in the host country. There are still a significant number of countries that require a Carnet, fortunately, that number is decreasing. As an odd development, Australia now requires it (as of 2009), unusual for a developed country, especially one without a land border. The Carnet is particularly relevant for travels in Africa, where its use is advantageous in many countries. When shipping to South Africa, a Carnet is compulsory. The Carnet is obtained through an automobile association and is financially secured with a cash bond, letter of credit from your bank, or an insurance policy. The insurance policy is the most common, although the most expensive choice. Depending on the country you are visiting, the bond can be up to 300 percent of the value of the base vehicle. Consider that before bringing your Unicat to Mongolia and take a KLR motorcycle instead.

Vehicle regulations will vary widely by country, but ensuring the vehicle looks sensible and is not overloaded is a good idea. Numerous countries (like Australia) have GVWR limits and will set up weigh stations on the side of the road. Avoid expensive lights all over the vehicle, as many countries also regulate driving lights. Placarding and reflector regulations also vary, so check the rules for the places you plan to visit. It is common to be checked for warning triangles and safety vests, so pack them regardless.

Vehicle insurance will likely be required, but it is a good idea to purchase it regardless. The insurance will most likely be liability coverage only, so do not expect your vehicle to be covered too. It is common for police officers to have random checkpoints where they may inspect the vehicle, search your contents, and review your documents. They are just doing their job, so smile.

Passports, Visas, and Vaccinations

With any international overland adventure, you must determine what visa requirements are needed for entry. These requirements vary widely by country and even by the home country of the visiting individual. For example, Mongolia does not require a visa for American citizens, but they do for someone from England (and most other countries). For US citizens, the most reliable source for this information is the Department of State. Based on the itinerary and duration of the trip, it is common to secure all visas before leaving your home country. This can be done using a visa service or by visiting the country's consular offices. The visa service does cost some money, but they are exceptionally efficient and know all the bureaucracy involved. However, on very long or loosely planned trips, obtaining the visas beforehand will not be practical and will need to be secured while on the trip, most often in the capital city of the neighboring country. E-visas have become commonplace in recent years, making the visa application process, payment, and receipt seamless. In most cases, the visa will be sent by email in a few days, and some can even be added to your Apple wallet and scanned via QR code at the border—progress!

We have found that a divided file folder is the best way to organize information, copies, and country-specific documents. I also keep a separate sleeve in the file folder with the originals, which I keep hidden, but accessible in the vehicle. My original passport always stays on my person and never in an easily accessible pocket. Several expedition-grade clothing companies design these pockets into their clothing. I keep a wallet in my front pocket with only enough cash for the day (usually about $100) and my international driver's license. Related, I also keep a USB drive with copies of all of the documents and a digital backup of my best photos from the trip.

When traveling, it is common for border officials to check your vaccination yellow card. In the years since the pandemic, some countries still request proof of a COVID-19 vaccination. The most common vaccination requirement is yellow fever, and many African countries will not allow entry without it. A visit to the CDC website is advised to confirm which vaccines are required and which are recommended by country. There are other vaccines that are worth considering based on your risks or goals. For example, it is worth researching the hepatitis A and B series, typhoid, and measles vaccines.

Crossing Borders

Depending on the border you drive up to, it might be order and efficiency or chaos. However, the process is almost always the same, so park the vehicle within sight of the customs and immigration buildings, grab your file folder, and lock the car. Carrying a camera with you is generally not recommended, so put that out of view. At many developing country borders, you will be approached by moneychangers and offers of "assistance." In most cases, exchanging money is fine, but should be done knowing the exchange rate (there are great apps for that) and only with smaller denominations. A fixer can be valuable and allow for some efficiency if you feel the person is trustworthy or recommended. As a rule, never give them any paperwork, but use their services to get from building to building and answer questions. It is important always to negotiate the fee upfront.

→

The Expeditions 7 Land Cruisers.

KNOW THE RESTRICTIONS

Many countries do not allow the import or export of large amounts of fuel or cash, and a pile of camera equipment will also raise suspicions. Most importantly, find out in advance if there are any restrictions on satellite phones, Starlink units, or other radio frequency devices. Drones have also become increasingly regulated or banned. Know the laws before you go.

You should also research if there are any restrictions on importing or exporting food products. It is disappointing to have to toss out a hundred dollars in food that was just purchased. Often, these restrictions are in place to control the movement of non-native species or diseases, so these requests should be respected. Some of the restrictions can also be quite humorous, like the ban on chicharrónes coming from Mexico to Belize (chicharrónes are fried pig skin).

BE ORGANIZED

Having your equipment organized and well-documented will greatly facilitate smooth border crossings. Make a list (with copies) of all electronics in the truck, including cameras, radios, computers, and so on. In my experience, we have never been hassled with having one camera and one computer for each of the vehicle occupants. At some borders, you will be required to complete a declaration document with a description of the equipment and its value. It is not uncommon for the border customs official to inspect your vehicle and verify that the declaration document is accurate. Honesty is important, but it can be useful to be somewhat cryptic in the description; for example, a satellite phone can be listed as a "Motorola 9555 phone," where it is properly declared but won't raise suspicion. The most important consideration at the border is to be patient and kind. You are visiting their country, and the border officials are just attempting to do their job. Respect and a smile will do wonders.

Tips for International Driving

One of the most dangerous things we do while traveling is driving, particularly at night. An accident can end a trip, so diligence of best practices and safety prevails. These tips focus on safety while also providing some tips and tricks for successful international driving.

1. Slow way down, it is not a race.
2. Expect the unexpected, always.
3. If you need to use your phone, stop and take a break.
4. The driver's primary job is the safety of the occupants.
5. The driver's secondary job is the safety of others around the vehicle.
6. All team members should be able to operate the vehicle.
7. Never drink and drive. Take a cab or walk.
8. Use extreme caution when passing to ensure sufficient sight distance.
9. Never give children candy or other items while sitting in the vehicle or on the road. It encourages them to run out when tourists approach.
10. Right on red is unique to the US; don't try it elsewhere.
11. Obtain an International Driving Permit. It is rarely required, but it looks impressive and is not your original should it be confiscated by police.
12. If you hit a goat, you just bought a goat. Stop and compensate the family, as the loss has a significant financial impact on them.
13. Never react in anger or road rage. That driver likely has cousins in the next town.
14. Slow down in every village. It will help prevent accidents, making you more likely to see that large, unmarked speed bump.
15. Learn what the traffic signs mean before arrival.
16. Consider picking up a local if they need a ride; you might need one next time.

← **Expect the unexpected,** always.

Travel Safety

The most common question I am asked about international travel is, "Is it safe?" Fortunately, the answer to that question is a resounding yes. Certainly, there are regions in some countries that should be avoided, but for the most part, each place is filled with people just like you, trying to provide for their family, enjoy a good meal, and have a laugh with their friends.

In many ways, safety while traveling is the same as safety in the city you live in. Avoid driving at night, don't get drunk, don't buy drugs, and don't hit on the police officer. In most cases, trouble can be avoided entirely by being observant, traveling with others, and not displaying wealth.

Pay close attention to your surroundings when walking or driving around. If something seems out of place, it probably is. It is important always to trust your gut and the intuitions of your travel companions. It is important to have a safety word that everyone in the group knows but does not raise suspicion. If someone says "rhubarb," everyone closes tight and starts moving immediately toward safety. Turn on location services and share your live position with others in your group and your emergency contacts back home. If cell coverage is limited, activate your inReach device and start the tracking mode.

Never carry a firearm when traveling internationally (unless permitted to do so) and use extreme caution even when carrying a knife. In most cases, bad guys in foreign countries attack with multiple assailants and have spotters nearby. According to the State Department, do not resist; lower your gaze and comply with their demands. The only time it is appropriate to resist is during a kidnapping attempt, which is extremely rare.

When staying in cities, use caution when accessing your hotel room. Wait to close the door until you have verified that the room is unoccupied. Always use the secondary lock once the door is closed and consider a door-stop alarm. For camping, the more remote, the better, and even then, consider pulling out of sight from the main roads and tracks. Overlanding is statistically safer than living in most cities in North America, but it helps to be mindful of the risks and take steps to avoid danger.

Fees, Fines, and Bribes

There are a few unavoidable discomforts with international overland travel, including corruption, bribery, and thinly veiled facilitation payments. The uninitiated will often decry that they would never pay a bribe, a convenience reserved for those who have never been face-to-face with the motivation an AK-47 can muster. Some with reasonable travel credentials will claim to have never paid a bribe when it is impossible to know exactly which taxes, fees, or fines are a bribe and which are not. We all must take the moral high ground and avoid these exposures to the extent we can. While I see it as possible to never knowingly pay a bribe, that is a rarity in the world of rough-and-tumble travel, particularly when you get deeper into Russia, Central America, or just about anywhere that recently experienced a coup or military conflict.

FINES AND TICKETS

A fine or ticket is the most likely bribe to pay knowingly or unknowingly. In some countries, it is common to make ticket payments directly to the officer, even on a portable credit card machine, to facilitate the process. The best place to start with these is to ask yourself, "Do I believe I did something wrong?" For example, were you speeding or running that red light? If the answer is yes, then you will likely need to pay a fine, and it is critical to understand to whom you will be paying that fine. Frequently, a pleasant conversation and some patience will reduce or eliminate the fine, but just as in other parts of the world, if you break the law, be prepared for the consequences. However, if you feel that there was no wrongdoing or they made up some obscure or petty infraction, be prepared with a plan upon which you and your travel partners all agree. Avoid giving the official originals of any of your documents. Have laminated copies of your driver's license on hand and high-quality duplicates of your vehicle documents. Once they have your originals, they have you.

With attempted extortion, several things will work in your favor, the first being a knowledge of the law and an awareness of how the process should go. Then, feel free to assert your innocence clearly and respectfully. Ask for the officer's full name or badge number. Ask the officer if you will receive a receipt for the fine that was paid. Then, the best plan is to wait. The official will already be put back by your declaration of innocence and the documentation you are beginning to gather about the exchange. But most importantly, a crooked official hates wasting time as much as you do, mainly because it exposes them to passersby and colleagues who could have a different view on corruption. The more they believe that a bribe is not likely, the easier it will be for them to move on to a more willing victim. In countries like Mexico, there are also tourist hotlines that you can call to have them speak directly to the officer. If it was an attempt at a bribe, just calling that number will send them on their way.

SHIPPING OFFICIALS AND BORDER CROSSINGS

The worst fleecing I ever experienced was in the Port of Buenos Aires, a beautiful city filled with amazing people and one of the most corrupt places on earth. Bribes (or *mordida*), in many cases better defined as facilitation payments, have become synonymous with getting anything done at the bureaucratic level in corrupt countries. The officials would intentionally delay or manipulate the system to put pressure on travelers so they would pay. This is where patience and having lots of spare time work. They will eventually run out of motivation and release the vehicle. The traveler must also be prepared to pay in other ways, as delays can result in costly hotel stays and taxi fares as the days mount.

At borders, the key is always to have a great attitude. I've never knowingly paid a bribe at a border, even after experiencing hundreds of crossings. My documents are always organized, and I research other travelers' experiences in detail. In many of these countries, those border officials are important people, used to being respected. I have found the more respect, kindness, and smiles I pay in their direction, the less they ask for money or time from me. As travelers, it is our responsibility to resist paying bribes as much as safety allows, but I would caution against being too critical of others who may have acquiesced to that pressure or fear.

Being a Gracious Guest

Once you cross the border, you are now a guest in that country. Being a gracious and generous visitor is important. This starts by researching the history of the country and learning their customs and cultural norms. Common practices may be offensive to you, but your role is as the observer. You do not need to agree with it, but it is often inappropriate or unsafe to intervene. It is also important to learn several common phrases in their language before arriving. This should include hello, goodbye, thank you, I am sorry, and of course, "Where do I find the best cappuccino?"

While traveling through the country, smile often and avoid sounding demanding or boisterous. Use caution with the volume of your voice, and do not expect that they owe you anything. Show respect at places of worship, cemeteries, and historic places. When taking photographs and videos, never capture an image of someone without their permission. Just imagine how odd it would feel if a car full of tourists pulled up in front of your house and wanted to photograph you mowing the lawn.

A Few Final Thoughts

Over the past few hundred pages, there have been many details and recommendations, but few are as important as reminding yourself to slow down, get good sleep, and stay connected with the people you love. Here are a few reminders from a fellow traveler.

1. Slow down . . . then slow down some more.
2. Sleep in sometimes.
3. Send postcards to your family.
4. Stay connected to your friends back home.
5. Be humble on social media when you share your experiences.
6. Make sure you are in the photos too (and not just selfies).
7. Make great meals in camp.
8. Say yes to that third cappuccino.
9. Bring comfy chairs and good pillows.
10. Take walks. It is so important to get away from the vehicle on foot.
11. You will wish you had more time. It is okay, we all do.
12. Travel will change you in ways you could have never imagined.

The Company We Keep

The most powerful takeaway I have experienced from my more ambitious overland adventures is the deep gratitude and respect for the individuals I have traveled with. Of any of the trips that went awry, it has always been attributed to the weakness in someone's character. Just like any organization, we all require a healthy, motivated, competent, and optimistic team. This was never more apparent than during the Expeditions 7 crossing of Greenland, where I had the pleasure of crossing the world's largest island with some of the most exceptional individuals of character I have experienced in my travels. Coming up with a great idea for an adventure is easy. Picking the right vehicle is even easier. But the company we keep during the trip will make all the difference.

Certainly, inspired ideas and innovative equipment add to the success and pleasure of an overland excursion, but what matters most is the experience of the collective whole. That can even mean going alone and the care we show ourselves on a solo journey. For me, any adventure is made sweeter by having others to share it with—the laughs and memories that come from the challenges and wonders along the way. Because of this, it is important to be deliberate about who we have along. The positive attributes of someone will likely shine on an adventure, while the negative traits will be amplified by the uncertainties and difficulties of life on the road. Some people thrive in harsh conditions, while others wither and retreat. I have seen both happen in the field, and it can significantly impact the enjoyment of everyone involved. One of the best ways to ensure a good team is to understand everyone's goals and expectations, a clear insight into what they hope to experience during the trip. If left undetermined, it can quickly lead to frustration and disappointment. For example, if one person loves to drive daily, and the other prefers to spend a few days in each location, a compromise must be identified early on. The secret is in the planning.

For my recent trip across the Altar Desert, I knew all but one of the travelers, and they were vouched for. In the case of Brian McVickers, Dave Harriton, and Chris Wood, I have known each of them for nearly two decades and have traveled extensively with them too. They are all levelheaded, respectful, and game for nearly any challenge. Some are better at planning, and some at execution, but all are as dependable as the day is long. Frustrations will invariably arise on any trip, so the company we keep will make all the difference when things go sideways. I remember the night when the sand blew so hard that our staked tents buckled and our sleeping bags filled with silica. There was not a single grumble from the group, and the hardship was addressed with self-deprecating humor and optimism. Egos had been checked at the border, and we all worked to make the trip a success for everyone.

During our travels, we often discover limits. We encounter the fringes of our character and the capability of our equipment. We think that buying more things will improve it, and going from 33-inch to 35-inch tires will somehow enhance the experience. It won't, and neither will another electronic gadget or pair of synthetic underwear. Overland travel has foundational principles for genuine adventure, and that comes down to visiting a place we are excited to see, bringing a vehicle and equipment suitable to the task, and being very, very intentional about the company we keep. After that, it is all about the journey.

←

The connections we make along the journey
remains the greatest blessing.

Top 10 International Overland Routes

1. The Silk Road—Central Asia

Distance: 4,000 miles/6,400 kilometers

Duration: 8–12 weeks

Difficulty: 5/10

One of the great historic overland trade routes, the Silk Road travels from Europe to China through the Middle East and Central Asia. Not restricted to a specific track, the modern traveler can choose numerous paths much like the traders of old. The route is a glorious meander along the steps of Marco Polo and the camel trains of yore.

2. The Pan-American Highway— Alaska to Argentina

Distance: 19,000 miles/30,000 kilometers

Duration: 1–2 years

Difficulty: 4/10

Traveling the Pan-American rewards the overlander with one of the longest routes in the world, spanning from the Arctic Ocean in the north to the Southern Ocean in the south. The traveler will experience every major climate zone and biosphere along the way and cross 17 borders. The most ambitious will consider including the Darién Gap.

3. London to Cape Town— England to South Africa

Distance: 10,000 miles/16,000 kilometers (varies by route)

Duration: 6–12 months

Difficulty: 4/10

London to Cape Town starts in the UK before crossing Europe, Turkey, and the Middle East into Egypt, pausing at one of the remaining ancient wonders of the world, the Pyramids of Giza. The rewards continue down the east coast of Africa and national parks filled with megafauna before arriving at one of the world's most beautiful cities, Cape Town.

4. The Canning Stock Route— Halls Creek to Wiluna

Distance: 1,150 miles/1,800 kilometers

Duration: 1–2 weeks

Difficulty: 6/10

With the distinction of being the longest unsupported overland track in the world, the Canning Stock Route follows the original cattle route through the Great Sandy and Gibson Deserts. There are 48 wells along the route along with an estimated 1,000 dune crossings, making it one of the most remote and challenging overland routes in the world.

5. Iceland and Vatnajokull Glacier—The Ring Road and Europe's Largest Glacier

Distance: 800 miles/1,280 kilometers

Duration: 1–2 weeks

Difficulty: 8/10

Crossing Vatnajokull is one of the few remaining high-latitude expeditions that are accessible to most travelers. It requires a specialized vehicle and days of effort to cross Europe's largest glacier. The trip should be capped off with a road trip around the Ring Road of this stunning and diverse country.

6. The Balkans— The Gem of Eastern Europe

Distance: 1,800 miles/2,900 kilometers

Duration: 2–3 weeks

Difficulty: 5/10

From the dramatic shoreline of the Adriatic to castles and even mountain hamlets, the Balkans are a feast for the traveler. Backcountry travel is permitted in most countries, and the routes can range from maintained to low-range rock crawling. This region is one of the best ways to overland in Europe.

7. Trans-Siberia and the Road of Bones—Crossing Russia to the Pacific Ocean

Distance: 5,000 miles/8,040 kilometers

Duration: 1–2 months

Difficulty: 5/10

Siberia spans nearly all of northern Asia, crossing from the Ural Mountains to the river Aldan, Lake Baikal, and the infamous Road of Bones. The driving is some of the most dangerous in the world and there are long stretches with limited resources or assistance. Winter travel will include the coldest city on the planet.

8. Cabo da Roca to Nordkapp—Traversing Western Europe

Distance: 3,600 miles/5,800 kilometers

Duration: 2 weeks

Difficulty: 3/10

From Portugal's beautiful and dramatic coastline to the shores of the Arctic Ocean, this south to north traverse of western Europe is a passage through time and ecology. Crossing through nine countries, it includes scaling the Pyrenees; touring the castles and museums of France, Amsterdam, Copenhagen, and Stockholm; and finally arriving at the northernmost road in the world.

9. West Coast of Africa—Cape Town to Tangier

Distance: 18,000 miles/29,000 kilometers

Duration: 4–10 months

Difficulty: 5/10 (dry season)

One of the most challenging overland routes in the world, the west coast of Africa will test the vehicle and driver, along with your capacity for border crossings and bureaucracy. The crossing of sixteen countries can result in thousands of dollars in visas and the expense associated with a vehicle Carnet. This route is the logistical Everest of overlanding.

10. Trans-Amazonian Route—Eastern to Westernmost Point in South America

Distance: 5,000 miles/8,000 kilometers

Duration: 6–12 weeks

Difficulty: 5/10 (dry season)

Beginning in Ponta do Seixas, Brazil, the route continues to the infamous Trans-Amazonian Highway (Rodovia Transamazônica BR-230), which permits side trips to the Amazon River. Deep in the jungle the route parallels Bolivia before crossing the border into Peru. The challenges continue over the Andes Mountains and into the small town of Nazca before turning north to the westernmost point of South America, Punta Balcones.

Top 10 North American Overland Routes

1. The TransAmerica Trail—Crossing the US on Dirt

Distance: 4,250 miles/6,800 kilometers

Duration: 4–6 weeks

Difficulty: 6/10

Pioneered by Sam Correro, this is one of the world's great overland tracks. Originally conceived for lightweight dual-sport motorcycles, most of this track can be driven by compact 4WD or larger adventure bikes. Crossing through nine states, the route includes technical tracks and high mountain passes, along with long stretches between resupply sites.

2. The Mid-Atlantic Backcountry Discovery Route—New York to North Carolina

Distance: 1,080 miles/1,730 kilometers

Duration: 7–10 days

Difficulty: 5/10

Universally, the Backcountry Discovery Routes (BDR) have become a badge of honor for overlanders, crossing many western states. There are also emerging routes on the east coast, like the Mid-Atlantic, which travels from the New York to the North Carolina border, mostly on dirt roads and trails, along with scenic sections of paved highways.

3. The Lost Coast— Hidden California Coastline

Distance: 121 miles/194 kilometers

Duration: 3–5 days

Difficulty: 4/10

The Lost Coast region is isolated, the terrain formidable, and the history of missing people, murders, and clashes between marijuana growers and ranchers is surprising. This area has the most bears and the highest rainfall in the state. All this variety and intrigue culminate into a calling card for exploration.

4. Big Bend— Traversing the Texas Borderlands

Distance: 116 miles/186 kilometers

Duration: 2–5 days

Difficulty: 5/10 (includes Black Gap Road)

Everything is bigger in Texas—including Big Bend National Park, which stretches for days along the border with Mexico. Starting in the picturesque town of Alpine, it takes nearly 100 miles to exit the pavement on Old Maverick Road. For a challenge, try Black Gap Road, which requires high clearance, but rewards with a dip in the Rio Grande.

5. The Utah Traverse— Saint George to Monticello

Distance: 600 miles/965 kilometers

Duration: 5–10 days

Difficulty: 6/10 (weather dependent)

Architected by Sinuhe Xavier, the Utah Traverse meanders from Mesquite, Nevada through Zion National Park in Utah and into the Grand Staircase-Escalante National Monument before descending the Burr Trail and Capitol Reef. After crossing Utah's highest road, it enters the Needles District and the infamous Elephant Hill. The route is simultaneously breathtaking and oblique, allowing for the traveler to turn where the weather and interests lead them.

6. The Baja Peninsula— Sonoyta to Todo Santos, Mexico

Distance: 1,210 miles/1,950 kilometers

Duration: 1–3 months

Difficulty: 5/10

I recommend starting in Sonoyta, Sonora and driving Mexican Federal Highway 2 through the Gran Desierto de Altar (the largest erg in North America). This also puts the route on the Gulf of California (also known as the Sea of Cortez). Highlights include Gonzaga Bay, Bahía de los Ángeles, Mission San Borja, San Ignacio, the old French hamlet of Santa Rosalía, and terminates in Todo Santos for its art and culinary treasures.

7. The Dempster Highway to Tuktoyaktuk—The Arctic Ocean Route

Distance: 900 miles/1,400 kilometers

Duration: 5–10 days

Difficulty: 3/10 (summer road)

The Dempster Highway is the gateway to the Arctic Ocean. Resupply in Whitehorse in Yukon, Canada before taking the side trip to Dawson City. Once on the Dempster, it is dirt all the way to the ocean, with few stops along the way and risk of whiteouts, ferry delays, and semi-trucks. The adventurous should consider the ice road in winter to Aklavik.

8. The Continental Divide Route— New Mexico to Montana

Distance: 2,500 miles/4,020 kilometers

Duration: 3–4 weeks

Difficulty: 6/10

The Great Divide Trail was originally pioneered by Tom Collins in 1989, combining the best of the Colorado high passes. It has since evolved to include backcountry tracks starting at the Mexico border and continuing through New Mexico, Colorado, Wyoming, and Montana. The route is ideal for 4WD enthusiasts and lightweight dual-sport motorcycles.

9. El Camino del Diablo— America's Longest Overland Trail

Distance: 156 miles/251 kilometers

Duration: 2–5 days

Difficulty: 5/10 (with Christmas Pass)

This prehistoric trail through the Sonoran Desert was first documented in 1540 during the Coronado Expedition and stayed in use as an alternate route for settlers traveling west. The remote track travels through Organ Pipe Cactus National Monument and the Cabeza Prieta Wilderness from Ajo to Yuma. A detour to Christmas Pass is recommended.

10. The Trans-Canada— Newfoundland to Vancouver

Distance: 9,500 miles/15,000 kilometers

Duration: 2–4 months

Difficulty: 7/10

Developed over five years with eight volunteers, the Trans-Canada Adventure Trail (TCAT) is a daunting route of nearly 10,000 miles of mostly dirt, mud, and deep-water crossings. Not for the faint of heart, this endeavor requires camping and technical riding skills, along with the likelihood of encountering bears and wolves along the way.

INDEX

US/Metric Conversion Charts

VOLUME CONVERSIONS

US Volume Measure	Metric Equivalent
⅛ teaspoon	0.5 milliliter
¼ teaspoon	1 milliliter
½ teaspoon	2 milliliters
1 teaspoon	5 milliliters
½ tablespoon	7 milliliters
1 tablespoon (3 teaspoons)	15 milliliters
2 tablespoons (1 fluid ounce)	30 milliliters
¼ cup (4 tablespoons)	60 milliliters
⅓ cup	80 milliliters
½ cup (4 fluid ounces)	120 milliliters
⅔ cup	160 milliliters
¾ cup (6 fluid ounces)	180 milliliters
1 cup (8 fluid ounces)	250 milliliters
1 pint (2 cups)	500 milliliters
1 quart (4 cups)	1 liter (about)
1 gallon	3.7854 liters

LENGTH CONVERSIONS

US Length Measure	Metric Equivalent
¼ inch	0.6 centimeters
½ inch	1.3 centimeters
¾ inch	1.9 centimeters
1 inch	2.5 centimeters
1½ inches	3.8 centimeters
1 foot	0.3 meters
1 yard	0.9 meters
1 mile	1.60 kilometers
50 miles	80.47 kilometers
500 miles	804.67 kilometers

WEIGHT CONVERSIONS

US Weight Measure	Metric Equivalent
½ ounce	15 grams
1 ounce	30 grams
½ pound (8 ounces)	225 grams
¾ pound (12 ounces)	340 grams
1 pound (16 ounces)	454 grams
50 pounds	22,680 grams
500 pounds	226.80 kilograms
1,000 pounds	453.59 kilograms
2,204 pounds	1 metric ton

ABOUT THE AUTHOR

Scott Brady is an adventure traveler, photographer, and publisher. He is the CEO of Overland International, the parent company of *Overland Journal* magazine, the *Overland Journal Podcast*, and the website *Expedition Portal*—the world's largest and most visited vehicle-dependent adventure community and overlanding editorial resource. Because of the large audiences of these outlets, Brady is often credited for popularizing overlanding in North America. As an overlander, Brady has circumnavigated the planet three times and was the first overlander to cross all seven continents. He was the expedition leader of the Expeditions 7 project, a three-year global adventure that was the first in history to take the same vehicle to all seven continents. *Top Gear*, the History channel, A&E, INEOS, Jeep, Land Rover, Toyota, and others have utilized his driving and expedition skills.

Overland Journal, the premier magazine for overland travel enthusiasts, blends adventure with sustainability. Circulating five times yearly, the publication provides readers with skill instruction, vehicle and gear reviews, route suggestions, backcountry cooking recipes, stories from the road, and more, with an emphasis on environmental responsibility. The publication is celebrated for its exquisite photography and in-depth writing. Parent company Overland International, which—in addition to the magazine—produces the *Overland Journal Podcast* and the *Expedition Portal* forum and YouTube channel, provides instructional content for the world's largest audience of vehicle-supported adventure travelers.